Other books by Gerald Weales

AMERICAN DRAMA SINCE WORLD WAR II

RELIGION IN MODERN ENGLISH DRAMA

A PLAY AND ITS PARTS

TALE FOR THE BLUEBIRD (NOVEL)

THE COMPLETE PLAYS OF WILLIAM WYCHERLEY (EDITOR)

EDWARDIAN PLAYS (EDITOR)

THE JUMPING-OFF PLACE

American Drama in the 1960's

GERALD WEALES

The Macmillan Company
Collier-Macmillan Limited, London

FIRST PRINTING

The Macmillan Company
Collier-Macmillan Canada Ltd., Toronto, Ontario

PRINTED IN THE UNITED STATES OF AMERICA

ACKNOWLEDGMENTS

Part of Chapter I is a revision of a USIA lecture which appeared under the title "Arthur Miller" in *The American Theater Today*, ed. Alan S. Downer, New York, Basic Books, 1967. Part of Chapter V appeared in the Fall, 1968, issue of *Shenandoah*, copyright © 1969 by *Shenandoah*: The Washington and Lee University Review. The ideas in Chapter VIII were first tried out in lectures at Bucknell University and Wilson College. I have borrowed freely from my reviews in *The Reporter*. The reviews there and in *Drama Survey* and my classes at the University of Pennsylvania provided an initial opportunity to come to conclusions about many of the plays discussed in this volume.

G. W.

Contents

Introduction

The working title for *The Jumping-Off Place*—"American Drama Since My Last Book"—began as a joke among my graduate students. Milked of its mockery, taken simply at face value, it is a useful description of the present volume, which is, in one way, an extension of *American Drama Since World War II*. Like the earlier book, which covered the years from 1945 to 1961, *The Jumping-Off Place* is a critical description of American plays. Although the two books are alike in intention and, to some extent, in method, it is the differences between them that say most about the present condition of American drama.

In *American Drama Since World War II* there was one chapter and a few scattered references to off-Broadway, which by that time was an established part of the New York producing scene but which had just begun to turn up new American playwrights. Inevitably, the book was about Broadway. The distinction between Broadway and off-Broadway—except in the technical sense so necessary to the decision makers at Actors Equity—was already beginning to disappear in 1961. Today, that distinction is so unimportant that I make no formal attempt to identify the playwrights according to place of production. Almost all of the dramatists discussed in *The Jumping-Off Place* and certainly those to whom I have given the most space have written partly or wholly for off-Broadway. Success in the traditional Broadway sense—money and fame (or notoriety)—still depends on New York production, on or off Broadway, but growing production opportunities—off-off-Broadway and in regional and university theaters—are making it increasingly possible for new plays to get a hearing and for dramatic reputations to begin to build outside the conventional framework of the commercial theater. In *Theatre World*, 1966–1967, John Willis devotes thirty pages to professional resident companies scattered throughout the country, and even his listings are incomplete. Most of these companies depend on the existing repertory, of course, but there is an obvious willingness to work with plays that have not received the New York seal of approval. Not that this is the theatrical millennium. Even sympathetic observers admit that much of the work of the off-off-Broadway theaters is inferior, and the regional companies—as Philadelphia, Pittsburgh, and Minneapolis demonstrated in 1967—are frequently beset by internal dissensions. It is clear, however, that what was only a possibility in 1961 is now a fact. American drama has spread out horizontally (across the country) and vertically (up and down town in New York). This may be a temporary development—although I hope not—but at the moment it is the prevailing one, which explains why *The Jumping-Off Place* is not Broadway bound.

One of the reasons it is no longer important whether or not a play is produced on Broadway is that there are fewer and fewer interesting new American plays done there. The success of Frank Gilroy's *The Subject Was Roses* only illustrates how uncongenial Broadway is to any play which makes a gesture, however limited, toward seriousness, for Gilroy's play had to be kept alive by artificial respiration until it became a sentimental cause in its own right. Even established playwrights are vulnerable; Tennessee Williams' *Slapstick Tragedy* was continually postponed during 1965, presumably because it could not find the backers to get into production, and its failure, when it finally opened in 1966, only confirmed the prejudices of the smart money. Except for occasional flukes, success on Broadway is limited to pre-sold European (largely English) imports, to light comedies, and to musicals. With a few exceptions (notably Frederick Knott's *Wait Until Dark*, 1966), even the standard commercial genres—mysteries, adaptations, sentimental dramas—have failed to draw audiences.

There were chapters on comedy and musical comedy in the earlier book because, at that time, they seemed to be very much part of the total context of American theater; today, they are more like specialty trades, marketing occasionally amusing products but without the vitality possible within the popular genres. The only news about Broadway comedy in the 1960's is the emergence of Neil Simon as *the* successful comedy writer of the decade. He has a knack for the proper use of stereotype and a winning way with standard devices, but for the most part he shares the prevailing Broadway attitudes of the naughty (Muriel Resnik's *Any Wednesday*, 1964) and nice (Jean Kerr's *Mary, Mary*, 1961) comedies which reflect sexual attitudes long since abandoned by the average junior-high student, a view of society and the family which seems to be based on a little Freud and the back files of the *Ladies' Home Journal*, and a reassuring belief that restrained eccentricity will allow one to conform happily ever after.

The musical comedy, which seemed to be developing into a forceful dramatic form in the 1950's, went completely soft in the 1960's. With the exception of Frank Loesser's nastily satirical *How to Succeed in Business Without Really Trying* (1961) and the bittersweet Harvey Schmidt–Tom Jones *The Fantasticks* (1960), which is in its eighth year off-Broadway as I write this, the musicals seldom manage to merge book and score into a piece that has a distinguishable tone of its own. Jerry Herman's *Hello, Dolly!* (1964) is more typical of the decade, a flashily empty show with only one good song, designed to celebrate its star; as Norman Mailer's throat-lumping tribute to Ginger Rogers in the introduction to *The Deer Park* indicates, it was the star, not the show, that audiences fell for; and that has been true for all the Dollys from Carol Channing to Pearl Bailey. In an article in *The*

Review of Economics and Statistics (February, 1966), Thomas Gale Moore, working from an audience sampling gathered in 1962, predicts that Broadway will continue to flourish; since he uses "quality" to mean "more expensive," his prophecy is of minimal aesthetic interest. Broadway, then, at least in its workaday role as dispenser of sanitarily packaged entertainment, has little place in a book that is trying to discover where American drama is now.

As the title of *The Jumping-Off Place* indicates, there is an implicit difference between it and *American Drama Since World War II*, but the difference may turn out to be more apparent than real. The body of dramatic material I dealt with in the earlier book is plainly in the tradition of American drama. My present title suggests an abrupt break denied by many of my comments in the chapters that follow; I am less convinced than many of the dramatists that the works discussed here represent radical departures in playwriting. Still, there is a genuine change in the feel of the theater in the 1960's, a sense of newness, of departure, of possibility. This derives, in part, from the altered face of American theater, the variety of producing organizations; to some extent, from the mixed-media games that have become popular and the experiments in ensemble playing developed in some of the off-off-Broadway workshops; and, in small part, to the apparent removal of all taboos on subject matter and language. It is possible that out of this atmosphere a new American drama will develop that is remarkably different in style and content; but, having learned from the history of drama that most departures are made with traditional material as baggage, I doubt it. When I put a name on this book, I was thinking not simply of the kind of jumping-off place from which pioneers moved into unknown territory, but my favorite jumping-off place in dramatic literature: that imaginary mountain in *King Lear* from which Gloucester threw himself.

G. W.

THE JUMPING-OFF PLACE

ONE

Williams and Miller

Perseverance, dear my lord,
Keeps honor bright; to have done, is to hang
Quite out of fashion . . .
  —ULYSSES IN *Troilus and Cressida*

One of the most talked-about productions in New York during the fall of 1967 was a gimmicky revival of Lillian Hellman's *The Little Foxes,* an all-star attraction in which the director, Mike Nichols, killed all of Miss Hellman's best effects, such as her carefully pointed curtain lines. Even so, the play was treated (or mistreated: a few critics decided that the revival was a good occasion to do in the collected works of Hellman) as an American classic and the playwright as a revered institution, a response which was not without its irony. Less than two years earlier, Miss Hellman had told a *New York Times* interviewer (February 27, 1966), "But I feel like a stranger in the theater now." Her alienation, if so fashionable a word can be used in a non-cosmic context, began, she said, long before the production of her last success, *Toys in the Attic* (1960). The failure of her most recent play, *My Mother, My Father and Me* (1963), an adaptation of Burt Blechman's novel *How Much?*, only confirmed what she was feeling. It is the audience that she finds strange—the Broadway audience, judging by her description of them ("Everyone seems to me old and square and rich")—but Miss Hellman is a stranger in another sense. Although the plays I describe in this volume recall, in many ways, earlier American drama, there is a style and tone about them that make the work of Miss Hellman—and of other playwrights whose reputations were made before or right after World War II—seem old-fashioned. When her *Toys* opened, most of the critics said that it reminded them of Tennessee Williams, the implication being that Miss Hellman was trying to find a new footing in a changing theater. Not long after that, Williams told Lewis Funke and John E. Booth (*Theatre Arts*, January, 1962) that his "style of writing for the theatre is on its way out."

Certainly, the 1960's was a bad decade for the older writers. S. N. Behrman contributed *But for Whom Charlie* (1964) to the first season of the Repertory Theater of Lincoln Center, but neither it nor the earlier *Lord Pengo* (1962), suggested by his *New Yorker* series on Duveen, attracted much attention. Group Theatre veterans Sidney Kingsley and Irwin Shaw made brief, unhappy appearances with *Night Life* (1962) and *Children from Their Games* (1963). Playwrights of the 1940's and 1950's—William Inge, Arthur Laurents, Garson Kanin, Paddy Chayefsky—also fared badly, although Chayefsky's Biblical play *Gideon* (1961) had some success in the *J.B.* league. The popularity of Thornton Wilder's *Plays for Bleecker Street* (1962) and Robert Anderson's *You Know I Can't Hear You When the Water's Running* (1967) probably reflect, at least in part, the acceptability of the short play during the 1960's. There seems little point in a detailed examination of these plays in this volume. It should be enough to consider what was going on with Tennessee Williams and Arthur Miller, who are, after all, the most eminent of our established playwrights. For one thing, they—like Miss Hellman —were being treated as historical figures. There was a twentieth-anniversary revival of *The Glass Menagerie* in 1965 and a production of *The Rose Tattoo* in 1966 that moved from the City Center for a brief Broadway run; *Death of a Salesman* was rediscovered by television in 1966, and *A View from the Bridge* ran for almost two years (1965–66) in an off-Broadway revival. Both playwrights published nondramatic work, Miller his first book of short stories—*I Don't Need You Any More* (1967)—and Williams his third—*The Knightly Quest and Other Stories* (1966). It is their work as active dramatists that concerns us here, however. The 1960's is the decade in which Tennessee Williams saw his winning streak as a popular dramatist come to an end, and Arthur Miller, wearing a new philosophical look, returned to the theater.

From the successful production of *The Glass Menagerie* in 1945 until well into the 1960's, Tennessee Williams averaged rather better than a play every two years, most of which had respectable New York runs—100 performances or more. Working for the most part in Southern settings and presenting somewhat lurid surface events, Williams told again and again the story of an outsider, one of the fugitive kind, who by virtue of his (or her) differentness—his artistic inclinations, his sexual proclivities, his physical defects—becomes a victim of an uncongenial society. As the number of plays grew, it became clear that, for Williams, all men are outsiders and the enemy is the character himself or time eating at him or a Godless universe, from which there is no escape, and the best he can do is to take what comfort he can from the temporary palliative, sex.[1] Although a persistent strain of social comment remained in his work, by the end of the 1950's he

[1] For a detailed examination of Williams' thematic and theatrical practices see my *Tennessee Williams* (1965), one of the University of Minnesota Pamphlets on American Writers.

had become a kind of existential melodramatist. From the beginning, Williams has been essentially a nonrealistic dramatist, using
everything from mechanical tricks (the television screen in *Sweet
Bird of Youth*) to artificial soliloquies (the set pieces in the same
play), from significant names (Val Xavier) to symbolic stage
sets (the body-soul balance in *Summer and Smoke*) to break out of
the realistic tradition of American drama, a tradition, incidentally,
in which he works extremely well (consider the breakfast scene in
The Glass Menagerie).

Williams' work in the 1960's begins with the highly deceptive
Period of Adjustment (1960), which many critics dismissed as
the Broadway marital comedy it pretended to be. On the surface it
looks like—and it is, to some extent—a conventional attack on
suburbia, making its satirical points while it tells the story of two
marriages, one brand-new and unconsummated, the other five
years old and teetering, both going through periods of adjustment.
The resolution brings both couples together in a curtain scene that
would be the familiar Broadway side-step if it were not that the
whole house shakes at this point, settling a little deeper into the
cavern over which the suburban development is built. The subtitle,
"High Point over a Cavern" (High Point is the name of the development), with its sexual *double-entendre*, suggests that the familiar
off-to-bed ending is not all that happy. The play is still another
instance, lightly disguised, of the Williams world in which men
live tentatively, in an unending period of adjustment, over an
abyss that is more than simply social. It is sprinkled with Williams
lines that help make the point ("The whole world's a big hospital,
a big neurological ward, and I am a student nurse in it") and, as
though the sinking house were not enough, he throws in an even
more apt image: the honeymoon car in which George and Isabel
arrive is a funeral coach.

Period of Adjustment is obviously an experiment for Williams,
an attempt to use a popular dramatic form for his own purposes;
it succeeded too well, for—in the original production, at least—it
came across as a heavy-handed light comedy, this despite the fact
that, in Isabel, Williams has created one of the best of his nervous

Southern women. "And I had the impression *Period of Adjustment* was a happy play," Williams told Funke and Booth in the interview quoted above, "but when I saw it this summer in the stock production with Dane Clark, I realized that it was about as black as *Orpheus Descending*." Black it is, certainly, but Williams' remark is an overstatement in the other direction. If we take the play seriously, it is possible to see the "happy" ending not simply as a joke but as a kind of assent to chaos rather than an attempt to escape it. In that case, the play is a first step toward what is genuinely new in Williams' work in the 1960's, a retreat from the inescapable violence of *Orpheus Descending* and *Suddenly Last Summer* to an acceptance of life and death, a resignation that is almost positive in its refusal to be sentimental or to indulge the self-pitiers. *The Night of the Iguana* (1961) and *The Milk Train Doesn't Stop Here Anymore* (1963) exemplify that change in Williams.

In *Iguana*, which gets its title and the name of its heroine and very little else from an early Williams story (in *One Arm and Other Stories*), the action takes place in a run-down hotel in Mexico. T. Lawrence Shannon, defrocked clergyman and alcoholic, comes running for shelter—dragging behind him a gaggle of outraged Texas teachers whom he is supposed to be taking on tour, including a sixteen-year-old he has seduced and her lesbian chaperone—only to find the hotelkeeper dead and his widow, Maxine, too eager to let him fill Fred's shoes. Hannah Jelkes pushes the wheelchair of her ninety-seven-year-old grandfather uphill through a rain forest to reach the Costa Verde, the last refuge for Nonno in a world through which he and Hannah have wandered, she making sketches, he reciting his poems to pick up the pennies that have kept them alive. So they arrive, priest, poet and painter, buffeted and suffering creatures, as the lines keep insisting, directly identified with the iguana tied under the porch, scratching in a vain attempt to escape before it is eaten. "At the end of its rope?" cries Shannon. "Trying to go on past the end of its goddam rope? Like *you!* Like *me!* Like Grampa with his last poem!"

Yet, this is not the usual Williams struggle in which the victims are destroyed by the ugly forces they face; this is a contest between Hannah and Shannon—oddly enough, a kind of conversion play. Shannon's view of the world is contained in his description of one of the sights he tried to force his "ladies" to see—a great pile of human refuse across which tattered beggars crawled, stopping to eat bits of still undigested food. His God, at once cruel ("stray dogs vivisected") and impersonal ("His oblivious majesty"), is embodied in the storm that strikes at the end of the second act ("Here is your God, Mr. Shannon"); the description in the stage direction, borrowed from the story ("like a giant white bird attacking the hilltop"), recalls Sebastian's God from *Suddenly Last Summer*, the birds diving on the young turtles. Shannon's reaction to the random cruelty of the universe and the ugliness of the world's inequities is to become cruel in his own right; like a child, he strikes out at everyone—Maxine, Hannah, the teachers for whom he has such contempt—wounding with words. He swims in self-pity. In the dark-night-of-the-soul scene in the third act, in which he is tied in a hammock, presumably to save him from suicide, Hannah taunts him: "Who wouldn't like to suffer and atone for the sins of himself and the world if it could be done in a hammock with ropes instead of nails. . . . Isn't that a comparatively comfortable, almost voluptuous kind of crucifixion to suffer for the guilt of the world, Mr. Shannon?" She suggests an alternative, an idea of God that she learned in the House for the Dying in Shanghai, the "little comforts beside the death-pallets" that the "children and grandchildren and the custodians" left there. Instead of forcing his God of "Lightning and Thunder" on others, even if He exists, she tells him to look into the longing faces and "Lead them beside still waters because you know how badly they need the still waters." If there is no comfort to be gained in heaven, there are "Broken gates between people so they can reach each other, even if it's just for one night only." This suggests the way characters in the earlier plays used sex—Blanche in *A Streetcar Named Desire*, Marguerite in *Camino Real*, Carol Cutrere in *Orpheus Descending*—and Hannah's description of the masturbating traveling salesman in Hong Kong intensifies that suggestion, as does Shannon's decision to stay with Maxine.

In the end, Williams goes beyond this limited sense of human contact. Hannah, who has thrown herself on Maxine's mercy in Act I, says, in effect, that if one cannot have God, then he must act like God. Shannon goes down and cuts the iguana loose, "because God won't do it." At this point, Nonno, just before he dies, finally finishes his poem about the orange branch in which growth is only half the story, decay the other, and the tree faces it "Without a cry, without a prayer,/With no betrayal of despair." Shannon's "spooks" and Hannah's "blue devils" are defeated, or at least held at bay, by an endurance that is strengthened by help given and help received. Since Shannon spends so much of the play fighting off Maxine, his staying (and there is no alternative) might be seen as his final destruction; if that were the case, Hannah's gentle God, like Dr. Sugar's in *Suddenly Last Summer*, would be as frightening as that of Shannon and Sebastian. This, however, is not the effect *The Night of the Iguana* finally conveys. Although there is something almost touchingly corny in the last exchange between Maxine and Shannon, in which she promises to help him get back up the hill and he "chuckles happily" (this being Maxine and Williams, it is also a sex joke), it is intended to convey that Shannon has found Hannah's "still waters," not undergone Dr. Sugar's lobotomy. Even Hannah's last scene, with the dead Nonno, is one of release, not defeat.

If, as Williams told Funke and Booth, *Iguana* is about "how to live beyond despair and still live," *Milk Train* is about how to go beyond despair and learn to die. It is an attempt to still that terrible cry Big Daddy makes at the end of the second act of *Cat on a Hot Tin Roof* when Brick forces him to face the fact of his death. *Milk Train* is based on the story "Man Bring This Up Road" (*Mademoiselle*, July, 1959; reprinted in *The Knightly Quest*), but the earlier fictional version, unlike the play, is not an exercise in *Iguana*-like theology. The much-married, fabulously rich heroine of the play, Flora Goforth, a Georgia swamp girl come up in the world, recalls Big Daddy in her vitality, her vulgarity, her sense of her own power; but also in her fear of death and her refusal to recognize the cancer that is killing her. She sits on an almost impregnable mountaintop in Italy, guarded by *lupos,* animal and human, and dictates her memoirs, from which she hopes to learn something about her life. "Sometimes I think, I suspect, that everything that we do is a way of—*not* thinking about it. Meaning of life, and meaning of death, too." Christopher Flanders, poet and mobile-maker, who is jokingly known as the Angel of Death because he has a habit of visiting old ladies just before they die, manages to invade the estate. Flora tries to make him sleep with her, but his job is to give the ladies "something closer to what they need than what they think they still want." He convinces Flora that she is not that self-sufficient, that "sooner or later, you need somebody or something to mean God to you," and, having taken him on his terms, not hers, she is ready to Goforth peacefully. She accepts the death that she could not escape in any case, recognizes it as simply the last of a great many moments that make up life, and, in doing so, alters her view of life itself. At the end, she asks Chris to help her into her bedroom ("I can't make it alone") and, thus, like Shannon in *Iguana,* comes around to Hannah's God.

Milk Train is an interesting play, particularly to anyone who has watched the subtle alterations and acceptances that have come to Williams over the last twenty years, but it is not a very good one. Even *The Night of the Iguana,* Williams' last popular success, suffers from a surfeit of argument. Williams has always been at his dramatic best when, as in *Streetcar* and *Cat,* character predominates over idea; when a too neat formulation (*Summer and Smoke*) or a too heavy mythic superstructure (*Orpheus Descending*) takes over, the characters have to fight for life. Although a sensitive actress can make something moving out of Hannah, as Margaret Leighton did in the original New York production, she is essentially nondramatic, a walking world view, and her third-act scene with Shannon is a little like a debate, artificially enlivened by his attempts at violence. Compare that vitally important scene with the business in the second act in which Maxine tempts Shannon with a rum-coco; the latter is much more dramatic, a confrontation of characters rather than ideas. Still, there is a genuine clash of ideas in *Iguana* and, for all that Hannah is a bit pale, they are given flesh enough to hold our attention, even to elicit our sympathy. This is not true of *Milk Train*. Flora is potentially a vibrant comic character, but except in some of her exchanges with her neighbor, the Witch of Capri, she operates in a vacuum. Chris is so bland a symbolic character that there is no conflict, no real abrasion, simply a reversal on Flora's part that is not presented dramatically or defined in any terms but philosophic generalization. The play is further hampered by the bogus Kabuki framework in which stage assistants set the scene and offer explanations where none are needed. *Milk Train* suggests *Camino Real* in its imaginative ponderousness, its determination to make its point, but, for all its obviousness, there is more fun in the early work.

The play I have been describing is the third—the published—version of *Milk Train*. It was first done at the Festival of Two Worlds in Spoleto, Italy, in the summer of 1962. It came to New York in January of the next year and ran for two months; in 1964, revised, it tried again and lasted for only five performances. Williams has always been a relentless reviser, turning stories into plays, short plays into long plays, old plays into new plays, but this was the first time that he brought the same material back so quickly, as though he were determined to say what is in this play. Its rejection, by critics and audience alike, marked a change in Williams' relationship to the American theater. He is still indisputably one of the leading American playwrights, but, as Broadway figures such things, he is no longer a safe property; the milk train doesn't stop here anymore.

In 1964, *The Eccentricities of a Nightingale* was tried out in summer stock but never came to New York, and it was published in a double volume with *Summer and Smoke*, of which it is a revision. Neater in action, simpler in theme, *Eccentricities* differs from the earlier play most importantly in that it allows Alma the temporary fulfillment of one night with John. Its best invention is Aunt Albertine, whose story Alma tells in Act II. Albertine lost her respectability and found happiness when she eloped with Otto Schwarzkopf, who ran the Musée Mécanique. On the night the Musée burned, Otto, who was drunk, would not leave the mechanical bird-girl, and Albertine, trying to save him, reached and got only a button. The moral, as Alma explains, is in her aunt's dying words, an echo from an early Williams story, "The Yellow Bird" (in *One Arm and Other Stories*): " 'Some people,' she said, 'don't even die empty-handed!' " In a note to the published play, Williams says that he wrote the revision to be performed in England but got to London too late, after the original *Summer and Smoke* was in rehearsal; that was presumably 1951. *Eccentricities,* then, does not really belong to Williams' work in the 1960's, except for the fact that he chose to release it almost fifteen years after it was written. It is, of course, a play about the "Broken gates between people" that Hannah speaks of in *Iguana*—a gentle, almost genteel example of one of Shannon's "One night stands."

During 1965, a bill of Tennessee Williams one-acters was repeatedly announced for production, but it was not until 1966 that *Slapstick Tragedy* finally got to Broadway. Even though the two plays—*The Mutilated* and *The Gnadiges Fraulein*—are minor Williams, "diversions," as he called them in his Preface when they were published in *Esquire* (August, 1965), it was surprising that the production lasted for only seven performances. In *The Mutilated,* the weakest of the two plays, two old friends, or friendly enemies, spend Christmas Eve trying and failing to find peace on earth for themselves. One of them is Trinket, who has had a breast removed because of cancer; the other is Celeste, a shoplifting, streetwalking wino who knows and threatens to divulge the secret of Trinket's mutilation. Much of the play deals with the quarrel between them, but it ends with their reconciliation on Christmas Day, when, in a haze of Tokay and sugar wafers, they have a vision of Our Lady, which, as Trinket says, takes away the pain. With the ironic religious experience, the omnipresent carolers chanting their miracle message *a cappella* ("I think the strange, the crazed, the queer/Will have their holiday this year") and some standard Williams comic lines, the whole thing should probably not be taken too seriously. It certainly should not be played for pathos, as it was in the original New York production.

The Gnadiges Fraulein is a grotesque comedy in which the heroine, down on her luck, is forced to compete with the cockaloony birds (the costumer's delight) for the fishing-boat rejects that provide her room and board. A decayed artist, recalling Alexandra in *Sweet Bird of Youth*, she is no match for organized parasites like the cockaloonies; the play is the account of how she fights the good fight for survival even though it sends her back to the docks, blind and bleeding. Her action forms the spine of the play, the flesh being the running commentary provided by Polly and Molly, the Greek chorus reduced to a comedy team. Williams has used this device before, as in *Orpheus Descending*, where the two comic sisters comment on the disastrous affair of Val and Lady, but now the comic duologue has stepped to the front of the stage and the suffering figure is reduced to an almost mute scarecrow, shivering on the periphery of the scene. Even so, in the last moment of the play, the comedy is upstaged; the final rush of the heroine, while Molly, Polly, and Indian Joe sit down to dinner in the background, should be frightening. Although the two plays have been published in separate acting editions, it is easy to see why Williams suggested, in his *Esquire* note, that they be performed together. The first is a sad and occasionally brutal work that ends on a note of ironic exaltation; the second is wild slapstick that finishes on a note of horror. "In production," Williams wrote, "they may seem to be a pair of fantastic allegories on the tragicomic subject of human existence on this risky planet." Since the heroine of *The Gnadiges Fraulein* provides a ludicrous example of the endurance Hannah embodies in *Iguana* and since the vision at the end of *The Mutilated* is a wine-soaked variation on the peace that Flora Goforth finds in *Milk Train*, the relation of *Slapstick Tragedy* to the more serious plays of the 1960's is a highly ambiguous one, particularly when one remembers that, as a double bill, the world ends not with Our Lady but with the cry of the cockaloony—*awk, awk, awk.*

Since the appearance of *Slapstick Tragedy*, Williams has published two short plays in *Esquire: I Can't Imagine Tomorrow* (March, 1966) and *Kingdom of Earth* (February, 1967). The second of these is still another grotesque comedy, suggesting *Baby Doll* rather than *The Gnadiges Fraulein*, in which an unlikely triangle is acted out in the face of an impending flood. The tubercular Lot comes back from Memphis with a new wife, Myrtle, and threatens the position of Chicken, his bastard half-brother who has been promised the farm when Lot dies. While Lot calls, then crawls for help, finally dying on the stairs, Chicken explains to Myrtle that only he can save her when the flood comes ("If you get on the roof tomorrow, it'll be Chicken, not Jesus, that gets you up there") and makes it clear that he wants her as much as she wants to stay with him. "There's nothing in the world, nothing in this whole kingdom of earth, that can compare with one thing, and that one thing is what's able to happen between a man and a woman, just that thing, nothing more, is perfect." At the end, he looks out at his land ("Chicken is king!") and then goes up to Myrtle, past the dead Lot, while outside we hear the "distant dynamite blast" which indicates that Mr. Sikes ("like God, he's got more to think about than people below him") has blown up one of his levees and the water is on its way. What the play has to say, beyond its anecdote, is that the only thing anyone can depend on is other people and, given "the scoop," as Myrtle has learned it ("The hardness of people"), this is at best a chancy dependence. The short story treatment of the same material, "The Kingdom of Earth" (in *The Knightly Quest*), is somewhat softer, partly because Chicken as narrator can carry us beyond Lot's death to their fructifying life together (Myrtle is expecting a child whom they will name either Lot or Lottie) and partly because there is no flood in the story and, therefore, no dynamite ending.

The *Iguana*-like choice of life over death is still implicit in the full-length version of the play—*The Seven Descents of Myrtle* (1968)—but it is no longer a neat if grotesque little parable. There are still the triangle, the shift in partners, and the flood, but the longer play has altered the characters. Chicken becomes a variation on the conventional Williams priapic figure, an uncomfortable compromise between a calendar-caressing recluse and the speaker of the salvational sex lines carried over from the one-act play. Lot is no longer simply tubercular. He is an impotent aristocrat of sorts (he cleans the crystal chandelier while Chicken works the land), ridden by the memory of his dead mother, whom he becomes in a rather trying transvestite death scene. There is no contest, then, for Myrtle. Inevitably she chooses potency over impotency, even if it means, as Stella's choice of Stanley meant twenty years earlier, the choice of vulgarity over gentility. Since Chicken is part Negro and he and Lot are half-brothers, Williams may intend some allegorical statement about racial changes abroad in the land, but such significance is finally irrelevant. What *Seven Descents* becomes is Myrtle and not much else. Most of Williams' invention in stretching his short play has gone into the creation of a Myrtle who is not so much a character of substance as a vehicle for a talented actress. If there is life at all in *The Seven Descents of Myrtle*, it does not come from character or theme or plot, but from an accumulation of funny bits.

Still another Williams play, *The Two Character Play*, opened in London in December, 1967. According to the reviews, it is about two performers, Felice and his sister Clare, who have been deserted by the other actors, who consider them insane; it takes place in the theater where, at Felice's insistence, they act out what is apparently their own story. David Wade, reviewing the play in the London *Times* (December 13, 1967) under the headline "Tennessee Williams's New Voice," compared Williams to Samuel Beckett. As long ago as the interview with Funke and Booth, Williams expressed his admiration for Harold Pinter. In the production of *Slapstick Tragedy*, directed by Alan Schneider, who made his reputation directing Beckett, Pinter, and Albee, *The Mutilated* nodded in the direction of Pinter, at least to the extent of being unspecific about Trinket's mutilation, which is clearly identified in the printed play; the acting edition offers variants for some of the speeches, showing how the definition was befogged. A hint of undefined terror, however, will not turn a Williams play into a Pinter play, particularly when the Williams play contains themes and devices that we have known as his for years; nor did Williams intend it to, for he said in the *Esquire* note, "They are not 'Theatre of the Absurd.'" If Wade is right, Williams may finally have moved tentatively in the Beckett-Pinter direction in *The Two Character Play*. If so, that would be somewhat ironic, like Hellman echoing Williams just at the moment when his voice was being drowned out by the absurdists. In any case, *The Seven Descents of Myrtle* is evidence that, come hell or high water, Williams, like Chicken, has no intention of abandoning familiar ground.

In 1964, after an absence of eight years, Arthur Miller returned to the New York stage. Within a year, he and the Repertory Theater of Lincoln Center offered two new plays—*After the Fall* and *Incident at Vichy*. The first of these is an excessively long self-analysis by a character whose biography so much resembles the playwright's that most critics take it as Miller's *Long Day's Journey into Night*. The second is a kind of roundtable discussion over a grave, during which one man finds the power to act. Although they are very different in superficial ways, the plays are alike in theme and tone. If they are inferior to the early plays—and I think they are—their shortcomings can best be seen in recognizing that there is not a complete break between early and late Miller. As a playwright concerned with both psychological man and social man (as his definition of social drama says that he should be), Miller is inevitably forced to deal with the problem of identity. This is what he has always written about, and it is as clearly the subject of *Incident at Vichy* as it is of *All My Sons*.

The basic premise of all his early work is that society is an image-making machine, a purveyor of myths and prejudices which provide the false faces and false values that modern man wears. The implication is that the individual has little choice—that he can conform and be destroyed, as Joe Keller (in *All My Sons*) and Willy Loman (in *Death of a Salesman*) are, or that he can refuse to conform and be destroyed, as John Proctor (in *The*

Crucible) and Eddie Carbone (in *A View from the Bridge*) are. Despite the blackness of this description, the plays are not pessimistic, because inherent in them is a kind of vague faith in man, a suspicion that the individual may finally be able to retain his integrity. This possibility appears, most conventionally, in the platitudes of Chris, the avenging idealist of *All My Sons*, and in the romantic death of John Proctor. In *A View from the Bridge* it lies outside the action of the play, in Miller's attempt, speaking through the narrator Alfieri, to engraft a ritual purity on Eddie: "not purely good, but himself purely." In *Death of a Salesman*, it does not lie in the "right choice" implied by Biff's "He had the wrong dreams." It certainly does not lie in Biff himself, in all those references to working with the hands, nor in the alternative suggested by Charley and Bernard. It is in Willy's vitality, in his perverse commitment to a pointless dream, in his inability simply to walk away. Willy Loman is a character so complex, so contradictory, so vulnerable, so insensitive, so trusting, so distrustful, so blind, so aware—in short, so human—that he forces man on us by being one.

Although *After the Fall* and *Incident at Vichy* end in positive acts, the new plays are a great deal more somber than the early ones. Quentin in *Fall* goes to meet Holga, ready to commit himself once again to a personal relationship, which we are to take as a commitment to life. The Prince in *Vichy* gives up the pass that would free him to save the life of Leduc. Despite these acts, the new plays embody a philosophic idea which belies the positive conclusions and which separates *Fall* and *Vichy* from the earlier plays. The difference lies in the way Miller uses the problem of identity. I do not mean that he has ceased to accept that men have images forced upon them. One of the lines of action in *Incident at Vichy*—although it might be called a line of inaction—has to do with the failure of the waiting men to resist what is being done to them. A great deal of the discussion concerns the way one should act in the face of his destroyers, what role he should play in an attempt to save himself. The implication is that the victims' failure to agree to attack the guard is their way of consenting to their own destruction. Lebeau, the painter, admits that he feels guilty although he knows he has done nothing wrong and is not ashamed of being a Jew. He can say, "Maybe it's that they keep saying such terrible things about us, and you can't answer." It is Leduc, the psychiatrist, who states the proposition formally: "So that one way or the other, with illusions or without them, exhausted or fresh—we have been trained to die." There is a relationship between this kind of thinking and the conception of Willy Loman as a man attempting to be the success his society admires, but there is a great difference too. Willy, as a consenting victim, is a product of Miller's observation; the consenting victims of *Incident at Vichy* are products turned out on the Bruno Bettelheim-Hannah Arendt line—explanations of totalitarian success which almost become apologies for it.

There is, then, a qualitative difference between the conceptions of society in *Death of a Salesman* and in *Incident at Vichy*. That difference, however, is not apparent if we look at *After the Fall* alongside *Salesman*. The pressures that beset Quentin and his friends and relatives are not necessarily the same ones that push Willy around, but they are the same kind. It is clear in *After the Fall* that much of Maggie's behavior is the result of her doing what is expected of her, and that Louise sees herself and Quentin in the roles that her psychoanalysis forces them to play. In the political subplot, Mickey testifies and names names partly because his new affluence requires that he should, and Lou, who makes a John Proctor refusal, admits that in the past he has compromised his sense of his own honesty and tailored himself to fit party requirements.

Yet *After the Fall* and *Incident at Vichy* are thematically two of a kind. The real split between these two plays and the earlier ones can be found in what the heroes are looking for—or, at least, in what they find. Like John Proctor and Eddie Carbone, both Quentin and Von Berg are concerned about their names. When Leduc seems surprised that Von Berg should take his title seriously, the Prince answers, "It is not a 'title'; it is my name, my family." Since he goes on to use words like *dishonor*, one might assume that *name* has the same value here as it does in *A View from the Bridge* or *The Crucible*. At this point in the play, it may have such value, at least for Von Berg, but the lesson that the play is going to teach him is to understand *name* as Quentin uses it when he keeps asking over and over in whose name one turns one's back. In the early Miller plays the quest for identity, for name, was a search for integrity. In *After the Fall* and *Incident at Vichy* that quest has become an attempt to find a workable definion.

In *After the Fall,* Quentin is faced with the problem of coming to some conclusion about himself which will make it possible for him to operate in the world. He is attracted to Holga, but he hesitates to commit himself to her, because so many of the commitments of his past—personal, political, and professional—have collapsed, leaving him nothing. The play is Quentin's look at that past, his attempt to find meaning in it. Early in the work, he says sadly, "I feel . . . unblessed." He is bothered throughout the play by a girl named Felice, whom he cannot get out of his mind. Once, casually, he did something that changed the course of her life, and he continually sees her, her hand lifted in benediction, saying, "I'll always bless you." At the end of the play, when he faces the figures from his past, like the director in Federico Fellini's 8½, he stops Felice from lifting her hand. He accepts that he is unblessed. What he learns in the course of the play is that he has spent his life trying, one way or another, to establish his innocence. The guilt that he feels about the way he has treated his family, about his two failed marriages, about his reluctance to defend his old friend has always been transferred to the other person in the relationship. At the end, he accepts that it is after the fall, that there is no innocence, that the guilt is his own. Earlier, Holga tells him her recurrent dream. In it, she has an idiot child, which she knows represents her life; she wants to run away from it, but she stays and finally brings herself to kiss it. In case Quentin or the audience has missed the point of the dream, she adds the moral: "I think one must finally take one's life in one's arms, Quentin."

Accepting one's life—at least in the context of *After the Fall*—

is more complicated than simply recognizing that any relationship implies responsibilities on both sides. The guilt that Quentin assumes is something very like original sin—an acceptance that he, and all men, are evil or have evil in them, the capacity to kill. This idea is presented several ways in the play. Verbally, in Quentin's statements about his failure to grieve for his dead—for Lou, for his mother, for Maggie. Visually, in the scene in which he begins to strangle Maggie and finds himself strangling his mother. Metaphorically, in the concentration camp tower that broods over the whole play. This is the element of the play that is most difficult to take, but it is a necessary part of the idea Miller has imposed on his work. Near the end, Quentin turns toward the tower and says, "My brothers died here . . ." and then, looking down at Maggie lying at his feet, adds, "but my brothers built this place." What is finally being said in *After the Fall* is not that Quentin's life shows him capable of cruelty, of murder even, but that he must accept his complicity in all the evil in the world. Holga, who carries the messages for Miller, says, ". . . no one they didn't kill can be innocent again."

Incident at Vichy comes to the same conclusion. In this case, it is not self-examination that brings self-knowledge to Von Berg; it is a lesson forced on him from outside by Leduc, who from the beginning of the play has accepted that man is inherently evil. When he says he believes the rumor that there are furnaces waiting to destroy them all, it is not because the destroyers are Germans or Nazis, but "It's exactly because they are people that I speak this way." Von Berg, on the other hand, believes that there are "certain people," not identifiable by race or class, through whom all that is best in civilization will finally survive. He imagines that his sympathy for the suffering of the Jews separates him from their tormentors. He is so horrified by what has happened in his native Austria that he has, as he says, "put a pistol to my head!" But he has not pulled the trigger, and, as Holga points out in *After the Fall*, by being alive he fails to be innocent. Leduc reminds him that the cousin he mentions early in the play, a man for whom Von Berg obviously feels affection, is a Nazi. "It's not your guilt I want," says Leduc; "it's your responsibility."

That line, however, is false—if not for Leduc, certainly for Miller. What he wants in this play is for Von Berg to recognize his guilt, as Quentin accepts his in *After the Fall*. In an article in *The New York Times Magazine* (January 3, 1965) called "Our Guilt for the World's Evil," Miller set out to correct some misconceptions that he felt had grown up around *Incident at Vichy*. He makes quite clear that, to him, the story is relatively unimportant and that Von Berg's heroic act at the end is gratuitous. "The first problem is not what to do about it," he says, "but to discover our own relationship to evil, its reflection of ourselves." If Quentin is a usable analogy for Miller himself, it would seem that the events of the eight years prior to 1964 made him find in himself qualities that he can accept only with difficulty. The accepting becomes possible, however, by extending the *mea culpa* to take in all men. He chooses to do this by embracing the commonplaces of contemporary psychology, but—since he is still a social dramatist— he uses the complicity gambit to turn personal guilt into public guilt. What this means to Miller as a playwright is that he no longer deals with man's struggle against the images being forced on him; instead, he becomes an image-forcer himself. After all the identity searching, the name that Quentin and Von Berg end up with is Everyman as Executioner. Both plays suggest—insist, really—that once this label is accepted, once the illusion of innocence is pushed aside, a man is free to act, even to act as a lover (like Quentin) or a martyr (like Von Berg). These positive acts, however, are simply the residue left by the burning away of the naive belief in man implicit in the early plays. In *After the Fall* and *Incident at Vichy*, the heroes are not in a struggle; they are in analysis. The analysis is successful when they accept that they fit the love-hate stereotype of the psychological man.

Although what Miller has to say in the new plays is philosophically suspect, it is not his theme but his commitment to it that has crippled his work. His new truth is not an impetus to creativity, but a doctrine that must be illustrated. In the past, he has occasionally been criticized for his didacticism, but in none of the early plays—not even in *All My Sons* and *The Crucible*—has he sacrificed action to argument. There are defects enough in those plays

—the hidden-letter trick in *All My Sons,* Elizabeth's loving lie in *The Crucible*—defects that grow out of a need to let the action make a social point. Even so, his main characters—even John Proctor—are more than one-dimensional vehicles. All of the early plays are attempts to understand man and his society by confronting a particular man with a particular situation. The generalizations to be made from that particularity lie outside the play—with the audience, with the critic, with the playwright in his theoretical writings. In the new plays, the situations and the characters are only demonstration models. The playwright has moved from the creation of character to the making of statements, from the concrete to the abstract. This can best be seen if we look at *After the Fall* alongside *Death of a Salesman,* the early play that it most resembles.

The first title for *Salesman* was *The Inside of His Head,* which would suit *After the Fall* just as well. According to the first stage direction of *Fall,* "The action takes place in the mind, thought, and memory of Quentin." Although the version of *Salesman* that finally reached the stage has objective scenes as well as subjective ones, both *Salesman* and *After the Fall* make use of the ideas and the devices of expressionistic theater. The barriers of time and space disappear. The skeletal set of *Salesman* and the free-form set of *After the Fall* were conceived to let Miller's heroes step freely from the present to the past or, particularly in the case of Quentin, from one moment in the past to another. Both plays are designed, then, to let the playwright (and his characters) escape the restrictions of conventional realism.

The difference between the two plays lies in the way the playwright uses his freedom. In *Salesman,* we follow Willy through the last desperate day of his existence, watching him clutch at impossible and mostly imaginary straws until, through Biff, he is able to find the release that will let him die. The jumble of memories that nag at him are not simply explanatory flashbacks, although there is exposition in them. Since they are as real to Willy as the immediate events, they contribute to his disintegration. In *Salesman,* then, all the scenes are part of the play's action. In *After the Fall,* this is hardly the case. In that play Quentin decides to go meet

Holga at the airport; the action, presumably, is his process of reaching that decision. When we see him at the beginning of the play, he is somewhat worried by the fact that hope keeps sneaking up on him even though he knews how awful everything is. The play uses his life to explain to him that he is the psychological stereotype discussed above. Then, perversely hopeful in a terrible world full of potential killers like himself, he goes off to meet the girl. Although there are lines to suggest that Quentin is undergoing some kind of torment, the pain of his self-analysis is belied by the discursive, man-to-man stance which he takes during the narrative sections of the play.[2] The remembered scenes, then, do not have the look of experiences being undergone, but of illustrations to prove a point. Even if we were to believe that Quentin is actually coming to conclusions as we watch him, those conclusions—his acceptance of himself—do not lead logically or dramatically to Holga. It is as though he stepped to the front of the stage and said, "I have a few hours to kill before I meet a plane. Let me spend them describing the human condition."

"Let me give you a piece advice," says Gregory Solomon, the aged furniture dealer in *The Price* (1968); "it's not that you can't believe nothing, that's not so hard—it's that you still got to believe it. *That's* hard." As this speech makes clear, Miller's most recent play is set in the same thematic country as *After the Fall* and *Incident at Vichy*. Here again are the rival brothers and, in the expositional past, the father whose business failed and the mother whose marriage did, elements already familiar from *After the Fall*. In *The Price*, Miller brings the two brothers—one a policeman, the other a successful surgeon—to the top floor of a brownstone house, the family home before 1929, where, surrounded by the furniture of the past, they try to face the mutual accusation that has dogged them for years, the last sixteen of which they have not

---

[2] Robert Anderson's most recent play, apparently an attempt to lay his own ghosts (as *Fall* must have been for Miller), suffers from the same problem. The narrator-protagonist of *I Never Sang for My Father* (1968), who feels guilty that he could never love his father, manages to reduce a human problem to a bromidic discussion, all the more unsatisfying because the old man is an admirable, unlikable, self-pitying bully, a character too idiosyncratic to fit the stereotyped pattern to which the play keeps reverting.

seen or talked to one another. Their encounter is a long, quarreling discussion, a kind of mutual analysis, which would be impossible (the characters are always saying that they want to get things clear, as though they were panel participants) if it were not that Miller so carefully builds the scene that the audience gets caught up in the self-justifying attacks, shifting allegiance from one brother to the other as new revelations, new modifications, new admissions are uncovered.

Victor, the policeman, blames Walter for not having lent him enough money to finish college and for having left him to care for the father, presumably broke and broken because of the crash. Walter accuses Victor of knowing that the father was not that helpless, at least financially, and of choosing his policeman's lot to keep Walter guilty. Although Miller says, in a "Production Note" to the published play, that a "balance of sympathy" in the playing of the brothers is a thematic and theatrical necessity, it is Victor, the conventional good son(whatever his motivation, he did look after the father) and the voice for the play's few social criticisms, who retains the sympathy of the audience. He is, after all, the protagonist. In an emotional paralysis as the play opens, he is unable to make a decision about his retirement from the force, an event toward which he and his wife once looked as a new beginning. Suspecting that his past has been meaningless and that his future can be no better, he hesitates to act, an indecision that is destroying his marriage. The play's action is to take him—as *After the Fall* takes Quentin—beyond all attempts to shift the blame for his life to his brother, his father, anyone outside himself. He learns to pay his own price for the choice he made, even though he recognizes that the choice was partly an accident of psychology and social situation. There is no grand revelatory moment as a result of his self-discovery. His wife does tell him not to bother to change out of his uniform as they go out to dinner and a movie, an acceptance on her part of what he is. No longer immobilized by the past, he is able not only to sell the furniture, but to take his fencing mask and foil as souvenirs.

If this were all there were to *The Price*, it would not be that welcome a change from *Fall* and *Vichy*. Its strength lies in the character of Gregory Solomon, who dominates the play when he is on stage and, through well-timed intrusions during the brothers' discussion, continues to be a formidable presence even when he has moved to the periphery of the central action. A man almost ninety years old, a retired appraiser, who finds in the furniture an opportunity to begin again, he is an embodiment of the idea that life is the product of belief beyond disbelief. More important he is Arthur Miller's first real comic character, a creation that realizes some of the possibilities implicit in Willy Loman's happier scenes. Solomon is a Russian-Jewish stereotype who escapes caricature and turns into a shrewd, garrulous, idiomatic, lovable old man. At the end of the play, he is left alone with the furniture. He turns on the Victrola and begins to play a laughing record from the 1920's that the audience has already heard. As the laughter begins, it has a sardonic quality about it, as though it were a comment on everything that the play has presented, but Solomon begins to chuckle, then to laugh with the record. The man swallows the machine, life pervades the stage, and *The Price* escapes being simply another demonstration about the nature of man.[3]

---

[3] I wrote this description of the end of the play after having seen the pre-Broadway tryout in Philadelphia, in which David Burns gave a remarkable performance as Solomon. When the play reached New York, the ending had been changed so that Solomon laughed alone. Whether it was a temporary change having to do with the replacement for Burns, who had become ill, or whether Miller imagined that he had improved his curtain, the new version was much less effective than the earlier one. The published play, which had been prepared for the press before the final changes were made (for instance, its two acts became one in New York), contains the original ending. Miller's description of the laughter, "howling helplessly to the air," suggests the double response I felt in Philadelphia. In that form, it is a superb miniature restatement of the play's theme.

TWO

Edward Albee:
Don't Make Waves

---

*Something tells me it's all
happenin' at the zoo.*
—SIMON AND GARFUNKEL

Edward Albee is inescapably *the* American playwright of the
1960's. His first play, *The Zoo Story*, opened in New York, on a
double bill with Samuel Beckett's *Krapp's Last Tape*, at the
Provincetown Playhouse on January 14, 1960. In his Introduction
to *Three Plays* (1960), Albee tells how his play, which was written in 1958, passed from friend to friend, from country to country, from manuscript to tape to production (in Berlin in 1959)
before it made its way back to the United States. "It's one of those

24

things a person has to do," says Jerry; "sometimes a person has to go a very long distance out of his way to come back a short distance correctly."

For Albee, once *The Zoo Story* had finished its peregrinations, the trip uptown—psychologically and geographically—was a short one. During 1960, there were two other Albee prouctions, largely unheralded—*The Sandbox*, which has since become a favorite for amateurs, and *Fam and Yam*, a *bluette*, a joke growing out of his having been ticketed as the latest white hope of the American theater. These were essentially fugitive productions of occasional pieces. In 1961, one of the producers of *The Zoo Story*, Richard Barr, joined by Clinton Wilder in the producing organization that is always called Theater 196? after whatever the year, offered *The American Dream*, first on a double bill with William Flanagan's opera *Bartleby*, for which Albee and James Hinton, Jr., did the libretto,[1] and later, when the opera proved

---

[1] According to a letter from Albee (October 13, 1966), Hinton, who was writing the libretto, fell ill and Albee finished the work; as he remembers it, he wrote the Prologue, the last scene, and did "considerable revision" on the other three scenes. The title page of the vocal score lists Flanagan with Hinton and Albee as one of the authors of the libretto. The opera, of course, is based on Herman Melville's "Bartleby the Scrivener." My responses are highly suspect since I did not see the opera in production; I read the libretto and listened to at least two of my friends—unfortunately, not at the same time— make piano assaults on the score. I would guess that the most effective scene, musically and dramatically, is Scene 2 in which Mr. Allan (the name given to Melville's nameless lawyer-narrator) goes to his office on Sunday morning and finds Bartleby there; his aria carries him from complacent Sunday-morning ruminations (mostly to slightly doctored lines from Melville) through the confrontation with Bartleby to his attempt to make sense of this clerk who will not do his work and will not go away. Bartleby's one-note "I would prefer not to" echoes in variations all through Allan's confusion in this scene. Less happy moments musically are church bells which chime in the piano part after they have been mentioned in the libretto and the calculated contrast at the end of Scene 3 when beyond the huffing-puffing violence can be heard the soprano of the office boy singing his way back on stage with the ballad-like song that identifies him. For the most part, the libretto is a softening of Melville's story. Since the Bartleby of the story makes a claim on the lawyer which cannot be (or is not) fulfilled, Melville's work has an obvious thematic relevance to Albee's. What is missing in the dramatization is Melville's superb ambiguity; there is not even an attempt in the opera to get the effect that Melville achieves when his narrator, who believes that "the easiest way of life is the best," manages to comfort himself by pigeon-holing Bartleby when the clerk is no longer alive and mutely accusing. The

unsuccessful, with an earlier Albee play *The Death of Bessie Smith*. During the next few years, there were frequent revivals of both *Zoo* and *Dream*, often to help out a sagging Barr-Wilder program, as in 1964 (by which time Albee had become a co-producer) when first *Dream* and later *Zoo* were sent in as companion pieces to LeRoi Jones's *Dutchman*, after Samuel Beckett's *Play* and Fernando Arrabal's *The Two Executioners*, which opened with Jones's play, were removed from the bill. Albee had become an off-Broadway staple.

By that time, of course, Albee had become something else as well. With *Who's Afraid of Virginia Woolf?* (1962), he had moved to Broadway and had a smashing commercial success. By a process of escalation, he had passed from promising to established playwright. After *Woolf*, Albee productions averaged one a year: *The Ballad of the Sad Café* (1963), *Tiny Alice* (1964), *Malcolm* (1966), *A Delicate Balance* (1966) and *Everything in the Garden* (1967). None of these were successes in Broadway terms (by *Variety*'s chart of hits and flops), but except for *Malcolm*, a gauche and imperceptive adaptation of James Purdy's novel of that name, which closed after seven performances, all of them had respectable runs and generated their share of admiration and antagonism from critics and public alike.

Although favorable reviews helped make the Albee reputation, critics have consistently praised with one hand, damned with the other.[2] If Harold Clurman's "Albee on Balance" (*The New York*

"Oh, Bartleby, Oh, humanity" that ends the opera is sentimental although it probably means to be something more exalted. The "Ah, Bartleby! Ah, humanity!" that ends Melville's story is ironic.

Flanagan, to whom Albee dedicated *The Zoo Story*, did the music for *The Sandbox*, *The Ballad of the Sad Café*, and *Malcolm*. Flanagan's music for *The Sandbox* is printed with the play in Margaret Mayorga's *The Best Short Plays*, 1959–1960.

[2] My own reviews, from *The Zoo Story* (*The Reporter*, February 16, 1961) to *Everything in the Garden* (*The Reporter*, December 28, 1967), have suggested with a decreasing amount of flippancy that there is less to Albee than meets the eye. Although my review of *Virginia Woolf* (*Drama Survey*, Fall, 1963) now seems unnecessarily condescending, my general misgivings about Albee as a playwright have not disappeared. What has disappeared, alas, is a letter that Albee sent to *The Reporter* to straighten me out after my review of *The Zoo Story*.

Times, January 13, 1967) treats Albee as a serious playwright and if Robert Brustein's "A Third Theater" (*The New York Times Magazine,* September 25, 1966) seems to dismiss him as a solemn one, only Broadway serious, the recent collections of their reviews—Clurman's *The Naked Image* and Brustein's *Seasons of Discontent*—indicate that both critics have had the same kind of reservations about Albee from the beginning. Albee, contrariwise, has had reservations of his own. From his pettish Introduction to *The American Dream* to the press conference he called to chastise the critics for their reactions to *Tiny Alice,* he has regularly used interviews and the occasional nondramatic pieces he has written to suggest that the critics lack understanding, humility, responsibility.

In spite of (perhaps because of) the continuing quarrel between Albee and his critics—a love-hate relationship in the best Albee tradition—the playwright's reputation has grown tremendously. It was in part the notoriety of *Who's Afraid of Virginia Woolf?* that turned Albee into a popular figure, and certainly the publicity surrounding the making of the movie version of *Woolf* helped to keep Albee's name in the popular magazines. Whatever the cause, Albee is now the American playwright whose name has become a touchstone, however ludicrously it is used. Thus, Thomas Meehan, writing an article on "camp" for *The New York Times Magazine* (March 21, 1965), solicits Andy Warhol's opinion of *Tiny Alice* ("I liked it because it was so empty"), and William H. Honan, interviewing Jonathan Miller for the same publication (January 22, 1967), manages to get Miller to repeat a commonplace criticism of Albee he has used twice before.

All this is simply the chi-chi mask over a serious concern with Albee. According to recent reports of the American Educational Theatre Association, Albee has been jockeying for second place (after Shakespeare) in the list of playwrights most produced on college campuses. In 1963–64, he held second place; in 1964–65, he was nosed out by Ionesco. The attractiveness of short plays to college dramatic groups—as Ionesco's presence suggests—helps explain the volume of Albee productions, but, with *The Zoo Story* invading text anthologies and *Virginia Woolf* climbing onto reading lists, it is clear that the interest in Albee in colleges is more than a matter of mechanics. More and more articles on Albee turn up in critical quarterlies—always a gauge of academic fashions—and those that are printed are only the tip of a happily submerged iceberg; Walter Meserve, one of the editors of *Modern Drama*, estimated in 1966 that 80 per cent of the submissions on American drama were about four authors: O'Neill, Williams, Miller, and Albee. The interest abroad is as intense as it is here. This is clear not only from the fact that the plays are translated and performed widely, but in the desire of audiences to talk or to hear about the playwright. Clurman, in that article in the *Times*, reporting on lecture audiences in Tokyo and Tel Aviv, says that there was more curiosity about Albee than any other American playwright. Albee's position, then, is analogous to that of Tennessee Williams in the 1950's. He recognizes this himself. When he wrote *Fam and Yam* in 1960, he let Yam (the Young American Playwright) bunch Albee with Jack Gelber, Jack Richardson, and Arthur Kopit. In an interview in *Diplomat* (October, 1966) he suggested that playwrights should be hired as critics; it was now Williams and Arthur Miller that he listed with himself.

In "Which Theatre Is the Absurd One?" (*The New York Times Magazine*, February 25, 1962), Albee wrote that "in the end a public will get what it deserves and no better." If he is right, his work may finally condemn or justify the taste of American theater audiences in the 1960's. More than likely, a little of both.

"I consider myself in a way the most eclectic playwright who ever wrote," Albee once told an interviewer (*Transatlantic Review*, Spring, 1963), and then he went on to make an elaborate joke about how he agreed with the critics that twenty-six playwrights—three of whom he had never read—had influenced him. Critics do have a way of getting influence-happy when they write about Albee—particularly Brustein, who persists in calling him an imitator—but they have good reason. There are such strong surface dissimilarities among the Albee plays that it is easier and in some ways more rewarding to think of *The Zoo Story* in relation to Samuel Beckett and Harold Pinter and *A Delicate Balance* in terms of T. S. Eliot and Enid Bagnold than it is to compare the two plays, even though both start from the same dramatic situation: the invasion (by Jerry, by Harry and Edna) of private territory (Peter's bench, Tobias's house). Yet, the comparison is obvious once it is made. Each new Albee play seems to be an experiment in form, in style (even if it is someone else's style), and yet there is unity in his work as a whole. This is apparent in the devices and the characters that recur, modified according to context, but it is most obvious in the repetition of theme, in the basic assumptions about the human condition that underlie all his work.

In *A Delicate Balance*, Tobias and his family live in a mansion in the suburbs of hell, that existential present so dear to contemporary writers, in which life is measured in terms of loss, love by its failure, contact by its absence. In that hell, there are many mansions—one of which is Peter's bench—and all of them are cages in the great zoo story of life. Peter's bench is a kind of sanctuary, both a refuge from and an extension of the stereotypical upper-middle-class existence (tweeds, horn-rimmed glasses, job in publishing, well-furnished apartment, wife, daughters, cats, parakeets) with which Albee has provided him—a place where he can safely not-live and have his nonbeing. This is the way Jerry sees Peter, at least, and—since the type is conventional enough in contemporary theater, from avant-garde satire to Broadway revue—it is safe to assume that the play does, too. Although Albee intends a little satirical fun at Peter's expense (the early needling scenes are very successful), it is clear that the stereotyping of Peter is an image of his condition, not a cause of it. Jerry, who plays "the old pigeonhole bit" so well, is another, a contrasting cliché, and it is the play's business to show that he and Peter differ only in that he does not share Peter's complacency. Just before Jerry attacks in earnest, he presents the play's chief metaphor:

> I went to the zoo to find out more about the way people exist with animals, and the way animals exist with each other, and with people too. It probably wasn't a fair test, what with everyone separated by

bars from everyone else, the animals for the most part from each other, and always the people from the animals. But, if it's a zoo, that's the way it is.

"Private wings," says Malcolm in the play that bears his name. "Indeed, that *is* an extension of separate rooms, is it not?" In a further extension of a joke that is no joke, Agnes, in *A Delicate Balance*, speaks of her "poor parents, in their separate heavens." *Separateness* is the operative word for Albee characters, for, even though his zoo provides suites for two people (*Who's Afraid of Virginia Woolf?*) or for more (*A Delicate Balance*), they are furnished with separate cages. "It's sad to know you've gone through it all, or most of it, without . . ." says Edna in one of the fragmented speeches that characterize *A Delicate Balance*, as though thoughts too were separate, "that the one body you've wrapped your arms around . . . the only skin you've ever known . . . is your own—and that it's dry . . . and not warm." This is a more restrained, a more resigned variation on the Nurse's desperate cry in *Bessie Smith*, ". . . I am tired of my skin. . . . I WANT OUT!"

Violence is one of the ways of trying to get out. The Nurse is an illustration of this possibility; she is an embryonic version of Martha in *Virginia Woolf*, with most of the venom, a little of the style, and practically none of the compensating softness of the later character, and she hits out at everyone around her. Yet, she never escapes herself, her cage. The other possibility is love (that, too, a form of penetration), but the Albee plays are full of characters who cannot (Nick in *Virginia Woolf*) or will not (Tobias, the Nurse) make that connection. The persistent images are of withdrawal, the most graphic being the one in *A Delicate Balance*, the information that Tobias in fact withdrew and came on Agnes's belly the last time they had sex. Although failed sex is a convenient metaphor for the failure of love, its opposite will not work so well. Connection is not necessarily contact, and it is contact—or rather its absence, those bars that bother Jerry—that preoccupies Albee. He lets Martha and George make fun of the lack-of-communication cliché in *Virginia Woolf*, but it is that cultural commonplace on which much of Albee's work is built. Jerry's story about his landlady's vicious dog—although he over-explains it—is still Albee's most effective account of an attempt to get through those bars, out of that skin (so effective, in fact, that Tobias uses a variation of it in *Balance* when he tells about his cat). Accepting the dog's attacks on him as a form of recognition, Jerry tries first to win his affection (with hamburger) and, failing that, to kill him (with poisoned hamburger: it is difficult to differentiate between the tools of love and hate). In the end, he settles for an accommodation, one in which he and the dog ignore each other. His leg remains unbitten, but he feels a sense of loss in the working arrangement: "We neither love nor hurt because we do not try to reach each other."[3]

"Give me *any* person . . ." says Lawyer in *Tiny Alice*. "He'll take what he gets for . . . what he wishes it to be. AH, it is what I have always wanted, he'll say, looking terror and betrayal straight in the eye. Why not: face the inevitable and call it what you have always wanted." The context is a special one here, a reference to Julian's impending martyrdom to God-Alice, who comes to him in the form or forms he expects. I purposely dropped from the Lawyer's speech the references to "martyr" and "saint" which follow parenthetically after the opening phrase, for as it stands above,

[3] One of the persistent—and, I think, unfortunate—ways of reading Albee is to assume that the animals and the animal imagery which figure in so many of the plays are being used to make some instructive point about man's nature. For instance, John V. Hagopian, in a letter to the *New York Review of Books* (April 8, 1965), insisted that the point of *Tiny Alice* is that "man must embrace his animal nature." It is true that Brother Julian has an abstraction problem in that play, but his acceptance of the world (and all the animals and birds that wander through the lines in *Alice*) is not—as the ambiguity in his death scene indicates—a sure sign of either health or reality. There is a certain amount of sentimentality in such a reading of the play, at least if the "embrace" is taken as positive rather than factual. In Albee's work there is a general equation between man and animal. This can be seen in *The Zoo Story*, not only in Jerry's dog tale and the zoo metaphor, but in the confusion of Peter's children with his cats and parakeets. Perhaps there is something ennobling, an up-the-chain-of-being slogan, in Jerry's comfort to Peter, "you're not really a vegetable; it's all right, you're an animal," but as Mac the Knife would say, "What's the percentage?" Albee's animals reflect the predicament of his men. There are still bars to look through, accommodations to be made.

the speech might serve as advertising copy for the Albee world in which his characters exist and—very occasionally—struggle. The too-obvious symbol of *The American Dream*, the muscle-flexing young man who is only a shell, empty of love or feeling, is, in Mommy's words, "a great deal more like it." *Like it*, but not *it*. Appearance is what she wants, for reality, as Grandma's account of the mutilation of the other "bumble" indicates, is dangerous.

The American Dream is a pat example of, to use Lawyer's words again, "How to come out on top, going under." Whether the accommodation is embraced (*Dream*) or accepted with a sense of loss (Jerry and the dog), it is always there, a way of coping instead of a way of life. It can be disguised in verbal trappings—comic (the games in *Virginia Woolf*) or serious (the religiosity of *Tiny Alice*, the conventional labels of *A Delicate Balance*). In the absence of substance, it can be given busy work; Girard Girard spells everything out in *Malcolm*: "You will move from the mansion to the chateau, and from the chateau back. You will surround yourself with your young beauties, and hide your liquor where you will. You will . . . go on, my dear." The unhidden liquor in *A Delicate Balance* (even more in *Virginia Woolf*, where it serves the dramatic action, as lubricant and as occasional rest) provides an example of such busyness: all the playing at bartending, the weighty deliberation over whether to have anisette or cognac, the concern over the quality of a martini. The rush of words (abuse or elegance) and the press of activity (however meaningless) sustain the Albee characters in a tenuous relationship (a delicate balance) among themselves and in the face of the others, the ones outside, and—beyond that—the nameless terror.

Implicit in my discussion of the separateness of the Albee characters and the bogus forms of community they invent to mask the fact that they are alone is the assumption that this is Albee's view of the human condition. The deliberate refusal to locate the action of his most recent plays (*Tiny Alice, Malcolm, A Delicate Balance*) strengthens that assumption. In fact, only two of Albee's settings can be found in atlases—Central Park (*The Zoo Story*) and Memphis (*Bessie Smith*). Even these, like the undifferentiated Southern town he borrowed from Carson McCullers for *The Ballad of the Sad Café* and the fictional New England college town of *Virginia Woolf*, might easily serve as settings for a universal drama. Yet, in much of his work, particularly in the early plays, there is a suggestion, even an insistence, that the problem is a localized one, that the emptiness and loneliness of the characters are somehow the result of a collapse of values in the Western world in general, in the United States in particular. *The American Dream*, he says in his Preface to the play, is "an attack on the substitution of artificial for real values in our society." Such an attack is implicit in the depiction of Peter in *The Zoo Story*.

It is in *Virginia Woolf* that this side of Albee's "truth" is most evident. He is not content that his characters perform an action which carries implications for an audience that far transcend the action itself. He must distribute labels. George may jokingly identify himself, as history professor, with the humanities, and Nick, as biology professor, with science, and turn their meeting into a historical-inevitability parable about the necessary decline of the West, but Albee presumably means it. Calling the town New Carthage and giving George significant throw-away lines ("When I was sixteen and going to prep school, during the Punic Wars . . .") are cute ways of underlining a ponderous intention. I would not go so far as Diana Trilling (*Esquire*, December, 1963) and suggest that George and Martha are the Washingtons, or Henry Hewes (*The Best Plays of 1962–1963*) that Nick is like Nikita Khrushchev, but Albee is plainly intent on giving his sterility tale an obvious cultural point. Martha's joke when Nick fails to "make it in the sack" is apparently no joke at all: "But that's how it is in a civilized society."

My own tendency is to brush all this grandiose symbol-making under the rug to protect what I admire in *Virginia Woolf*. If we can believe Albee's remarks in the *Diplomat* interview, however, all this comprises the "play's subtleties"; in faulting the movie version of his play, he says, "the entire political argument was taken out, the argument between history and science."[4] The

---

[4] Perhaps we cannot believe him. In an article on the making of the movie (*McCall's*, June, 1966), Roy Newquist quotes Albee: "They had filmed the

chasm that confronts the Albee characters may, then, be existential chaos or a materialistic society corrupt enough to make a culture hero out of . . . (whom? to each critic his own horrible example, and there are those would pick Albee himself), or a combination in which the second of these is an image of the first.

There is nothing unusual about this slightly unstable mixture of philosophic assumption and social criticism; it can be found in the work of Tennessee Williams and, from quite a different perspective, that of Eugène Ionesco. The differentiation is useful primarily because it provides us with insight into the shape that Albee gives his material. If the lost and lonely Albee character is an irrevocable fact—philosophically, theologically, psychologically —if all that *angst* is inescapable, then his plays must necessarily be reflections of that condition; any gestures of defiance are doomed to failure. If, however, the Albee character is a product of his societal context and if that context is changeable (not necessarily politically, but by an alteration of modes of behavior between one man and another), then the plays may be instructive

---

play, with the exception of five or ten minutes of relatively unimportant material." Although I quote from a number of interviews in this chapter, I am aware that interviews, at best, are doubtful sources of information and opinion. There are the obvious dangers of misquotation and spur-of-the-moment remarks which are untrue (is *The Ballad of the Sad Café* an earlier play than *Virginia Woolf*, as Albee told Thomas Lask in a *Times* interview, October 27, 1963, or are we to believe the dates accompanying the Atheneum editions of his plays?) or only momentarily true (the conflicting opinions about the movie version of *Woolf*). Beyond that, it is clear that Albee, when he is not on his high horse, likes to kid around. I am not thinking of an occasion like the joint interview with John Gielgud (*Atlantic*, April, 1965), where the chummy inside jocularity masks what must have been a major difference of opinion over *Tiny Alice*, but of an interview like the one in *Transatlantic Review*, in which Albee is very solemn and still sounds as though he is putting Digby Diehl on. Or the one in *Diplomat* that got me into this footnote in the first place, for in that one Albee uses what I assume is a running gag, of which Otis L. Guernsey, Jr., never seems aware. In three variations on a single line, he ponders whether or not *Woolf*, *Alice*, and *Balance* are comedies on the basis of whether or not the characters get what they want or think they want. The joke, of course, is that the line comes from Grandma's curtain speech from *The American Dream*: "So, let's leave things as they are right now . . . while everybody's happy . . . while everybody's got what he wants . . . or everybody's got what he thinks he wants. Good night, dears."

fables. He has dismissed American drama of the 1930's as propaganda rather than art, and he has disavowed solutions to anything. Still, in several statements he has suggested that there are solutions—or, at least, alternatives. Surely that possibility is implicit in his description of *The American Dream* as an "attack." In the *Transatlantic Review* interview, he said that "the responsibility of the writer is to be a sort of demonic social critic—to present the world and people in it as he sees it and say 'Do you like it? If you don't like it change it.'" In the *Atlantic*, he said, "I've always thought . . . that it was one of the responsibilities of playwrights to show people how they are and what their time is like in the hope that perhaps they'll change it."

Albee, then, shares with most American playwrights an idea of the utility of art, the supposition not only that art should convey truth, but that it should do so to some purpose. There is a strong strain of didacticism in all his work, but it is balanced by a certain ambiguity about the nature of the instructive fable. In interviews, he harps on how much of the creative process is subconscious, how little he understands his own work, how a play is to be experienced rather than understood. Insofar as this is not sour grapes pressed to make an aesthetic (his reaction to the reviews of *Tiny Alice*), it may be his way of recognizing that there is a conflict between his attitude toward man's situation and his suspicion (or hope: certainly *conviction* is too strong a word) that something can, or ought, to be done about it; between his assumption that this is hell we live in and his longing to redecorate it.

Whatever the nature of the chasm on the edge of which the Albee characters teeter so dexterously, to disturb the balance is to invite disaster or—possibly—salvation. If the conflict that I suggest above is a real one, it should be reflected in the plays in which one or more characters are willing to risk disaster. *The American Dream* and *The Sandbox* can be passed over here because, except for the sentimental death of Grandma at the end of the latter, they are diagnostic portraits of the Albee world, not actions performed in that setting. *The Death of Bessie Smith* and *The Ballad of the Sad Café* are more to the point, but they are also special cases. Although risks are taken (the Intern goes outside to examine

Bessie; Amelia takes in Cousin Lymon in *Ballad*), the plays
are less concerned with these acts than they are with the kind
of expositional presentation—not particularly satirical in this
case—that we get in *Dream*. Even so, the Intern's risk is meaningless since the woman is already dead; and Amelia's love is necessarily doomed by the doctrine the McCullers novella expounds—
that it is difficult to love but almost impossible to be loved—and
by the retrospective form the play took when Albee saddled it with
a maudlin message-giving narrator. *Tiny Alice* and *Malcolm* are
two of a kind, particularly if we consider them as corruption-of-
innocence plays, although there is also a similarity of sorts between Malcolm's attempt to put a face on his absent father and
Julian's attempt to keep from putting a face on his abstracted
Father. They are even similar in that Albee, sharing a popular-
comedy misconception about what that snake was up to in the
Garden, uses sex as his sign of corruption—ludicrously in *Alice,*
snickeringly in *Malcolm.* Traditionally, one of two things happens
in plays in which the innocent face the world: either they become
corrupted and learn to live with it (the standard Broadway
maturity play) or they die young and escape the corruption
(Synge's *Deirdre of the Sorrows* or Maxwell Anderson's *Winter-
set*). In the Albee plays, both things happen. Julian dies after
accepting the world (edited to fit his preconceptions about it) and
Malcolm dies, muttering "I've . . . lost so much," and loss, as the
plays from *The Zoo Story* to *A Delicate Balance* insist, is what
you gain in learning to live with it. There are extenuating circumstances for the deaths in these plays (Julian's concept of God is
tied in with his desire to be a martyr; Malcolm's death is borrowed
from Purdy, although Albee does not seem to understand what
Purdy was doing with it in the novel), but these plays, too, are
illustrations of the Albee world, and the deaths are more sentimental than central. *Everything in the Garden* is such an unlikely
wedding of Albee and the late Giles Cooper, whose English play
was the source of the American adaptation, that it is only superfi-
cially characteristic of Albee's work.

It is in *The Zoo Story, Who's Afraid of Virginia Woolf?* and *A*

Delicate Balance that one finds dramatic actions by which the ambiguity of Albee's attitudes may be tested. In *The Zoo Story*, so goes the customary reading, Jerry confronts the vegetative Peter, forces him to stand his ground, dies finally on his own knife held in Peter's hand. In that suicidal act, Jerry becomes a scapegoat who gives his own life so that Peter will be knocked out of his complacency and learn to live, or LIVE. Even Albee believes this, or he said he did in answer to a question from Arthur Gelb (*The New York Times*, February 15, 1960): "Though he dies, he passes on an awareness of life to the other character in the play." If this is true, then presumably we are to take seriously—not as a dramatic device, but for its content—Jerry's "you have to make a start somewhere" speech in which he expounds the steps-to-love doctrine, a soggy inheritance from Carson McCullers ("A Tree. A Rock. A Cloud.") and Truman Capote (*The Grass Harp*). That the start should be something a great deal less gentle than the McCullers-Capote inheritance might suggest is not surprising when we consider that violence and death became twisted life symbols during the 1950's (as all the kids said after James Dean's fatal smashup, "Boy, that's living") and, then, turned literary in the 1960's (as in Jack Richardson's *Gallows Humor* and all the motorcycle movies from *The Wild Angels* to *Scorpio Rising*).

The problem with that reading is not that it is awash with adolescent profundity, which might well annoy some of the audience, but that it seems to be working against much that is going on within the play. Although Albee prepares the audience for the killing, it has always seemed gratuitous, a melodramatic flourish. The reason may be that it tries to suggest one thing (salvation) while the logic of the play demands something else. Except for a couple of expositional lapses, Jerry is too well drawn a character —self-pitying and aggressive, self-deluding and forlorn—to become the conventional "hero" (Albee uses that word in the Gelb interview) that the positive ending demands. He may well be so aware of his separation from everyone else that he plans or improvises ("could I have planned all this? No . . . no, I couldn't have. But I think I did") his own murder in a last desperate

attempt to make contact, but there is nothing in the play to indicate that he succeeds. At the end, Peter is plainly a man knocked
off his balance, but there is no indication that he has fallen into
"an awareness of life." In fact, the play we are watching has
already been presented in miniature in the dog story, and all Jerry
gained from that encounter was "solitary but free passage."
"There are some things in it that I don't really understand," Albee
told Gelb. One of them may be that the play itself denies the
romantic ending.

Virginia Woolf is a more slippery case. Here, too, the play
works against the presumably upbeat ending, but Albee may be
more aware that this is happening. According to the conventions
of Broadway psychology, as reflected, for instance, in a play like
William Inge's *The Dark at the Top of the Stairs*, in a moment of
crisis two characters come to see themselves clearly. Out of their
knowledge a new maturity is born, creating an intimacy that has
not existed before and a community that allows them to face their
problems (if not solve them) with new courage. This was the
prevailing cliché of the serious Broadway play of the 1950's, and
it was still viable enough in the 1960's to take over the last act of
Lorraine Hansberry's *The Sign in Sidney Brustein's Window* and
turn an interesting play into a conventional one. *Virginia Woolf*
uses, or is used by, this cliché.

Although the central device of the play is the quarrel between
George and Martha, the plot concerns their nonexistent son. From
George's "Just don't start on the bit, that's all," before Nick and
Honey enter, the play builds through hints, warnings, revelations
until "sonny-Jim[5] is created and then destroyed. Snap, goes the
illusion. Out of the ruins, presumably, new strength comes. The
last section, which is to be played "very softly, very slowly," finds
George offering new tenderness to Martha, assuring her that the
time had come for the fantasy to die, forcing her—no longer
maliciously—to admit that she is afraid of Virginia Woolf. It is

[5] One of the "echoes"—to use Albee's word (*The Best Plays of 1964–1965*) for the unanchored allusions in *Tiny Alice*—must surely be a song that
little boys used to sing: "Lulu had a baby,/Named it Sonny Jim,/Threw it
in the piss-pot/To see if it could swim."

"Time for bed," and there is nothing left for them to do but go together to face the dark at the top of the stairs. As though the rejuvenation were not clear enough from the last scene, there is the confirming testimony in Honey's tearful reiteration "I want a child" and Nick's broken attempt to sympathize, "I'd like to. . . ." Then, too, the last act is called "The Exorcism," a name that had been the working title for the play itself.

As neat as Inge, and yet there is something wrong with it. How can a relationship like that of Martha and George, built so consistently on illusion (the playing of games), be expected to have gained something from a sudden admission of truth? What confirmation is there in Nick and Honey when we remember that she is drunk and hysterical and that he is regularly embarrassed by what he is forced to watch? There are two possibilities beyond the conventional reading suggested above. The last scene between Martha and George may be another one of their games; the death of the child may not be the end of illusion but an indication that the players have to go back to go and start again their painful trip to home. Although there are many indications that George and Martha live a circular existence, going over the same ground again and again, the development of the plot and the tone of the last scene (the use of monosyllables, for instance, instead of their customary rhetoric) seem to deny that the game is still going on. The other possibility is that the truth—as in *The Iceman Cometh* —brings not freedom but death. To believe otherwise is to accept the truth-maturity cliché as readily as one must buy the violence-life analogy to get the positive ending of *The Zoo Story*. My own suspicion is that everything that feels wrong about the end of *Virginia Woolf* arises from the fact that, like the stabbing in *Zoo*, it is a balance-tipping ending that conventional theater says is positive but the Albee material insists is negative.

In *A Delicate Balance*, the line is clearer. The titular balance is the pattern of aggression and withdrawal, accusation and guilt which Tobias and his family have constructed in order to cope with existence. Agnes suggests that Tobias's "We do what we can" might be "Our motto." When Harry and Edna invade the premises, trying to escape from the nameless fears that have attacked them, they come under the white flag of friendship. Tobias must decide whether or not to let them stay, knowing that the "disease" they carry is contagious and that infection in the household will likely upset the balance. His problem is one in metaphysical semantics, like Julian's in *Tiny Alice*, although God is not the word whose meaning troubles him. "Would you give friend Harry the shirt off your back, as they say?" asks Claire, before the invasion begins. "I *suppose* I would. He *is* my best friend," answers Tobias, and we hear echoes from *The American Dream*: "She's just a dreadful woman, but she *is* chairman of our woman's club, so naturally I'm terribly fond of her." *Dream*'s satirical fun about the emptiness of conventional language becomes deadly serious in *Balance*, for Tobias must decide whether the meaning of *friendship* is one with substance or only surface—whether *friendship* is a human relationship implying the possibility of action and risk, or simply a label, like *marriage* or *kinship*, to be fastened to a form of accommodation. As Pearl Bailey sang in *House of Flowers*, "What is a friend for? Should a friend bolt the door?" Tobias (having failed with his cat as Jerry failed with the dog) decides to try doing more than he can; in his long, broken speech in the last act, he displays his fear, indicates that he does not want Harry and Edna around, does not even like them, "BUT BY GOD . . . YOU STAY!!" His attempt fails because Harry and Edna, having decided that they would never risk putting real meaning into *friendship*, depart, leaving a depleted Tobias to rearrange his labels. He will have the help of Agnes, of course, which—on the balance—is a great deal, for she finds the conventional words of goodbye: "well, don't be strangers." Edna, who not many lines before made the "only skin" speech, answers, "Oh, good Lord, how could we be? Our lives are . . . the same." And so they are.

Thematically, *A Delicate Balance* is Albee's most precise statement. The gesture toward change, which seemed to fit so uncomfortably at the end of *The Zoo Story* and *Virginia Woolf*, has been rendered powerless within the action of *Balance*. Not only are Albee's characters doomed to live in the worst of all possible worlds; it is the only possible world. The impulse to do something about it can end only in failure. Yet, Albee cannot leave it at that. He cannot, like Samuel Beckett, let his characters turn their meaninglessness into ritual which has a way, on stage, of reasserting the meaning of the human being. He almost does so in *Virginia Woolf,* but his suspicion that games are not enough—a failure really to recognize that games are a form of truth as much as a form of lying—leads to the doubtful exorcism. Although the *angst*-er in Albee cannot let Tobias succeed, the latent reformer cannot help but make him heroic in his lost-cause gesture. He becomes an older, wearier, emptier Jerry, with only the unresisting air to throw himself on at the end.

"Better than nothing!" says Clov in *Endgame.* "Is it possible?" Out of the fastness of his wasteland, and against his better judgment, Albee cannot keep from hoping so.

In my critical and psychological naivety, I assume—as the paragraphs above show—that Albee's plays are really about the accommodations forced on man by his condition and his society. It is impossible, however, to get through a discussion of Albee without facing up to what might be called—on the analogy of the fashionable critical term *subtext*—his sub-subject matter. That is the "masochistic-homosexual perfume" that Robert Brustein found hanging so heavily over *The Zoo Story.* It is a perfume of little importance except insofar as it throws the audience off the scent of the play's real quarry.

A student stopped me on campus a few years ago, hoping I would be able to confirm the story that *Who's Afraid of Virginia Woolf?* was first performed by four men in a little theater in Montreal. When I expressed my doubt, he went off to call a friend in New York who knew someone who knew the man who had been stage manager . . . although somehow he never got the confirmation he wanted. Except for the circumstantiality of this account (why Montreal?), it was a familiar rumor. Albee, in the *Diplomat* interview, explained that it was a letter to the *Times* that started the whole thing, that from there it passed into print elsewhere, first as rumor, then as fact. "I know the difference between men and women," he said, "and I write both characters." The more sophisticated interpreters simply step over Albee's denials and assume that the play, whoever it was written for, is really about a homosexual marriage. The reasoning here is that homosexual marriages, lacking the sanctions of society, are extremely unstable and that to survive at all they must create fantasy devices to bind the couple together. Hence, the imaginary child—for what other kind of child could come from the union of two men? There is a kind of specious logic in operation here. The flaw in it, however, is the refusal to recognize how much fantasy is a part of any relationship, how two people who are close (husband and wife, lovers of whatever sex, good friends) invent private languages, private rituals, private games which set them off from the others. Jimmy and Alison play at squirrels-and-bears in John Osborne's *Look Back in Anger*, and Sid and Iris play wild-mountain-girl in *The Sign in Sidney Brustein's Window* without either couple being taken as surrogate homosexual unions. My own inclination would be to let Martha and George have their "little bugger," as they call the nonexistent child, without insisting that they have a big one.

I have heard the play praised for the clarity with which it presented a homosexual couple, but, for the most part, such readings are based on a rejection of the possibility that George and Martha may have a representative heterosexual marriage. A similar rejection takes place when the play is dismissed as a kind of homosexual denigration of conventional marriage. Surely the castrating female and the dominated male are such commonplace psychological stereotypes—on and off stage—that their appearance need not be taken as an indication of a perverse attempt to do in all the Darbys and Joans who provide America's divorce statistics. Besides, Martha and George do not really fit those stereotypes. They appear to at the beginning, but as the play goes on it becomes clear that they are really very evenly matched in a battle that has been going on seriously since Strindberg's *The Dance of Death* and comically since *The Taming of the Shrew*. Albee's male wins, as in Shakespeare, but only tentatively, as in

Strindberg. Not that Albee is particularly interested in the battle of the sexes as such. He has his own use for it, which is not to attack heterosexuality, but to present one of his many accommodation images: a well-matched pair of antagonists form a balance of sorts.

If a play like *Virginia Woolf* could call up the homosexual echoes, it is not surprising that *Tiny Alice* set them roaring. The opening scene between Cardinal and Lawyer is an exercise in bitchiness, primly nasty and insinuating, a marked contrast to the verbal exchanges between Martha and George. It passes from Lawyer's sneering comment on the caged cardinals ("uh, together . . . in conversation, as it were") to a variation on the old joke about the suitability of a boy or a clean old man, to hints of a schoolboy affair between the two men (Lawyer: "I'll have you do your obeisances. As you used to, old friend"), to mutual accusations in which Lawyer becomes an anus-entering hyena and Cardinal a mating bird. The business of the scene is apparently expositional, setting up the donation that will send Julian to Alice, so the tension between the two characters and the implication of their past relationship is gratuitous. So, too, is Lawyer's calling Butler "Darling" and "Dearest." The homosexual overtones in Julian (his attraction to the Welsh stableman, his kissing Miss Alice's hand "as he would kiss a Cardinal's ring," and the sensuality of his martyrdom dream in which the lion seems to mount him and he lingers over the entrance of the gladiator's prongs) might be more legitimate, a suggestion of the ambiguity of celibacy. Still, since he is sacrificed to heterosexuality—in that ludicrous scene in which he buries his head in Miss Alice's crotch, a cunnilingual first for the American stage—there is justice in Philip Roth's celebrated attack on "The Play that Dare Not Speak Its Name" (*New York Review of Books*, February 25, 1965). Roth accused Albee of writing "a homosexual daydream" about the martyrdom of the celibate male and disguising it as a metaphysical drama. Several weeks later (April 8, 1965), a letter to the editor insisted that there was no disguise at all in the play because a "tiny alice" is homosexual jargon for, as the writer so coyly put it, "a masculine derrière." Acting on this information, Bernard F. Dukore added an ingenious footnote to an article in *Drama Survey* (Spring, 1966) in which he considered that Julian, Butler, and Lawyer, all lovers of Miss Alice, might really be lovers of "tiny alice" and the opening doors at the end an anus symbol, but—as he went on to complain—a play that depends on a special argot for its symbolism is lost on a general audience. If "tiny alice" really is a gay word for anus and if Albee is using it consciously, he may be making an inside joke which has some relevance to his presumed serious play. If one of the points of the play is that all concepts of God (from Julian's abstraction to the mouse in the model) are creations of the men who hold them, a sardonic joke about God as a "tiny alice" is possible. Certainly, Albee has made that joke before, casually in *Virginia Woolf* (where George speaks of "Christ and all those girls") and more seriously in *The Zoo Story* (where one of the suggestions in Jerry's where-to-begin-to-love speech is "WITH GOD WHO IS A COLORED QUEEN WHO WEARS A KIMONO AND PLUCKS HIS EYEBROWS . . ."). On the other hand, the phrase could turn the play into an audience put-down such as the one described by Clay in *Dutchman*, in which he says that Bessie Smith, whatever the audience thought she was doing, was always saying, "Kiss my black ass."

This kind of speculation, hedged in as it is by *ifs* and *maybes*, is finally pointless. I almost wrote *fruitless*, but I stopped myself, assuming that my use of "inside joke" earlier is contribution enough to a silly game. How cute can a critic get without his tone corrupting his purpose? This question has relevance for the playwright, too. The problem about *Tiny Alice* is not whether there is a hidden homosexual joke and/or message, but that the obvious homosexual allusions seem to have little relevance to the plot device (the conspiracy to catch Julian), the play's central action (the martyrdom of Julian), or its presumed subject matter (the old illusion-reality problem). Unless Roth is right, the homosexual material is only decoration, different in quantity but not in kind from the additions and emphases that Albee brought to the already campy (old style) surface of Purdy's *Malcolm*.

The Zoo Story is the only Albee play in which a homosexual reading seems possible and usable in terms of what else the play is doing. It is, after all, the account of a meeting between two men in Central Park ("I'm not the gentleman you were expecting," says Jerry), in which one lets himself be impaled by the other, who has a phallic name. Jerry, dying, says, "I came unto you (*He laughs, so faintly*) and you have comforted me. Dear Peter." Jerry's casual references to the "colored queen" and the police "chasing fairies down from trees" on the other side of the park; his story of his one real love affair with the park superintendent's son, whom Otto Reinert (in *Modern Drama*) identifies with Peter by virtue of Peter's "proprietary claim" to the park bench; the implications in Jerry's "with fury because the pretty little ladies aren't pretty little ladies, with making money with your body which is an act of love and I could prove it"—all contribute to the possibility of this being a homosexual encounter. If it is, then much of the verbal and physical business of the play—Jerry's teasing, his wheedling, his tickling, the wrestling struggle for the bench—can be seen as an elaborate seduction which, since Jerry forces his partner to hold the knife, can only be summed up as getting a rise out of Peter. The dramatic fable can be read this way and still be relevant to the thematic material discussed earlier in this chapter. The problem comes when we consider the end of the play. If it is the positive ending that Albee suggested in the Gelb interview, if Jerry has passed on his "awareness of life," it must be Peter's initiation, and that, as Jerry says earlier, is "jazz of a very special hotel." On the other hand, as John Rechy keeps insisting in his seemingly endless novel, *City of Night*, a homosexual pickup in a park is a particularly workable image for the failure of contact between people.

"You know, I almost think you're serious," says Nick about something other than drama criticism, and George answers, "No, baby . . . *you* almost think you're serious, and it scares the hell out of you."

I feel a little that way about my very plausible reading of *The Zoo Story* in the section above. For if I am willing to accept the possibility of Peter as phallus, how can I deny all the interpreters who insist on seeing Jerry as Christ and Peter as the rock upon which to build his church? At least, the analogy of the homosexual pickup works comfortably within the action of the play and, less comfortably, with the thematic material. Despite the Biblical echoes ("I came unto you" again), the Christ-Jerry analogue is possible only to the extent that every sacrificial victim is a Christ figure, but that is a tautology which contributes nothing to an understanding of the play. If we see Jerry's suicidal finish as a sacrifice, we learn precious little about his action by nodding wisely and saying: oh, ho, Christ. We might as well say: oh, ho, Sydney Carton. Still, writers will use mythic and historical identifications for their characters (Tennessee Williams in *Orpheus Descending*), and critics will go myth-hunting and trap the slippery beasts. It has now become customary to dive into the underbrush of each new Albee play and bring them back alive.

Albee is partly to blame. He uses obvious symbols such as the muscular young man who is *The American Dream* and the athletic death figure in *The Sandbox*. He asks Julian and Miss Alice to form a pietà in *Tiny Alice* and the dying Julian to spread his arms to "resemble a crucifixion." In some notes prepared for a press conference, later printed in *The Best Plays of 1964–1965*, Albee said of *Tiny Alice*: "The play is full of symbols and allusions, naturally, but they are to be taken as echoes in a cave, things overheard, not fully understood at first." I take this to mean that they have no functional use in the play, in relation to either character or action, and that at best they provide a texture as allusive words do in some poetry. In a play, as in a poem, an allusion may uncover another realm of possibility (for instance, the ironies that keep emerging in *Peer Gynt*), but it can do so only if it does not wreck itself on the dramatic facts of the play. Take that pietà, for instance. It must either make clear something in the relationship between Julian and Miss Alice that has been implicit all along, or it must seem—as it did on stage—an exercise in literary pretentiousness.

Tiny Alice is the most blatant, but all the Albee plays insist on suggesting that there is more there than meets the eye and ear. This can be seen in the way Albee appears to be playing with the significance-seekers. In Agnes's "We become allegorical, my darling Tobias, as we grow older." In George's "Well, it's an allegory, really—probably—but it can be read as straight, cozy prose." Of course, Albee may mean this, too. In either case, he deserves to have the significant-name game played in his dramatic front yard. So Jerry becomes not only Christ but Jeremiah, and Julian not only Christ but Julian the Apostate. The Washingtons and the Khrushchevs get into *Virginia Woolf*. When Agnes, commenting on how much Claire has seen, says, "You were not named for nothing," she is presumably making a nasty crack about *claire* as an adjective meaning *bright*.[6] Yet audiences came out of the theater asking questions about St. Clare, St. Agnes, the Apocryphal Tobias, and even Miss Julie.

Albee may be fond of symbols and allusions, echoes and things overheard, but he plainly does not work—as the search for mythic analogies suggests—with dramatic images that come from outside his plays. This does not mean that he is the naturalist he occasionally claims to be, as when he told a *New York Times* interviewer (September 18, 1966) that even *Tiny Alice* was naturalistic. Even in *Virginia Woolf*, which is certainly the most naturalistic of his plays, the situation is basically unrealistic; the drinking party is a revelatory occasion, not a slice of life in a small New England college. For the most part, his characters have neither setting nor profession, and when they are defined by things, the process is either conventionally (Peter's possessions) or unconventionally (the contents of Jerry's room) stereotypical, so obviously so that realism is clearly not intended. Nor do the characters have biographies, at least of the kind one has come to expect from the psychological naturalism of the Broadway stage. *Virginia Woolf*, harping as it does on the parental hang-ups of its two principals, comes closest to that pattern, but it is never very clear in this play how much of the memory is invention, which of the facts are fantasy.

---

[6] According to my French dictionary, *claire*, as a feminine noun, means "burnt bones or washed ashes used for making cupels." Chew on that.

If *Virginia Woolf* and *The Zoo Story* are, at most, distant cousins of naturalistic drama, how much more remote are Albee's plainly absurdist plays (*The Sandbox, The American Dream*), his "mystery" play with its label-bearing characters (*Tiny Alice*), his drawing-room noncomedy (*A Delicate Balance*).

A close look at Albee's language provides the clearest indication of the nonrealistic character of his plays. *A Delicate Balance* is the most obvious example. The lines are consciously stilted, broken by elaborate parenthesis ("It follows, to my mind, that since I speculate I might, some day, or early evening I think more likely—some autumn dusk—go quite mad") or pulled up short by formal negative endings ("Must she not?"; "is it not?")—devices that call for inflections which stop the natural flow of speech. There are lines that are barely comprehensible ("One does not apologize to those for whom one must?"), which cannot be read without great deliberation. The verbal elaboration has particular point in this play since the language itself becomes a reflection of the artificiality of the characters and the setting, a pattern in which form replaces substance. This can best be seen in the play's most intricate digression. "What I find most astonishing," Agnes begins as the play opens, only to interrupt herself with her fantasy on madness. Her thought meanders through Tobias's practical attempt to get the after-dinner drinks, and we are fifteen speeches into the play, past two reappearances of the "astonish" phrase, before her opening sentence finally comes to an end. Seems to end, really, for the phrase recurs just before the final curtain, as Agnes goes her placidly relentless way—"to fill a silence," as the stage direction says—as though the intrusion of Harry and Edna and Tobias's painful attempt to deal with it were an easily forgotten interruption of the steady flow of nonevent.

In the *Atlantic* interview, explaining why he felt that English actors were needed for *Tiny Alice*, Albee said that he had moved from the "idiomatic" language of *Virginia Woolf* to something more formal. *A Delicate Balance* is a further step in elaboration. Yet, the language of the earlier plays, however idiomatic, is plainly artificial. Albee has used three main verbal devices from the beginning: interruption, repetition, and the set speech, the last of which makes use of the first two. The set speeches are almost formal recitations, as the playwright recognizes in *The Zoo Story* when he lets Jerry give his monologue a title: "THE STORY OF JERRY AND THE DOG!" There are similar speeches in all the plays: Jack's "Hey . . . Bessie" monologue which is the whole of Scene 3 of *Bessie Smith*; the Young Man's sentimental mutilation speech in *The American Dream*; George's "bergin" story and Martha's "Abandon-ed" speech in *Virginia Woolf*; the narrator's speeches in *Ballad*; Julian's dying soliloquy in *Tiny Alice*; Madame Girard's Entre-Scene monologue in *Malcolm*; Jack's direct address to the audience in *Garden*. Although Albee does not direct the speaker to step into a spotlight—as Tennessee Williams does with comparable speeches in *Sweet Bird of Youth*—he recognizes that these are essentially solo performances even when another character is on stage to gesture or grunt or single-word his way into the uneven but persistent flow of words. Of Tobias's big scene at the end of *Balance*, Albee says "This next is an aria."[7] In *The Zoo Story*, Jerry does not use a simple narration; his story is momentarily stopped for generalizing comments ("It always happens when I try to simplify things; people look up. But that's neither hither nor thither") and marked with repeated words ("The dog is black, all black; all black except . . .") and phrases ("I'll kill the dog with kindness, and if that doesn't work . . . I'll just kill him"). The word *laughter* punctuates the "bergin" story the way laughter itself presumably broke the cocktail-lounge murmur of the bar in which the boys were drinking.

It is not the long speeches alone that are built of interruption and repetition; that is the pattern of all the dialogue. On almost any page of *Virginia Woolf* you can find examples as obvious as this speech of George's: "Back when I was courting Martha—

---

[7] Albee's one attempt at fiction—the beginning of a novel which *Esquire* (July, 1963) printed as one of a group of works-in-progress, a fragment that was probably written for the occasion—is essentially a long speech like the ones in the plays. *The Substitute Speaker*, a play that Albee has been announcing since 1963, will contain the granddaddy of the solos if it really has in it the forty-minute speech Albee once promised.

well, don't know if that's exactly the right word for it—but back when I was courting Martha. . . ." Then comes Martha's "Screw, sweetie!" followed by another attempt from George, more successful this time, "At any rate, back when I was courting Martha," and off he goes into an account which involves their going "into a bar . . . you know, a *bar* . . . a whiskey, beer, and bourbon *bar*. . . ." Sometimes the repetitions become echoes that reach from act to act as when Martha's "snap" speech in Act Two is picked up by George in the snapdragon scene in Act Three. From *The Zoo Story* to *Everything in the Garden*, then, Albee has consciously manipulated language for effect; even when it sounds most like real speech—as in *Virginia Woolf*—it is an exercise in idiomatic artificiality.

At their best, these artifices are the chief devices by which Albee presents his dramatic images. Neither naturalist nor allegorist, he works the great middle area where most playwrights operate. He puts an action on stage—an encounter in a park that becomes a suicide-murder, a night-long quarrel that ends in the death of illusion, an invasion that collapses before the defenders can decide whether to surrender or to fight—which presumably has dramatic vitality in its own right and from which a meaning or meanings can emerge. The central situation—the encounter, the relationship implicit in the quarrel, the state of the defenders and the invaders —is defined almost completely in verbal terms. There is business, of course, but it is secondary. Jerry's poking and tickling Peter is only an extension of what he has been doing with words; George's attempt to strangle Martha is a charade not far removed from their word games. When events get more flamboyant—the shooting of Julian, Julia's hysterical scene with the gun—they tend to become ludicrous. The most obvious example in Albee of physical business gone wrong is the wrestling match between Miss Amelia and Marvin Macy in *The Ballad of the Sad Café*; the fact that it is the dramatic climax of the play does not keep it from looking silly on stage. Ordinarily, Albee does not need to ask his characters to *do* very much, for what they *say* is dramatic action. "The old pigeonhole bit?" says Jerry in *The Zoo Story*, and although it is he, not Peter, who does the pigeonholing, the accusation and the mockery in the question is an act of aggression, as good as a shove for throwing Peter off balance.

In the long run, Albee's reputation as a playwright will probably depend less on what he has to say than on the dramatic situations through which he says it. The two Albee plays that seem to have taken the strongest hold on the public imagination (which may be a way of saying they are the two plays I most admire) are *The Zoo Story* and *Virginia Woolf*. The reason is that the meeting between Jerry and Peter and the marriage of George and Martha, for all the nuances in the two relationships, are presented concretely in gesture and line; they take shape on the stage with great clarity. *Tiny Alice*, by contrast, is all amorphousness. It may finally be possible to reduce that play to an intellectual formulation, but the portentousness that hovers over so many lines and so much of the business keeps the characters and the situation from attaining dramatic validity. *The Zoo Story* is more successful as a play, not because its dramatic situation is more realistic, but because it exists on stage—a self-created dramatic fact.

A Delicate Balance is a much stronger play than *Tiny Alice*. As the discussion early in this chapter indicates, it is probably Albee's most perfect combination of theme and action, and its central metaphor—the balance—is important not only to the play but to Albee's work as a whole. Yet, compared to *Virginia Woolf*, it is an incredibly lifeless play. The reason, I think, is that the Martha-George relationship has dramatic substance in a way that the Tobias-Agnes household does not. Too much has been made—particularly by casual reviewers—of the violence, the hate, the anger in the Martha-George marriage. It is just as important that the quarrel be seen in the context of the affection they have for one another and the life—even if it is a long, sad game—which they so obviously share. One of the best inventions in all of Albee is the gun with the parasol in it, for what better way of seeing the relationship of Martha and George than in terms of a murderous weapon that is also a sheltering object; the instrument is a metaphor for the marriage, and its use is a preview of what will happen in the last act.

From the moment the play opens, from Martha's challenge,

"What a dump. Hey what's that from?" it is clear that Martha and George play the same games. He may be tired at first, not really in the mood for a session of name-the-movie, or he may be faking indifference because he cannot remember that the "goddamn Bette Davis picture" Martha has in mind is *Beyond the Forest* (1949), but there is companionship in the incipient quarrel that will not disappear as the argument grows more lethal. It can be seen directly in several places. Near the beginning of the play, after a mutual accusation of baldness, they go into a momentary affectionate scene in which his "Hello honey" leads to her request for "a big sloppy kiss." Almost the same phrase, "C'mon . . . give me a kiss," is her compliment for his having been clever enough to introduce the parasol-gun into the game room. Much more important than the grand games to which he gives labels—Humiliate the Host, Get the Guests, Hump the Hostess—are the small games that they play constantly—the play-acting routines, the little-kid bits, the mock-etiquette turns, the verbal games. The whole force of the play depends on their existence as a couple, a relationship made vivid in moments such as the one in Act III when Nick, humiliated at his sexual failure, begins angrily, "I'm nobody's houseboy . . ." and Martha and George shout in unison, "Now!" and then begin to sing, "I'm nobody's houseboy now. . . ." Their closeness is important if we are to recognize that George can be and is cuckolded. This event takes place on stage in Act II when Martha and Nick dance together sensuously and, speaking in time to the music, she tells about George's abortive attempt to be a novelist. It is at this moment that their marriage is violated, that George's anger shows most plainly, that he initiates a game of Get the Guests. "Book dropper! Child mentioner!" accuses George, and we see—perhaps before he does—the connection that forces him to carry "the bit about the kid" to its murderous conclusion. One may come away from *Virginia Woolf* suspicious of the end of the play and its presumed implications but never in doubt about the dramatic force of either characters or situation.

A *Delicate Balance* provides a marked contrast. We learn a great deal about the antipathy between Agnes and Claire, the sexual life of Agnes and Tobias, the marriage problems of Julia, the nameless fears of Edna and Harry, but the situation is explained more than it is presented. Some of the language is witty, some of it—particularly Agnes' lines—is quietly bitchy, but speeches do not pass from one character to another, carving out a definition of their relationship; lines fall from the mouths of the characters and shatter on the stage at their feet. Thematically, this is fine, since separateness is what Albee wants to depict, and he is ingenious in the way he lets the artificiality of his language contribute to the general sense of empty façade. Unfortunately, the characters are defined only in terms of their separateness, their significance as exemplary lost ones. Not so indeterminate as *Tiny Alice, A Delicate Balance* still lacks the kind of concreteness that comes from a dramatic image fully realized on stage. The characters are given a little biography, a few mannerisms, a whisper of depth, but they remain highly articulate stick figures moving through a sequence of nonevents to a foregone conclusion.

Unless Edward Albee is on some unannounced road to Damascus, there is not much doubt about what he will be saying in the plays that lie ahead of him. It is how he chooses to say it that will be important. In the face of his most recent work, in which significance seems to be imposed from the outside instead of meaning rising from within, we have every reason to be afraid, not of, but for *Virginia Woolf*.

THREE

Front Runners, Some Fading

*Depending on circumstances, tragedy
will prevail over comedy or vice versa.*
—GUILLAUME APOLLINAIRE

"The new generation's knocking at the door," says the Famous American Playwright in *Fan and Yam*. "Gelber, Richardson, Kopit . . . Albee. . . ." This roll call is more than an Albee joke, for in the early 1960's these names formed, at least in the pages of the popular press, a group on which the future of the American theater presumably rested. "All we have in common is that we got produced off-Broadway," complained Jack Gelber to an interviewer from *Newsweek* (December 18, 1961), trying to separate himself from Albee and Jack Richardson. "None of us has written a play at all resembling the others," Kopit told the guest editors for the college edition of *Mademoiselle* (August, 1962). The first produced play of each of these playwrights brought its author a great deal of publicity, but, with less fanfare, other names— Arnold Weinstein, Frank D. Gilroy, William Hanley, Murray Schisgal—were added to the great-expectations list. Albee, alone, made the transfer safely from YAM to FAM, but several of the others—Richardson, Hanley, Gilroy, Schisgal—moved on to Broadway with varying degrees of success. The others have continued their work off-Broadway.

There is no sensible way of talking about these playwrights as a group. To each man, then, his own critique.

JACK GELBER

When *The Apple*, Jack Gelber's second play, opened in New York, he was quoted in the *Newsweek* interview mentioned above: "I don't believe I have the kind of talent that can produce a straight play in the nineteenth-century sense, which is what they are doing today." The remark had minimal relevance in a season in which few such straight plays were produced and even less were successful. If we accept the end of his sentence as the excessive statement of a man with a crying need to separate himself from a semifictional "they" and if we take the rest of the quotation as true after a fashion (like the strippers in *Gypsy*, he has to have a gimmick), his idea of his work is still false in a very basic way. All three of his plays—*The Connection* (1959), *The Apple* (1961) and *Square in the Eye* (1965)—make desperate attempts to shatter theatrical illusion, to force the actors and the audience into one another's arms, but behind his manipulation of devices a very conventional playwright is at work.

Gelber's sense of character, dramatic situation, emotional effects is stereotypical, even sentimental. Perhaps this quality can be seen more clearly in his nondramatic work where there are no audible jazz combos or visible movie screens (the jazz and movie references are there, of course) to obstruct the view of his soft-centered world. Take, for instance, "Neal vs. Jimmy the Fag," a story that appeared in *Evergreen Review* (December, 1964), a confrontation tale in which an aging ex-con, with only his need to offer, tries and fails to take a young woman away from the titular faggot. "This is your last chance," comes Neal's final cry and then, "He could not control the shame he felt for his own pitifulness and did not wait for an answer, slamming the door." If it were a play instead of a short story, that would be a *schmaltz* curtain, all the more obvious because the whisper of low life—the criminal-homosexual subculture—is still as hokily romantic as it was at the turn of the century. To be fair to Gelber, although he clings to a semi-Bohemian milieu, he goes out of his way—particularly in *The Connection* and in his novel *On Ice* (1964)—to insist that there is no qualitative difference between the square and the hip worlds. "There are lousy hipsters and lousy squares," says Cowboy in *The Connection*. Even if this disavowal is taken as genuine, if Gelber's addicts (*The Connection*), actors (*The Apple*), and painters (*Square in the Eye*) are stripped of any implicit romanticism, Gelber cannot pull away the vestigial threads of ordinary stage psychology that—behind the bead curtains of avant-garde theatrics—can be seen clinging to them.

In his favorable review of *The Connection* (in *Seasons of Discontent*), Robert Brustein wrote, "The only false note of the evening is struck by your own conventional expectation, conditioned by years of phony drama and sociological indoctrination." Although Gelber is plainly suspicious of easy explanations of human behavior and overly neat formulations of human action, perhaps because he believes in the "random universe" that besets Manny Fells, the hero of *On Ice*, the note that Brustein heard at *The Connection* never sounded false to me. The conventional expectations—of character, plot and theme—are fulfilled. Not conventionally, of course, because Gelber's use of the play-within-a-play device and his on-again-off-again parodic stance let him back away from the characters and situations he is dealing with. *The*

Connection tells how a producer brings together a group of addicts and has them improvise a scenario prepared by a sympathetic playwright and how—reality being stronger than art—the action on stage destroys any attempt to control it. This is obviously a workable dramatic metaphor for a statement about the inadvisability of putting labels on life, but there is a producer (Julian Beck) and a playwright (Gelber) beyond the fictional ones, and this fact—which not even the panhandling actor-addict in the lobby can hide—adds a probably unintentional ambiguity to the statement.[1]

Jaybird, the fictional playwright, has presumably assigned characters to each of the main performers. In the first act, while they wait for the heroin to arrive, each of them is expected to do a revelatory turn, spelled by the jazz combo. At the beginning of the play, when the introductions are made, labels are distributed lightly, as the producer, joking ponderously, calls Ernie "our dope-addict psychopath" and Sam "our expert in folk lore." Presumably Gelber is playing with popular psychology when he plants references to Ernie's cruel father and Leach's orphanage upbringing, as though they were causes for a situation which he thinks cannot be explained in those terms. Yet, his and Jaybird's characters overlap. When Jaybird loses control of his play, when presumably it passes into the addicts' hands, Ernie is still the psychopath, Solly still the intellectual, Sam still the uneducated wiseman, Leach still the female male, at once mothering and accusing. In the same way, Gelber both has his plot and dismisses it. Much of the activity in the play seems almost random—beginnings that are

---

[1] In a USIA lecture on off-Broadway (in Alan S. Downer's *The American Theater Today*), Bernard F. Dukore has an ingenious theory about how Gelber's Pirandellian theatricality works. Whenever the characters in the frame play break into the action, they remind the audience that it is looking at characters on stage, but, since they are supposed to be played by addicts rather than actors, the audience realizes that it is "watching reality." For Dukore's explanation to be convincing, one must assume that this is indeed the audience's realization. For me, this is not the case. The obvious theatricality strengthens my sense of the characters as stereotypes, not of the actors as addicts, and it is this, not my own willful or over-conditioned refusal to take part, that makes me constantly aware that I am watching Gelber's play rather than Jaybird's.

going nowhere, exchanges that are only isolated bits. This desultory quality is so strong that, at first glance, Roger Shattuck's description of the play as "the long ineptly timed *coitus interruptus*" (in his poem "New Years Afternoon 1961") seems as apt as it is clever. In fact, there are two conventional plots— one for each act—and both of them build to climax. The first has to do with the waiting, which is not an enclosed action, as it is in *Waiting for Godot*. Here the settlers (the addicts), trapped in the fort (Leach's room), wait for the arrival of the cavalry (the connection) so that they can be saved from the Indians (turned on). In naming his connection Cowboy, Gelber pays mock tribute to the plot he is using, and he lets Solly explain it to the audience. "So we wait for the trustworthy Cowboy to gallop in upon a white horse," he says, and then, for those who do not get the joke, he adds, "Gallant white powder."

In the second act, the fort having been saved (Sister Salvation arrives with Cowboy), there is a turning-on celebration, during which the second plot goes into operation. When Brustein says that Gelber is "never guilty of Pirandello's operatic plot construction," and Nat Hentoff (*Evergreen Review*, January, 1960) talks about "the non-end of the anti-play," I have the feeling that I must have seen some other *The Connection*. Leach's overdose and the business about who will desert and who will try to help him is the purest melodrama, and it works in those terms even though Gelber uses Jaybird to belittle the convention. Through much of the play, Jaybird worries about his plot and his characters. "This part was to be blood and guts drama," he says near the end of the play, after he has turned on too, and a few speeches later, "I wrote a play with four heroes. . . . You are all heroes. I mean in the theatrical sense. Cowboy, can't you act like a hero?" It is at this point that Leach begins to go for the overdose, and within a few minutes the stage is deserted by all but the four heroes (Leach and the three men who stick by him—Cowboy, Solly, and Sam) and the playwright who will speak the nonheroic benediction over them: "No doctors, no heroes, no martyrs, no Christs." As a comment on addiction, the line may be valid. As a description of the drama, it is like a denial of operetta to the tune of "The Blue Danube."

Aside from what the play is trying to say about the distance between life and sociological, psychological, artistic descriptions of it, it has a conventional social point to make. As Zero Mostel's old night club act had it in more innocent days, "We're all a bunch of aspirin eatin' wrecks." Gelber uses his collection of addicts to remind the audience that we are all in search of some connection by which we may be, in Sam's words, "redeemed. From my eternal suffering I am redeemed! Like a pawn ticket." The analogy between the two worlds is made verbally in speeches by Cowboy (the one about lousy hipsters and lousy squares), by Sam (who describes working, worrying people as "hooked worse than me"), and by Solly ("You are your own connection"). It is made dramatically in the scene in which Solly joins Sister Salvation in an evangelistic exchange, music under, and sentimentally in the discovery that Sister Salvation is also on dope. It is illustrated when the line between the two plays disappears, when Jaybird and one of the photographers, who is supposed to be filming the play, take heroin. The juxtaposition of "eternal suffering" and "pawn ticket" in Sam's speech indicates what is implicit throughout the play— that whatever connection is made, the salvation is temporary. Only the need is permanent. Gelber, then, uses Leach's microcosmic pad to make a statement that is almost as formulistic as the sociology and psychology that the play ostensibly denies.

In *The Apple* a group of actors are supposed to be improvising a play. They are interrupted by a drunk who, like Sam in *The Connection*, annoys the audience in the lobby. He is aggressive, disruptive. It is never quite clear whether the actors' treatment of him as an outsider is part of the improvisation or part of the acting situation. If it is the latter—and I suspect that it is—the play is apparently making some kind of comment about the uses of theater. The play is full of real apples (bitten, passed around, the cores used as missiles) and verbal ones (Iris: "I'm whatever you want me to be . . . I'm your apple, baby"). In his speech at the end of the play, Ace explains that Ajax, who is somewhat grander in his concepts, would tell the audience "that this apple is a golden Chinese apple and stands for knowledge," a description that recalls the desire of Jabez to "Start from the beginning. Do the Adam and Eve bullshit." Ace settles for pointing out that "a lot of people wanted this apple" and ends by urging the audience to come back but not "without wanting something." Commenting on another actor and on the interrupting drunk, Ace says, "Stark would turn into an apple for you. And the madman would throw the apple at you." The assumption—at least, my assumption—is that this sentence and the whole knockabout evening is saying that the theater both gives an audience what it wants and confronts it with its desires.

In trying to fasten a specific label to *apple*, I may be imposing my own sense of order on a play that wants none of it. "Art is precision," says Jabez early in the play. "Control, control every gesture, every word." Ace says, "Relax. There isn't any grand design." What the audience gets from the play are the suggestion of conventional relations among the actors, a series of supposedly improvised sketches, a great deal of free-floating aggression, and many apparently random comments on death and art as well as on apples and wants. Except that the idiom is American and that there is a complete absence of delight for its own sake, the play suggests the kind of surrealist-dadaist theatrical games that were played in France at about the time of the First World War. Since the parts of the play, which are perhaps not supposed to make a whole, are not very interesting and since there is such an air of earnestness in its fun, I assume that Gelber wants the play to make a statement. If the audience (a random collection of shifting desires) dictates the performance, as one might assume from my definition of *apple* and from Ace's long theater-eye metaphor in which "The light from the outside comes through the eyeball [the audience] and focuses on the stage," then the statement may be no more than Jabez's answer to Ace, "No design is grand design." My own answer would have to be to Iris: not my apple, baby.

With *Square in the Eye*, we are back on familiar Gelber ground. This is a fairly obvious story disguised by machinery (movies and slides sharing stage with live actors), by antirealistic staging (entrances and exits through the audience, monologues in the style of the stand-up comedian), and by structural games (the story told out of sequence). In Act I the protagonist (if that is a possible word to use in talking about a Gelber play) appears to be Ed Stone, a would-be-artist schoolteacher who blames his wife, his family, the politics of the art world for his lack of success. At the end of the act, freed by the death of the wife, he is marrying a rich girl: "So I don't paint. Big deal. Or I do. That's my choice now."

In Act II, as we move back in time, the focus shifts from Ed to Sandy, the dying wife. In the long sequence in the hospital room she confronts all her failures—as daughter, as wife, as mother, as friend, as lover, as art critic, as crusader. The family and friends who body out these failures are obvious clichés—from the comic you-should-eat-something Jewish mother to the young daughter who does the Electra bit—but in expressionistic plays, too often, "That's the way it really is." Sandy's sense of loss, her unfulfilled desire for something more than she has had, is presumably to be taken seriously, which means sentimentally, and there is no way of avoiding the syrup of the ending. As Ed goes out through the audience, his and Sandy's voices can be heard on tape, ending with her declaration of love and "Don't go—Don't Ed."

Presumably this ending is supposed to be put in perspective by the first act. There is a long sequence in Act I in which, without a break, the scene shifts from the hospital corridor where Sandy's parents and Ed learn of her death, to the funeral parlor, to the funeral itself. This scene is played for satirical effect, the main device being the single actor who plays the doctor, the funeral director, and the rabbi, whose indifference in each case is presumably masked but actually emphasized by the jargon of his trade. In retrospect, in the light of the second-act hospital scene, this satiric material is probably supposed to take on another quality, to suggest that it is a social reflection of a failure of contact which is much more basic, which finally condemns Sandy to die alone. Unfortunately, in that last scene Gelber goes for easy ironies that misuse the material of the first act. For instance, Sandy predicts, "It'll be just your luck to marry some vapid rich doll and her docility will be the death of Ed Stone, the painter." If Gelber is prepared to work for that level of perception, there is little point in going in search of more subtle effects. One might as well take straight the tears in the last moments. In any case, it is difficult to escape the feeling that Sandy and Ed, their family and friends, are escapees from the William Inge world of the fifties, trying to pretend that they are at home in the setting Gelber has given them.

At one point in *On Ice*, Gelber begins to bring Manny Fells and a girl together; their approach is tentative, circumlocutory. "Louise interposed a complicated story, painting mechanistic sketches of the dramatis personae and elaborating the relationships based on incredibly subtle banalities." That line, when I read it, broke loose from the novel and took on a critical life of its own. Gelber, as playwright, refuses to use Louise's method, but—even in his best work, *The Connection*—he is working from the same base.

JACK RICHARDSON

In "Jack's First Tape," a self-interview in *Theatre Arts* (March, 1962), Jack Richardson, with two modestly successful off-Broadway productions behind him, tried—his tongue only slightly in his cheek—to define himself as a playwright. In the process, he commented on the dramatists and the movements most talked about at the time, neatly summing them up, placing them in his own perspective.[2] Jean Genet, he wrote, "has a genius for avoiding the right words, but his insights are interesting." That phrase, wrenched out of context and turned upside down so that the words mean what I want them to mean, might serve as a description of Richardson as playwright—in his off-Broadway plays, *The Prodi-*

[2] His comments indicate what has become increasingly clear since 1966, when he became regular reviewer for *Commentary*—that Richardson is an extremely perceptive critic.

gal (1960) and *Gallows Humor* (1961), and in his resounding
(and undeserved)[3] Broadway flops, *Lorenzo* (1963) and *Xmas
in Las Vegas* (1965).

"Insight," in Richardson's case, has less to do with the penetration to some underlying truth than it does with the metaphorical
invention, the intellectual construction through which he attempts
to present his recurring sense of the relationship between man and
life, between order and disorder. "A definite statement," he says
in the self-interview, "always smacks of the inchoate truth and the
hysterical insight." Smack as they will, definite statements (about
indefinite matters, it is true) are made in all of the Richardson
plays. To reduce the plays to statements is only to cut away what
is least there, for Richardson's problem about the "right words" is
not simply verbal—although it is that too—but the failure of flesh,
an inability to create characters with strength enough to rise out of
the concepts that fathered them and, as the old actor says in *The
Fantasticks*, to "press the stage."

In *Uncle Vanya*, Sonya replies to Elena's compliment about her
hair: "When a woman is not beautiful, they always say: 'You
have beautiful hair, you have beautiful eyes.'" At the risk of
sounding like Elena, I have to say that, for all his limitations as a
dramatist, Richardson is the most intellectually engaging of the
young playwrights, the one whose play of mind is most interesting.
In his novel *The Prison Life of Harris Filmore*, the warden is a
seven-foot ex-basketball player who once, jumping higher than
usual, got a perspective on the "sweaty scramble" that took in
game and spectators alike and sent him finally to the security of
the prison. This kind of invention, at once serious and comic, can
be found in all the plays and in his other work, fiction and nonfic-
tion alike. "Do you distrust metaphysics?" he asks himself in
"Jack's First Tape," and answers, "Do you mean would I lend it
money?" This gag is not only an example of a kind of serious

---

[3] I am judging from having read the plays—the manuscript of *Lorenzo*,
the published *Xmas in Las Vegas*. The plays on stage may have been different
from the ones I read, or the productions may have been bad, but neither of
them lasted long enough for me to get to them to find out.

playfulness, which unfortunately does not always come off in the plays, but it is also an indication of the attitude of mind—the distrust of systems—that lies behind all the metaphors with which Richardson works. For him, life is a confusion, a constant surprise, an unpredictability which man, if he is to be truly alive, must embrace; it is a struggle in which inevitable defeat and loss (mortality is, after all, part of the bargain of life) is balanced against "the sense of possibility." Man, however, suspicious of the "sweaty scramble," commits metaphorical suicide by retreating into the illusory order of systems of philosophy, legal constructs, books of rules, conventional expectations, received opinions, private worlds of love or work, private rooms. At the end of "Grace Through Gambling," a confessional article that appeared in *Esquire* (April, 1967) and from which I borrowed the phrase about "possibility," Richardson, a compulsive gambler (to use a redundancy), a fat advance from a publisher in his pocket, is about to set off on a trip that will let him gamble his way around the world. The night before his departure, he lies awake and considers what he will be leaving:

> Work on the table; a loved girl in your bed; and rooms you fashioned to be your sanctuary. . . . I admitted that all the chaos I was going into frightened me and that I knew I would someday grow numb even to the pleasures of gambling. I was going west in the morning so that the peace that was around me would never be my final end.

All the Richardson plays, one way or another, are about avoiding or seeking that peace.

In *The Prodigal,* in which Richardson, like Giraudoux and Sartre before him, turns the *Oresteia* into a contemporary philosophical play, Orestes attempts to escape involvement in the conflict between Agamemnon and Aegisthus, a struggle that is more basic than one for political control of Argos. Agamemnon's is the heroic view, the idea that man is—or can be—a little larger than life; it is a faith which has sent him "halfway around the world correcting the injustices done to" man. There is the suggestion here of an attitude uncomfortably close to the one that keeps the United States, always acting on the highest moral principles, involved in small and not-so-small wars all over the world, but Richardson is not after narrow satirical references. Agamemnon's belief is balanced against that of Aegisthus, which sees man as insignificant, the victim of the gods and not their potential challenger. Both philosophies define man in terms of prior concepts and both, when they attain power, resort to violence. Orestes, finding nothing to choose between them, takes refuge first in cynicism (a pose of indifference which may be a first step toward commitment) and, when that fails, tries to set up housekeeping in Voltaire's garden, which sounds as though it grows on Sweeney's cannibal isle, to "watch conception, birth, decay, and death, and to give myself to the same process." Since the Orestes legend will not let its hero escape his mythic (that is, his societal) role, he goes back to Argos to commit his murders—forced there by Electra's, by society's, by his audience's need for a hero.

On the face of it, *The Prodigal* seems to be about the way society keeps the gentle princes of the world from living the simple life, but the attraction of the play is that it is not that conventional. As the farewell scene with Praxithia indicates, Orestes is no man to find his vegetating peace in a garden; as the title suggests (the prodigal son, after all, went home to escape the unfamiliar), he will, for all his protests, find some comfort in the demands of the world "that we inherit the pretensions of our fathers, that we go on killing in the name of ancient illusions about ourselves." Orestes in the garden and Orestes as "the popular and typical hero" are two of a kind, the play suggests, for it does busy itself with being openly didactic. Richardson, in "Jack's First Tape," says, "I am concerned that man seems determined to learn nothing from history." Orestes, early in *The Prodigal*, suggests that he and Pylades go down to the beach and play with the slave girls, pretend to give them freedom, accept the reward of their magnanimity, and then lock the girls up again: "We'll call the game 'history.'" Cassandra, at the end of the play, hoping for "an audience other than the one we play for now," looks for a society that "will demand something better for your consent than edgeworn ideals and dramatic necessity." In *The Prodigal*, then, which is still the most interesting of Richardson's plays, he is concerned as much with society, which offers only life-inhibiting choices, as with Orestes, the chooser. In the plays that follow, the focus shifts slightly; that evanescent "sense of possibility" becomes increasingly important.

Gallows Humor is much too neat. It consists of an unnecessary prologue, in which an actor, as death, explains that he is outdated because the "one-time basic distinction between the quick and the dead has become far too abstract today," and two short plays that illustrate the point. In the first, Walter, waiting to be executed for the murder of his wife, is content in his tidy cell with its ascertainable bounds, its comforting routines, until Lucy, the state-provided prostitute ("an innovation in our penal program," says the Warden), arrives to reintroduce the disorder that Walter is trying to escape. Outside, he had lived a life governed by habit and by law until his world fell to pieces on the day a client of his, unable to control her hiccoughs, set the courtroom to laughing and lost what should have been an open-and-shut case for damages. After that, irrationality invaded his life until he smashed his wife's head with a golf club and found his way to the cell, free of "the dizziness on the other side of those walls," where he can die, happily, on schedule. "Dying with your point of view really makes me sick to my stomach," says Lucy, and she proceeds to litter the cell with cigarettes and chicken bones, providing the setting in which they finally make love: "You'll be living again when you strangle." In the second play, the executioner, Phillip, formerly a creature of routine, has just reached Walter's post-hiccough state of comic chaos, but he fails to go beyond that, proves unable to kill his wife, and goes meekly off to the execution. The two women parallel the men they affect. Lucy compares Walter to "a *happy* 'still-life' whore," the end-of-the-line in her profession, one who just lies back, an instrument, and receives her customers without recognition; Lucy's behavior in the cell is an attempt to escape that fate as well as to save Walter from it. Martha, the apparently assertive wife of the second play, has her chance to break out, a possible affair with the Warden, but neither of them can work an assignation into their busy schedule.

The play is funnier in conception than it is in fact and, for all its shortness, remarkably repetitious. By comparison, *The Prison Life of Harris Filmore* is a much more successful treatment of the same theme. The novel, which was not published until 1963, was presumably written at about the same time as, or before, *Gallows Humor*; the copyright date is 1961 and a note identifying Richardson in the Spring, 1960, *Transatlantic Review,* in which he had a story, indicates that the novel, in some form, existed at that time.

Harris Filmore, like Walter, "had always assumed the rules, laws, and customs of his society were by no means acts of whimsy," until his conviction for bank fraud—a technical error called a crime. In fear of the unknown, not hearing the hints of the priest ("a modern monastery") and the doctor ("the peace of your own little cell"), Filmore goes off to prison not expecting the shelter that it turns out to be. The novel is the education of Harris Filmore, his coming to accept philosophically what he has accepted instinctively from the moment the comfort of prison routine began to close around him. When Harris' cellmate releases the pigeon he has nursed back to health, it flies hesitantly, still unused to its wings, up, out, over the prison walls where a hawk pounces on it. "There is always a hawk for pigeons that want to be free as a bird," says MacIntyre, the prison guru, and he adds, "For hawks, there are eagles." By the time the prison outbreak takes place, Harris has so adjusted that Radigan, one of the incorrigibles too alive to settle for the peace of the prison, with the choice of Harris or the Warden, shoots his fellow prisoner. "He wanted, at that moment, to blow the prison up in bits," says the Warden, "so he shot at *you!*" Harris' wound brings him parole, but by that time he has come to see parole as the Warden sees it, an opportunity to commit another crime that will bring him back for a longer stay. In the last chapter of the novel, he robs a Salvation Army meeting and shoots one of the sisters.[4] As the book closes, the outraged voices of the police above him, "he

---

[4] He uses a tiny pistol "you couldn't hurt a cat with," so that no serious damage is done to his victim. Although violence and murder provide the life images in the novel and in *Gallows Humor,* the murders are always described as having happened, never performed in the present. It is as though Richardson were afraid that for his audience, as for Pegeen in *The Playboy*

tucked his knees in close to his chest, rested his head on the cement pavement, stretched his shackled arms luxuriously, and fell immediately to sleep." The charm of the novel is that, although it is in the third person, it is written from Harris' point of view. The representatives of the outside world—Harris' wife, his lawyer, the visiting ladies, Radigan—are all ugly, strident, grotesque—while the insiders are almost saintly; and yet the final effect is that prison is a kind of death. Ironically, the novel conveys this idea dramatically, but the drama, *Gallows Humor*, is forced to reiteration.

Lorenzo was an unlikely play for a young dramatist to use in his first assault on Broadway. It provided an opportunity for handsome costumes, and the flamboyance of its actors' rhetoric[5] might have been expected to have a surface appeal. Still, it is a play that uses its historical setting not for romance, but as a vehicle for ideas; heavy with argument and touched with ambiguity, it could hardly have what *Time* (February 25, 1963) called "crowd lure."[6] In short, it was not an assault on Broadway at all; it was a typical Jack Richardson play. Set in "a small war of the Renaissance," it is a story of a troupe of actors ("We are no one's enemy") caught between sides in a conflict which would have been at home in the politics of *The Prodigal*. The benevolent Duke of Milan, intent on draining the dangerous swamps of Italy, finds that he must conquer the countryside before he can cure it; he is egged on by his Chancellor, who is in love with history, and by Van Miessen, the general whose mercenaries provide the army.

---

of the Western World, "there's a great gap between a gallous story and a dirty deed."

[5] It may have been the rhetoric that made the play and the part of Lorenzo attractive to Alfred Drake, but Drake is more than a musical comedy star turned Shakespearean. In 1952 he helped adapt and starred in Ugo Betti's *The Gambler*, and Betti is the recent European dramatist most like Richardson. Both Betti and Richardson are dramatists of ideas who are more often intellectually fascinating than they are dramatically effective.

[6] The *Time* review is a good example of the kind of ambiguous response that Richardson is likely to elicit. The reviewer, faced with all those words (he imagines the play is in verse) and all those ideas, declares it "ambitious, daring, and gratifying" and manages to convey the impression that he did not much like it.

Lorenzo, the director of the Theatre of the First Dove (that, I take it, is a peace joke), insists that this is not the actors' war, that their world of make-believe is the real world, their refuge against the chaos which threatens to and finally does break in on them. At one point, Lorenzo reminds Antonio (the troupe's villain who, at the end of Act I, out of character, dies a conventional hero) of the meaningless wars of their youth: "No, Antonio, an artist is under obligation to pay high tribute to man's suffering, not, unless he's presumptuous, to change it." The cannons, however, sing siren songs to Lorenzo's son and daughter. Tired of playing virgins, Laura becomes Van Miessen's mistress. Tired of mock heroism, Giorgio (wearing his Alexander the Great helmet) goes off to fight against the Duke of Milan. Reality so far invades the fantasy camp of the actors that Lorenzo's wife admits that she is old and Ricardo, who plays heroes, that he is a coward.

It is Lorenzo, however, whose decision is important. It quickly becomes clear that the play is a conflict between Lorenzo and Van Miessen, between the escape into art and the willingness, as Van Miessen says of Giorgio, to pay "the price for taking breath on this planet." Having offered only a stage lament over the real body of Antonio, Lorenzo, moved by the news of his son's presumed death, finally decides to fight. Donning Giorgio's helmet ("The pity is that all men who fight Van Miessen must look a little ridiculous"), recognizing that he loses even if he wins (for Van Miessen has forced him off stage), Lorenzo, after an actor's flourish, attacks and is quickly killed. "Welcome back to the world, actor," says Van Miessen. In the last scene, Giorgio, who is after all not dead, returns, appalled that the army he fought with is as indiscriminately cruel and destructive as the one he fought against. Convinced now that his father was right, he rides over the protests of the others, who insist that Lorenzo had changed, and sets out to recreate the actors' unreal world.

George Wellwarth, the most sympathetic of Richardson's critics, suggests, in *The Theater of Protest and Paradox*, that in Richardson's view illusion is preferable to reality, but surely he is mistaken; that last scene must be ironic. Unless the final scene is taken at face value, the play is apparently saying that man cannot escape (by fantasy, by art, by dream), that he is in the world and that this fact sometimes demands an act—even when failure is implicit in the action. In the context of Richardson's work as a whole, the implication is that Lorenzo is most alive when he dons the helmet and draws the sword, steps from the comfortable conventions of art to the killing confusions of life.

"After *Xmas in Las Vegas*," one of Richardson's early and most ardent admirers told me, "I give him up." The implication was that Richardson had traded his serious intentions as a playwright for the hope of Broadway success. Yet *Xmas in Las Vegas* is as unlikely a Broadway comedy as *Lorenzo* is a Broadway costume drama. When the curtain comes down on a Broadway comedy, the complications have been smoothed, the confusions sorted out, the impending disasters avoided; the characters settle for conventional marriage, normality, the quiet life—what the audience takes as a happy ending. Even when Tennessee Williams worked in the genre, in *Period of Adjustment*, he covered his sardonic ending with the surface suggestion that all was right with the world. Richardson's hero, Edward Wellspot, having lost his last blackjack game, will be forced to settle for the conventional life ("Now, Eleanor, we can put our lives in order, stop chasing aces and sleep in separate beds to get as much rest as possible"); as the play ends, he puts a pistol to his temple and then lowers it on his wife's words, "Edward, won't going back to Boston accomplish the same thing?" This is the bleakest final curtain—at least, the bleakest intentional one—that I can remember for a Broadway comedy. Richardson is up to his usual philosophical business, differentiating between chaos (life) and order (death), and once again he is trying to force a dramatic form to his own purposes. If the *Esquire* article on his gambling habits is biographically exact, 1965 was the year he began gambling in earnest; his choice of gambling as his chaos-life image may, then, be a reflection of his immediate preoccupation, but his use of it recalls all the earlier plays.

Xmas is the story of an unsuccessful assault on Olympus. The

Wellspots have come to Las Vegas, as they do every Christmas, so that Edward can attempt once again—this time his last—to beat Spiros Olympus at blackjack, to make the big killing that is always just out there for the gambler. Edward needs the victory to save not only himself but his family. Eleanor, who remembers when "you were young, with new decks of cards, and I thought you would never lose," has taken to seeing naked angels, disaster signs, calling them back to Boston and security. Emily (the daughter), four times married, always disappointed, has taken refuge in sleep, has settled for erotic dreams. Lionel (the son), a perennial graduate student, ineptly suicidal, is attracted to despair on a grander scale. "I realized the world was divided into two tragic camps," he says, summing up his sister and himself, "one suffering from post-coital depression, the other, from post-Copernican." Michel (the uncle), an old jazz man who thinks of himself as a big sex performer, begins to wheeze at the slightest memory and is forced "to swap innuendoes with a lady bass player who looks like she was never laid in her life." By the end of Act I, Edward has convinced the family—except Lionel—that this time he has found his unbeatable luck (a widow from New Rochelle who cannot lose). For a first act curtain, Lionel is lured off the balcony from which he threatens to jump in a scene that recalls the awakening of Isabel in Jean Giraudoux's *Intermezzo*. The sounds that call Isabel back, however, are those of ordinary life; since ordinary life is death in *Xmas*, Lionel has to be attracted by the lurid, slightly comic come-on of material and erotic fantasy ("It's every dream I ever had," says Mrs. Simon, the luck from New Rochelle).

When Mrs. Simon turns out to be human—when she loses—Edward returns to his family and plays a savage Santa Claus scene in which he gives Lionel a pistol, Emily sleep shades, Eleanor and himself two tickets to Boston. By this time, however, Lionel, who has had a successful night with a Vegas show girl, wants "everything you coaxed me off that balcony with," and so rejects the pistol. "Well, there he goes," says Edward. "Next up at the table." Early in the play Lionel says, "If there's any sign in the heavens it should be 'You can't beat the house.'" Olympus, in his long story about Tallahassee Slim and the marked dice game, implies that, win or lose, you lose. Elsewhere, however, he explains why he likes Edward: "If I were sentimental, I'd say I envied his stubbornness, his dry throat, his wet hands—all the palpable signs of life you lose when you're the house. . . .". In *Xmas in Las Vegas*, as in the other Richardson plays, no one can beat the system, but there is something positive, something alive in trying; something sad in being past trying; something sadder in simply copping out. If Richardson had really been intent on a popular success, he would have ended the play with Lionel's assertion and not with Edward's loss, which has Lionel's loss implicit in it; but his plays are controlled by ideas and not by generic forms or audience demands.

If I have managed to convey how interesting I find Richardson's work, I have probably been misleading about the quality of the plays. There is still the problem of the missing "right words," the verbal awkwardness and the sense of abstraction that rob the plays of the substance that would transform them from conceptions to creations. The language difficulties are the easiest to illustrate. Richardson's lines make unnecessary demands on the actor and on the audience—the demands not of subtle thought or clever word play, but of awkward syntax. How can a performer read or an audience hear a line like Clytemnestra's "Our love is a born talent, and is present before we, by practicing upon men, begin to expand and polish it into an art," or, even worse, Aegisthus' "The moment you speak of, if, as you say, it is a great one, it will also be, I promise you, short." This is excessive, of course, and the examples are from Richardson's first play, but the insensitivity to the sound of words implicit in those lines can be found in all the plays. Michel says, "When I left home, a hot trombone player with bright red hair parted in the middle and played in a band that wore checkered vests and tight sharkskin suits, I glowed." This line is formed, in part, by Richardson's concept of humor, which hangs heavily, although sometimes amusingly, over *Xmas in Las Vegas* and *Gallows Humor*. It depends on the piling up of detail, usually incongruous, to create a description or an anecdote that is not funny in itself but by virtue of the verbal decals that decorate it. It is the method of S. J. Perelman and—as his *The Beauty Part* (1962) illustrates—it is a kind of comic excess that works better on the page than it does on stage, except in the hands of a comic writer like Oscar Wilde (see the account of the finding of Jack in *The Importance of Being Earnest*) who understands that the details exist not only for themselves but as part of a complete rhetorical build. Too often—even when the lines are neither difficult nor excessive in their quest for laughs—they are undistinguished as language and undistinguishing as a means of characterization. For instance, in Electra's dream of Agamemnon's return, waves are "indifferent," the sky is "limitless," boats seem "insignificant," waves break, and soldiers press eagerly. It might be argued that Electra is a little girl who can see a homecoming only in conventional language, but the bulk of the play is colored by such usages. Aegisthus, for instance, calls any truth man might strive for "pompous dung . . . merely the leftover droppings of the gods," paying no attention to Orestes' accurate comment, "Your choice of metaphor leaves something to be desired, Aegisthus." Whether Orestes is faulting Aegisthus for lack of gentility or for banality (which he should be), his own rejoinder founders under the weight of "leaves something to be desired."

Occasionally one of Richardson's metaphors works in a variety of ways. Just before Antonio is killed in *Lorenzo*, he insists that the world is not brutal, that it is "foolish and clumsy, like a fat man making love." The metaphor itself is not particularly impressive, but it does describe the world as the play reveals it. More than that, however, the phrase has dramatic value. Antonio is a fat man, and his attempt to persuade Laura not to leave with Van Miessen is his way of making love. Seldom, however, does a Richardson line work so well; when it does, the pleasure in it is tempered by the fact that it shows up the limitations of so much of the language. In *Lorenzo*, for instance, the hollow rhetoric of the actors might serve the play as a whole, but only if it could be differentiated from the hollow rhetoric of everyone else.

In part, the language difficulties in Richardson's plays are a reflection of a larger problem; the dead verbal metaphors are a token of his failure to give life to his dramatic metaphors. In a review in *Commentary* (March, 1967), he said of the kind of play that tries to get by on a single visual image for our times, "the audience may grow restive unless the ensuing play adds some intelligent, humorous, or tragic flesh to that metaphor." He has tried, in his own plays, to give metaphor (an intellectual conceit in each case, not a visual image) a dramatic situation to live in and characters to live it. In a review of *Danton's Death* at Lincoln Center (*Commentary*, January, 1966), he says that "the mind has its personality and the intelligence its passions" and complains that Herbert Blau "seems to respect thought so much that he hardly considers it a human process." Yet for all that he understands the connection between thought and emotion, Richardson cannot create characters that compel an audience, that serve as more than points of view or illustrations in the argument. There are moments when one character or another flickers into life, but during the debates, the discussions, the intellectual confrontations, when life is most needed, the plays become expository rather than dramatic. In an essay on Hubert Humphrey in *Esquire* (November, 1966), Richardson wrote:

> in America at least, politicians have only two public arrangements of features: one—grave, frozen with portent and seriousness; two— jovial, beaming with one-of-the-boys humor. The thousand nuances between these extremes appear to be off-limits to public scrutiny, perhaps because they seem indecisive, perhaps because they do not give a reassuringly clear notion of the attitude behind them.

Is there a message here for the playwright?

ARTHUR KOPIT

When *Oh Dad, Poor Dad, Mamma's Hung You in the Closet and I'm Feelin' So Sad* was published in 1960, Gaynor F. Bradish, who as tutor of Dunster House, Harvard, got Arthur Kopit started as a playwright, wrote an introduction in which he called Kopit

"Harvard's most successful undergraduate playwright." Six years later, in "Thank You, Annette Funicello," an article in *The Saturday Evening Post* (July 16, 1966), Kopit, defending the "hard-won jersey" which proclaimed him "Mr. Volleyball," cutely cleared the sport of the charge that it "belongs to the pop world of saddle shoes, soda pop and Batman." Kopit seems to be in the tradition of those playwrights who create (with very little effort in his case) images which obscure their work. "Undergraduate" is still the critics' favorite pejorative word for Kopit, a way of dismissing whatever seriousness lies behind the clever surface of his plays. There is some justice in that dismissal, too, for Kopit is still the playful beginner. There is nothing in *The Day the Whores Came Out to Play Tennis and Other Plays*, a collection of short plays published in 1965, that shows an advance over *Oh Dad*, which was written in 1959, the year Kopit graduated from college.

So much fun has been had with or at the expense of *Oh Dad* (summer stock productions, an unbelievably terrible film version, jokes about the title) that it has become the clown play of the decade—at once a successful sick joke and a good clean American absurdist comedy. All this fashionable chi-chi, however, should not be allowed to hide what is best and strongest in the play, Kopit's ability both to use and to make grotesque fun of popular psychological ideas about American society and their representation on stage. When Jonathan takes out the fire axe, chops up his mother's Venus's-flytraps, and kills her piranha fish, Rosalie, standing amid the debris, says consolingly, "There's something bothering you, isn't there?" Her words pull us away from the comic exoticism of the setting, back to the conventional psychological melodrama where we have heard that line so many times before. Jonathan is, after all, the frustrated adolescent who finally breaks out into murder. Here, and throughout *Oh Dad*, the play makes use of cliché—both social and dramatic—and suggests that just beyond the laughter the cliché turns back again into truth. "You take the most serious thing you can think of," Kopit told *Mademoiselle*, "and treat it as comically as you can."

The theme, of course, is that favorite American one—the

emasculation of the male. Madame Rosepettle, who cannot remember the name of the son she dotes on, is a real American Mom (*Suddenly Last Summer* division), intent on protecting her boy's purity, dead certain that he is a winner ("Mother says I'm going to be great. . . . Of course, she doesn't know ex-actly what I'm . . . going to be great *in* . . ."). "Did I say cage?" she asks when the Commodore interrupts her story of Jonathan's birth. "I meant crib. I put him in a crib. . . ." As though to prove that there is more than one way to skin a kid, the play provides, as thematic balance to the dominating Madame Rosepettle, the offstage parents of the children for whom Rosalie is babysitter: "They're never home. They just mail me a check every week and tell me to make sure I keep the children's names straight."

Madame Rosepettle's entourage includes not only her stuttering son, but the dad of the title, the stuffed corpse of her husband ("He's my very favorite trophy"), for Madame Rosepettle is not only a mother; she is a woman as well. She is a familiar type, the iron maiden with the come-hither look. In her long monologue, she describes how she shut herself in a room, ignored the lusting males who came scratching at the door, opened only for Jonathan's father when he said the magic words ("Will you please marry me?") and then opened only once, which is how she had Jonathan. In the elaborately staged champagne supper, the hint of willing femininity quickly disappears and, using the waltz as though it were a weapon, she reduces the Commodore to a wheezing wreck who is barely able to crawl to safety. Rosalie is a complementary American type, the child seductress.[7] She is at her

---

[7] A girl in one of my classes complained about my use of "American" in this context, but I think of all the characters in Kopit's play as being American types, perhaps because of the idiom. Although Kopit dresses Rosalie in "childish pink," as though she were a ten-year-old, in my mind she is the sweater-and-skirted girl who once (when Kopit was in college, in fact) flourished on campuses and in the pages of *Mademoiselle* and *Seventeen*. With the pseudonursery styles that became popular in the mid-1960's, Rosalie's costume suddenly was transformed from a joke to a kind of incipient realism. In any case, for the student, who probably should have been complaining as a woman rather than as an American, I will admit that both Rosalie (the knowing innocent) and Madame Rosepettle (the seductive virgin) may be international female types. Still, they do seem very American to me.

best in the scene in which she attempts to seduce Jonathan on his
mother's bed, only to have the stuffed father come falling out of
the closet. "Who the hell is this!?" she asks matter-of-factly, and as
the horrified Jonathan tries to stutter out a reply, she adds, "What
a stupid place to keep a corpse." Although this is a hard-as-nails
parody of the mandatory tea-and-sympathy scene in which the shy
boy is helped to manhood, Rosalie is as much a devourer as the
mother she is trying to replace. Madame Rosepettle, recalling her
first glimpse of her husband, says that she knew "Albert would
be mine, all mine—mine to love, mine to live with, mine to kill;
my husband, my lover, my own . . . *my very own*." Rosalie says to
Jonathan, "I want you . . . all for myself. Not to share with your
mother, but for me, alone. . . ."

At first glance, *Oh Dad* appears to be a serious play trapped in
a pastiche of parody and nonsense. For this reason, presumably,
Martin Esslin (in *The Theatre of the Absurd*) seems to hear
Kopit saying, "Don't take this seriously, I am only piling on the
horror for the sake of fun!" In returning to the play, I find that,
the surprise having gone out of many of the lines, the fun is less
funny and the literary jokes (the "Rose" names kidding *The Rose
Tattoo*, the two Venus's-flytraps to the one in *Suddenly Last
Summer*) are very strained. Yet, much of this is less gratuitous
than it first appears. Kopit uses the chatter in Scene 1 about
stamps and coins and books, about plants and fish and the effi-
ciency of bellboys, not simply as a comic turn, but to establish
both Madame Rosepettle and Jonathan. Neither in this play nor in
the ones that follow can Kopit quite resist a joke when it occurs to
him, but it is a mistake to assume that any Kopit play is only the
sum of its jokes.

Aside from *Oh Dad*, the only other Kopit plays produced in
New York are *The Day the Whores Came Out to Play Tennis* and
Sing to Me Through Open Windows, two one-acters which were
offered on a short-lived double bill in 1965. *Sing* was first written
when Kopit was still in college and, as he says in the introduction
to *Whores*, "has been extensively and frequently rewritten." It was
used as a curtain-raiser during previews of *Oh Dad* but was withdrawn before the play opened in New York. It is a fantasy play

involving three characters—a boy, an old magician, and a clown —and its point is an ambiguous one, depending on which character is taken as the center of the play. Andrew, the boy, comes to see Ottoman, the magician, as he has every year for the past five years. Before their meeting, the Clown, who is actually some kind of servant dressed as a clown, awakens the protesting Ottoman by throwing open the windows. An exchange between the magician and the boy establishes that Andrew has grown, put on weight, graduated from public school. Ottoman performs a trick that the boy expects, pulling a rabbit from a hat, but this time the rabbit is dead. The Clown then forces the magician to play several "little games" with him, in each of which he menaces the old man, and at last performs a vanishing trick in which he does not vanish because the box is too small. Finally Andrew, who wishes he could stay, has to leave (they play this scene in the third person), Ottoman collapses, and the Clown packs him away in his own trunk.

Ottoman's lines are full of references to change, disappearance, fear; if the play is his, the menacing clown, who cannot be made to vanish in the box trick, must be death. Yet the play begins and ends with the boy. His opening lines establish a vaguely remembered time, and the magician's room materializes on stage; he is the last to leave the bare stage after the room disappears. There is a verbal connection between him and the Clown (the repeated line, "Five years, sir. To the day") which suggests that what the Clown does at the end is in some way connected with the boy. The implication, of course, is that Andrew is outgrowing childhood, that Ottoman represents a world of imagination that he must leave, however reluctantly, and that he is the death of the old man. *Sing*, then, is a play about age and death or about childhood —I prefer the latter view—but its weakness as a play does not lie in this problem of interpretation. Although its visual images—the mimetic scenes with the Clown—are sharp and forceful, the language is dull—either flatly sentimental ("he knows at that moment that he will soon be gone from there and will not see the magician again, ever again") or clumsily ornate for Ottoman

("Which is: that sometimes, Loveless, I am of the feeling that you open my windows solely in the hope that I might, as a result, contract what constitutes a death of cold"). The purity speeches in *Oh Dad,* with all their parodic overtones, are more genuinely lyrical than anything in *Sing to Me Through Open Windows.*

The Day the Whores Came Out to Play Tennis is a comedy designed to make a social point. It takes place in the Nursery of a private country club, where the governing committee has taken refuge, powerless to deal with the "catastrophe" that has befallen them. The club has been invaded by eighteen women, who arrive in two Rolls Royces decorated with raccoon tails and snappy sayings ("Doris Loves Dick") and who are now playing championship tennis on the club courts, wearing brightly colored tennis dresses and no pants at all. When the club president protests, they fart in unison; when another official tries to stop them, they beat him with tennis rackets and send him back inside with a note that says simply "Whores." While the attack from outside is under way, there is revolution within, for Duncan, the club's English servant, refuses to do what he is asked, talks back to the protesting members, finally deserts (wearing the president's tennis outfit) to join the ladies outside. As the play ends, the committee crouches inside while the tennis balls drum against the shutters which they hurriedly close when the first balls begin to smash through the windows.

"Clearly I had something besides country clubs in mind," Kopit told a *New York Times* interviewer (January 31, 1965). Clearly, he did. The club obviously represents a self-contained life, full of its own corruptions, with its own rules and its own defenses, suddenly menaced from outside. The committee members, who cover three generations, include a young man who spends most of the play sitting on a hobbyhorse and who cries at the possibility that he may be a cuckold; an old man who indulges in pointless practical jokes and who cheats to lose at gin rummy so that he can find someone to play with; the club wolf who is a predator only on safe home grounds; a childless man ("Anyway, as it turns out, we *both* were sterile. The doctor said we were a perfect pair") who worries about whether or not he is properly dressed. As though all this were not perfectly clear, the rummy-playing old man, one of the founders of the club, is named Old Gayve, a name that suggests Gayev, the ineffectual brother of *The Cherry Orchard*. The end of Kopit's play is almost a parody of Chekhov's if we take the committee as a kind of many-headed Firs. The committee, like Firs, is shut in, presumably to die (or to be replaced). The president's "With nothing to do. And *that's* the crying shame of it. Nothing to do. But sit in the Nursery like little children . . . and watch what we built collapse all about us" recalls Firs's "There's no strength left in you, nothing's left, nothing. . . ." The last words in Kopit's play are Old Gayve's barely audible "Tsk-tsk-tsk-tsk-tsk-tsk-tsk," while the tennis balls, like Chekhov's axes, sound in the audience's ears.

The difficulty with *Whores* is not that the Chekhov analogy is cleverer than it is necessary, but that the lines are only occasionally funny and the social point gets lost in the surface presentation of the characters. Judging by the names (and by the comedians who performed the play in New York: Phil Foster, Lou Gilbert), *Whores* is supposed to be a Jewish character comedy, less obvious in its idiom than the kind of play Gertrude Berg used to do. Perhaps Kopit intends that they should have no more specific significance than his bare-assed tennis players or his ungentlemanly gentleman's gentleman, but it is difficult to escape the suburban Jewish milieu and the suspicion that this play is not making a general social point but some kind of oblique comment on the Negro middle-class exodus, following the sons and grandsons of immigrants into the safe suburbs.

The other plays published in the collection to which *Whores* gives its title include *The Questioning of Nick* (1957), Kopit's first play, a very efficient realistic play in which the police get a confession from a boy by playing on his vanity and insecurity; *The Conquest of Everest* (1964), a "divertissement," in which an American tourist couple, intent on the sunset or love, beat a Chinese soldier to the top of Mount Everest; and *The Hero* (1964), a mime play in which a woman shares a man's billboard oasis and

rock-hard sandwich, smiling as though they had found comfort in
the approaching darkness. *Chamber Music*, the only other play in
the volume, is somewhat more ambitious. It was half of a program
called *Asylum*, originally scheduled for production in 1963 but
withdrawn before it could open. Now rewritten, *Chamber Music*
presents a chaotic ladies' committee business meeting in an insane
asylum. Chaired by a woman who thinks she is Susan B. Anthony
and with Gertrude Stein taking minutes,[8] the ladies (Osa Johnson, Pearl White, Amelia Earhart, St. Joan, Queen Isabella,
Mrs. Mozart) have to decide what to do about "the various feelings of hatred, hostility, jealousy, be-lli-gerency and revenge"
which they decide cannot come from them (although the meeting
displays such feelings in almost every line) and so must emanate
from the Men's Ward. After several presumably unworkable suggestions, Susan B. Anthony comes up with the idea of sending a
body as a warning. The ladies kill Amelia Earhart and promptly
forget why, each returning to her own delusion. What the play, at
least at this point, seems to be saying is that a nonexistent danger
can become so commanding that it can force an action, however
pointless, and that this action, if we believe Susan B. Anthony's
words ("If that didn't work, we could send another one in the
afternoon, then perhaps another the following morning") is subject to escalation. If Kopit seriously intends the play to give this
implication, he probably should have ended with the death or at
least the mad ritual over the body, but the play goes on to let us
(with Mrs. Mozart) hear music from the sky and to allow one of
the staff to make a long speech which pulls the attention away
from the women altogether. A good part of the play, of course, is
taken up with jokes (some of them funny) based on the characters the women think they are, but Kopit's invention becomes

[8] These two characters, plus a specific reference to the opera, suggest that
Gertrude Stein's *The Mother of Us All* may have somehow led Kopit to this
play. Not that there is any noticeable verbal or thematic connection between
the two works unless one wants to play with the lines in Stein's prologue,
"Pity the poor persecutor . . . . Because the persecutor gets persecuted." One
of Kopit's jokes about Stein contains incipient literary criticism. He provides
the character with Jonathan's stutter and then, in a Steinesque passage, suggests that Stein's style is only an extended stutter.

quickly repetitious (perhaps because that is the nature of delusion) and the serious core of the play is smothered in presumably comic detail. As in *Oh Dad*, Kopit is still walking the fine line between facility and substance.

ARNOLD WEINSTEIN

Arnold Weinstein's reputation as a playwright rests on a single play, *Red Eye of Love* (1961). It is a chaotic triangle play in which Wilmer Flange, the young idealist ("What would the world do without our type of people, people who stop to watch a girl dance in the street like this?"), struggles with O. O. Martinas, the meat tycoon ("You don't acquire delicatessen departments watching people dance in the street"), for the love of Selma Chargesse, who wants to dance in the streets (as she does in Scene 1) and to have security as well ("I only did it for the money"). While Wilmer searches for the key to the universe (it is variously bookkeeping, movies, dolls, being a traveling Santa Claus, military history, musicology, and meat) and O. O. builds extra stories on his meat department store, Selma passes back and forth between them until, toward the end of the play, the three get together in a meat-chopping *ménage à trois*. At the very end, Wilmer, still key-shopping, sets off "to live way out there among the Navaho," joined by Selma and O. O., who brings down the curtain on his plans for a fish department store: "First floor, flounder; second floor, sea bass. . . ."

The action, which is set in no particular time, is spread over years—including a depression and a war—but some characters age ("What are we getting so old about?" asks Selma) and some do not. As it was played in New York, *Red Eye* recalled the naive earnestness of the silent movie; on the page, it suggests an Horatio Alger story in reverse. "After years of failure—" says the First Policeman of Wilmer, and the Second Policeman finishes the sentence, "—he finds real failure." My description imposes on the play a stronger sense of order than the playwright does, for

Weinstein seems to be interested primarily in kidding around. He uses all kinds of gags, visual and verbal—blackouts, running gags, language games. He parodies Broadway chichés of frustration, sex confession, lostness ("Lost touch. *You* talk about lost touch! I've lost such touch!"), and the child as monster. He calls for projections on the curtain (a Brechtain device, although, considering his preoccupation with film, he is probably thinking of silent movie titles), but he will settle for the cards once used to announce vaudeville acts. Vaudeville, in fact, may be the key— to Weinstein, if not to the universe. At his best, he has a strong satirical imagination which can be seen not only in the not quite realized commercial-violence image of the meat department store, but in Wilmer's attempt to invent a doll that can get sick and die: "Kids would love that. Real live death to play with." Yet, the play never quite works at that level. It makes fun of everything from deodorants to war in the same tone of voice and ends by becoming amiable. Being funny would be enough if *Red Eye of Love* did not keep hinting that it wanted to be something more than that.

Most of the Weinstein work following *Red Eye of Love* opened and closed with such rapidity that I did not have a chance to see it, and none of it—aside from *Red Eye*—has been published. *Fortuna*, a musical based on an Eduardo de Filippo play, with music by Francis Thorne, and *The Twenty-five Cent White Cap*, a one-acter, played a few performances off-Broadway in 1962. Another short play, *They*, was done at Philadelphia's Theater of the Living Arts in 1965. It is a satirical piece which divides its attention between who "they" are and why one should worry about them (" 'They say that falling in love is wonderful.' Who's *they* in that song?") and the conventions of party-giving in which one invites strangers in the hope of return invitations. Except for a few provocative lines ("They set up burning voices on nearby lawns"), the play is a less funny attempt to utilize the not-quite-realistic sincerity that worked much better in *Red Eye*.

In 1964, *Dynamite Tonight*, a satirical musical for which Weinstein did the words and William Bolcom the music, played for one performance in an off-Broadway Actors Studio production. In 1967, after playing at the Yale School of Drama, a revised version of the show (among the revisions, *Tonight* became *Tonite*) tried off-Broadway again; this time it lasted a few performances longer. It is a pacifist play—very reminiscent of the 1930's—which takes place in a supply bunker underneath a battlefield after twenty years of fighting. Most of the songs are nonmelodic talk songs in which there is much repetition of lines, sometimes by one person, sometimes picked up by others; much of it suggests the kind of musical cartoon Marc Blitzstein wrote in *The Cradle Will Rock*. The basic satiric joke is the contrast between the situation of the soldiers and their complaints, lines about war being tough enough without having to eat at bad restaurants or without commercial films plunging to a new low. There are also extensive parodies of the kind of operetta Jeanette MacDonald and Nelson Eddy used to do in the movies. Much of it, like the satire of war in *Red Eye*, is both too obvious and too gentle. It is only with Smiley's song in the second act—in which, having lost his sight, he sings about how much he will miss the movies—that the show becomes horrifying as well as funny. That surely was the intention of the work as a whole. Although there is much inventiveness in *Dynamite Tonite*, most of it seems familiar in a way that *Red Eye of Love* does not; that play uses the familiar to surprise.

In *The History of America*, a sketch published in *Kulchur* (Spring, 1963), a group of men, each in a different hat with a personality to match, asks the bare-headed New Man, whom they all call Bill, to do something for them. He has the last line: "My name's not Bill." Weinstein is most effective with such understated neatness (the sketch is only two pages long), but too often his successful bits are surrounded by a kind of straining which suggests the busy bird in his poem "The Hysterical Parrot" (*Between Worlds*, Spring-Summer, 1961). It "forgot it had forgot how to fly."

FRANK D. GILROY

In a cartoon by Joseph Mirachi (*Harper's*, September, 1966), a solid, heavy-faced, moustached man sits in an audience, staring in disbelief at the program; the caption: "Expanded from a script for a television play! Oh, my God!" Although I looked in vain for a similar declaration in the program for Frank D. Gilroy's *That Summer—That Fall* (1967), his retelling of the Phaedra legend seemed more video than Greek in its origins. The thirteen brief scenes suggested the fragmented dramatic action that comes so naturally to television. Then, too, the play lasted no more than an hour and a half, even though it had been lengthened unnaturally by perilous pauses after every line. It was as though director Ulu Grosbard's rehearsal practices had been carried into the final production. In *About Those Roses*, Gilroy's day-by-day account of the difficulties in getting *The Subject Was Roses* on stage, he quotes Grosbard's words to the cast: "I don't care if you take three minutes between lines." Walter Kerr (*The New York Times*, April 2, 1967) is more kindly in the face of what used to be called "significant silences" when one talked about Maeterlinck; he assumes that Gilroy "undoubtedly intended that the empty spaces should be filled with passion all the more intense for being unspoken," but he admits that the spaces remained empty.

Finally, however, it was neither the many scenes nor the suspicious length that suggested television; it was the tone of the play. For me, there has always been something slightly soap-operatic about the unhappy classical triangle of father, son, and young stepmother (it probably has something to do with Madeleine Carroll in *My Son, My Son!*). Although Euripides, Racine, and even Robinson Jeffers manage somehow to save Phaedra from the limitations of domestic drama, Gilroy's Angelina (the Greeks have become Italians in lower Manhattan) is a heroine-victim in a more familiar tearful tradition. This is hardly surprising, for Gilroy's earlier plays, *Who'll Save the Plowboy?* (1962) and *The Subject Was Roses* (1964), are small, thin, naturalistic plays that go for simple character points and sentimental effects. The ghost of Greek tragedy hovering over *That Summer—That Fall* makes it ludicrous, and the earlier plays are never that. At worst, to get back to Gilroy's affinity for television, they are plays, as Arthur Laurents said of *Roses* (*The New York Times Magazine,* September 11, 1966) "so tiny they belong on the tiny screen where they will not be attenuated by an extra hour of padding."

What Larry Doyle wants to find out in *Who'll Save the Plowboy?* is whether or not Albert Cobb (the Plowboy) is happy. Larry is dying of a wound he got fifteen years earlier, saving Albert's life on the battlefield, and he hopes to discover that his death has some point. In the course of the play, he learns that Albert's life is totally empty; his child was born a monster, his marriage has collapsed into mutual recrimination, his job is meaningless drudgery. "The best thing you could have done was let him die that night," says Albert's wife. "He'd never admit it, but he feels that way himself." He says as much, obliquely, at the end of Act I when, drunk and maudlin, he pleads: "Take me to Florida. Give me a job. Talk to me. Help me, buddy. Save the Plowboy again."

The play is excessively expositional, carefully explaining what everyone needs to know so that it can build to the final scene, one which is effective as a strange mixture of horror and sentimentality. Albert, unaware that Larry has found out that the child who was named after him is a monster, comes in with an eleven-year-old boy who has been bribed with the train that Larry brought for his namesake's Christmas, and the four characters play a painful charade in which Albert tries to be the father, the boy is interested only in the train, and Larry and Albert's wife, in an abrupt change of character, attempt to protect the Plowboy in his deception. The situation is so contrived that the play seems less a drama involving the three main characters than it does an illustration of how bad things can be. In someone else's hands, the work might have become sardonic, an act of heroism and friendship that in retrospect becomes a foolish, even destructive gesture. Gilroy, who brings down the curtain as Albert switches on the train, offers the audience the comfort of tears.

Pat Hingle was among the many actors who read *The Subject Was Roses* before it came to production. Gilroy records his opinion in *About Those Roses*: "He liked the script, but thought Broadway had priced itself out of the luxury of such plays." Gilroy lets Hingle's appraisal, and others like it, stand in the printed diary—mild ironies from the reader's after-the-fact vantage point. The real irony, however, is that Hingle was right, and the painfully won success of *Roses* is a fluke that proves nothing about Broadway. No brave little band of small but sincere plays has arisen to challenge the musicals, the light comedies, the English imports, the star vehicles that dominate the commercial theater in New York in the mid-1960's. The success of *Roses* is unusual, not instructive. When Gilroy says that he is offering his diary "for those who like fairy tales," he is saying less about the diary itself (it is largely a collection of names, most of them unfamiliar) than he is about the aura that has grown up around the play. The play's success touches theater fans on that sensitive spot which, in the late 1930's, was tickled by film and stage musicals in which show-biz kids, against all obstacles, finally get their show open; one almost expects Gilroy to come on singing, "They call us babes in arms/But we are babes in armor."

The story is an attractive one. Financed by small contributions, mostly from friends; produced, directed, designed, and managed by men who had never done those jobs on Broadway before; acted by performers who were not stars; kept open with borrowed money when the favorable reviews (three raves, two mixed, one pan, but one of the raves from the powerful *Times*) failed to send audiences running to the theater; *Roses* held on, slowly built its audience, played to its first full house on its 136th performance, went on to win the Pulitzer Prize and the Drama Critics Circle Award and to run for almost two years. *Reader's Digest*, with an audience attuned to little people and big success, ran an article (June, 1966) on the *Roses* phenomenon and called it, inevitably, "The Subject Was Faith."

That *Roses*—like *Abie's Irish Rose* and *Tobacco Road* before it—made its own way against unlikely odds is fascinating (perhaps even admirable), but the telling of its tale does get in the way of any approach to the play itself. John Cleary, in *Roses*, is a self-made, up-from-the-slums boy, easy in manner in the outside world, defensively impersonal at home; his wife is shabby genteel with a bad family hang-up. Each has developed a manner (she martyred, he aggressive) that keeps them, except in rare moments, from getting through to one another. In the play, which is set in 1946, their son Timmy comes home from the war, able now to understand some of the things that are wrong with his parents' marriage and—unable to change them—sets out on his own with their blessing. The action, insofar as there is one, lies in Timmy's arrival at understanding. A mother's boy when he left home, her ally in the family quarrel, he returns in Act I intent on making it up to his father, only to learn before Act II is over that there is no point in choosing sides: "When I left this house three years ago, I blamed *him* for everything that was wrong here . . . When I came home, I blamed *you* . . . Now I suspect that no one's to blame . . . Not even me."

The play is not sentimental in the traditional way; that is, Timmy's coming home does nothing to solve his parents' twenty-year-old difficulties. Richard Watts, Jr. (New York *Post*, May 26, 1964) and John McClain (New York *Journal-American*, same date), the authors of the mixed reviews, both had misgivings about the play's resolution. McClain seemed to be looking for the standard happy ending, but Watts's doubts were more complicated and never very clear in the review itself. In his feeling that the end "seems ineffectual," Watts may have been onto something, because the resolution is a false one. Too honest to use his returning veteran as a marriage counselor, Gilroy shifts his focus from the failed marriage to the relationship of son to parents. It is the business of the last two scenes to let Timmy give and receive declarations of love (obliquely in the father's case, of course) so that his departure is not a rupture but a release. Yet Gilroy has established the characters of the parents so effectively, has so carefully indicated that their love for Timmy is hopelessly muddled in their use of him as a weapon, that the ending—particularly the big scene between Timmy and his father—seems not to grow from the characters but from some need outside the play.

Although I dislike the kind of criticism that confuses biography with the work under discussion, I do not see how it can be avoided in this case. Gilroy has too often announced that the play is based on his own family. In *About Those Roses*, after a worried call to Jack Albertson assuring him that they were about to go into rehearsal, he asks his diary: "Am I overly solicitous of Jack because he is the father? Am I trying to do something for him that I never had the chance to do for my own father?" The *Reader's Digest* article, which calls the play "a poignant letter of love to his parents," quotes Gilroy: "This is my way of saying how I came to love them. I wish I'd had the understanding and compassion for them when I was young that I have now." Unlike Eugene O'Neill, who never gave to Edmund in *Long Day's Journey into Night* the "deep pity and understanding and forgiveness" which were his own, Gilroy gets his wish and lets Timmy have that "understanding and compassion." The last two scenes—particularly the final one—seem to be a self-indulgence on the author's part. It would make little difference if it were not that those scenes soften the portrait of the marriage, asking for affectionate sympathy where something more austere might have been possible. The psychological and societal exposition that explains the differences between the parents is of little dramatic value, but their quarrels—the best thing in the play—are effective because they reflect patterns of conflict that are habitual, repeated arguments in which the participants use ordinary things (expenses, say) as the means of voicing a division that is deeper, about which they cannot speak. In the end, Gilroy erases that effectiveness. Having had his big love scene between father and son, he lets the family settle into a morning routine in which the father's curtain line, another complaint about the coffee, reduces the revelation of good naturalistic drama to the lump in the throat of kitchen comedy.

In his review of *Roses* (New York *Herald Tribune*, May 26, 1964) Walter Kerr speaks of "alienation" and "estrangement" but, slipping into his favorite anti-intellectual pose, goes on to talk happily of Gilroy's decision "to let the cosmos go hang." The terms are a bit grandiose for Gilroy's plays, but they do suggest an attitude that underlies all his work. All three of these plays are about marriages in which the participants cannot speak to one another and in which there is not even the comfort of sex; there are rejection scenes in each of them. Even in "Far Rockaway," the playlet that Gilroy wrote for the Lincoln Center's look-at-us television special (Fall, 1965), the hero is a man to whom no one can or will listen. Although *The Only Game in Town* (1968) ends, as Broadway comedies should, with the incipient sound of wedding bells, it is a soapy rather than a comic account of two people who overcome their fears of committing themselves and agree to a marriage ("the only game in town") even though they know, perhaps because they have seen the earlier Gilroy plays, that it is a "feeble and wheezing institution." Implicit in all these plays is a sense of things as bleak as that in Albee. Yet, bleakness is not Gilroy's subject. Nor does he seem to be able (or to want) to create characters with the power and the validity to light the darkness. Instead, he stays close to stereotype and manipulates his situation, however depressing, so that at the final curtain he backs away from the implications of his material and asks the audience to cry and to smile through its tears. After the first preview performance of *Roses*, he wrote in his diary: "Many tearful faces coming up the aisle after the play. I suspect this play may appeal more to the public to the critics." He may have been wrong about the reviewers, who are after all only extensions of the public, but he had taken the measure of his own talent.

WILLIAM HANLEY

William Hanley made his off-Broadway debut in 1962 with a pair of one-actors, *Whisper into My Good Ear* and *Mrs. Dally Has a Lover*. With the first of these, the first of his plays accepted for production, he had already found the form—the revelatory conversation—that he has used in all his dramatic work to date. *Whisper* is a desultory discussion between two old men, during which they decide not to carry out the double suicide that they have planned. The title derives from Max's account of his father,

who was deaf in one ear and into whose good ear he whispered his
secrets until the day that he heard his mother and father laughing
over his discovery of girls. The point, made explicitly (as always
with Hanley), is that if one has something important to say, he
need not shout, as Charlie suggests, but whisper into the good ear
if he can find it. Charlie is Max's good ear, the one he can trust
(he admits his homosexuality to Charlie), and Max's reluctant
decision not to kill himself at the end ("I don't want to do it
alone") is presumably his recognition that, bleak though their
lives may be, they are friends, and that is something of value. In
reducing the play to the few lines above, I have attempted to
avoid the kind of adjective which might evoke the sound of hearts-
and-flowers music, but, even so, the play's central situation stands
exposed as a sentimental commonplace. Hanley's characters—in
this play and the later ones—are close to stereotype; Max, the
presumed realist, is the sentimental person, and the romantic
Charlie is the practical one. Such characters are least interesting
when they are most aware of themselves and trying to convey that
awareness to one another (*i.e.*, to the audience). Hanley's work is
most attractive when his dialogue is apparently aimless, when its
meanderings in fact form a pattern through which the characters
emerge.

Mrs. Dally Has a Lover is a much more interesting play, both
in its strengths and in its weaknesses. In this case the conversation
is post-coital, with the middle-aged Mrs. Dally and Frankie, her
eighteen-year-old lover, talking while she gives him coffee and
sews the buttons back on his shirt. That she tore them off in her
eagerness, fortunately before the curtain went up, may push the
affair in the direction of *Alfie*, but Hanley presumably, and rightly,
wants her to be busy at a maternal action while the play is going
on. We learn a lot about Mrs. Dally and her marriage—from her
standpoint only; her husband cheats on her and makes fun of her
sensitivity ("No class. The brute") and they once had a child who
drowned while her husband was flirting with a girl and who, had
he lived, would now be Frankie's age. This biographical material,
typical of Hanley's preoccupation with excessive motivation, is

much less important than the situation presented on stage; it is in the here-and-now of his characters that Hanley shows his greatest talent. Mrs. Dally is continually aware of the difference in age between her and Frankie and the necessary effect that will have on their affair (she understands the implications for them of the Donne poem "The Good-morrow," which she recites), and she cannot be comfortable with what she has. Frankie, on the other hand, cannot understand what disturbs her. He is instinctively gentle, capable of surprise sweetnesses or insights which touch her, but he is also potentially the husband (as in his reaction to the sweater Mrs. Dally bought and her husband rejected) and is always eighteen. When they part at the end of the play, at the end of their afternoon, nothing much has happened except that she has tried to make him see the world as she does.

The best thing about the play is that Hanley recognizes that Mrs. Dally is a difficult woman, demanding and self-preoccupied for all her presumed understanding, and, for this reason, the conversations involve patterns of approach and withdrawal which are at once accurate and moving. One example should serve. She has just finished an excited description of the Cellini cup in the Metropolitan Museum, and Frankie responds with genuine admiration, "Sometimes you look happy about the damnedest things." She cannot leave the response alone, accept it as an instance of affection and bewilderment; she must believe that "you ain't as dumb as you think you are." So she pushes, wanting to know what makes Frankie happy. Unsure of what she is after, he retreats in embarrassment, unwilling to risk looking foolish. By the time he can speak, expressing his pleasure in watching his sisters ("I felt happy when the kids were going for their candy"), she has retreated in her turn, hurt that he resisted her, and can only respond by flattening what she has conjured. "You asked me, I'm tellin' ya," he says, and she answers, "Okay. You want a sandwich?" For several lines, she tries to use food to stop the words in his mouth, until they work back around to her, to them, and she is involved again. It is in moments like this that the play rises above the burden of literary device and idea with which Hanley weighs it down.

The first problem with the play is Mrs. Dally herself. She is the wife of a taxi driver, living in a shabby railroad apartment and speaking the vernacular of her surroundings. She is also an incipient intellectual, a reader of Donne, a confirmed museum-goer. I do not deny that there are women who are both, but they are difficult to believe on stage. The artistic life of Mrs. Dally is familiar Broadway shorthand for sensibility, and it must be taken that way or else as a sign of pretentiousness on her part. In either case, it detracts from the portrait of a sensitive woman in a milieu that makes her vulnerable, one which Hanley draws most effectively in the moments when Cellini and Donne are forgotten.

The play's chief difficulty, however, is not the slightly false veneer on Mrs. Dally; it lies in a conflict between the action and the messages the work tries to carry. It is excessively explicit about the difficulty of communication and the need, in the face of the transitoriness of love, to learn to carry what is best in one relationship into the next, to "pass it on," as the children's game puts it. It would be comforting if we could take this sentimentalization only as Mrs. Dally's, for she is the character who makes the points, but the total impression is that the ideas are important to Hanley too, and his other plays confirm that kind of softness. Without them the play exists simply as a presentation of character, the present uncertainties and inevitable end of an affair, the demands and comforts of love, and the frightening effects of a difference in ages. For that, it needs no packageable concepts and fewer conventional literary indicators.

Hanley told a *New York Times* interviewer (December 13, 1964) that he wrote *Mrs. Dally* when the producer asked for a play to pair with *Whisper*. It is not *Whisper*, however, but *Today Is Independence Day*, published with the two earlier plays in *Mrs. Dally Has a Lover and Other Plays* (1963), that is the companion piece to *Mrs. Dally*. It is another conversation, this one between Mrs. Dally (Evalyn) and Sam, the husband, the "brute." It is far less intricate than *Mrs. Dally*, less interesting as characterization, for what is implicit in the dialogue of the earlier play is here carefully labeled. As Sam keeps saying, Evalyn is a trial because she wants to change people and because she wants to get inside them, to understand their motivations. We saw this in *Mrs. Dally;* in *Independence Day* we hear too much about it.

The action is a simple one; Sam almost leaves her but does not. Her attempts to keep him fail because she can change the color of her hair (she dyes because "When I was a blond we used to have a lot more fun") but not the complexion of her mind. "Oh, Jesus," says Sam at the beginning of the play when she insists that he means *innuendo*, not *implication*, "flashing your brains around so early in the morning?" It is the news that she is going to a psychiatric clinic—the last intellectual outrage—that sends him to the door, where he is stopped by a box of flowers, his birthday gift to her. Marriage, the play implies, is a business of accident and habit as much as of understanding and passion. Fortunately, the idea is not explicitly spelled out, but neither is it embedded in character as the transitory nature of the affair is in the earlier play. *Independence Day* remains primarily a trick. It is presumably designed to stand alone, but whatever ironies it carries arise from the fact that we know it is taking place after the affair with Frankie (one line indicates this) and that much of the incidental information is already known in another context.

With *Slow Dance on the Killing Ground* (1964), Hanley made the transition to Broadway.[9] At the end of Act One of this play, the first full-length Hanley play to reach New York, the playwright introduces a third character into his familiar two-person discussion, but the entrance of Rosie does not herald a new departure in dramaturgy for the author. The action is still primarily talk, but in this case the revelation is much more formal (each of the three

---

[9] There was an earlier attempt, *Conversations in the Dark* (1963), which closed during its Philadelphia try-out. According to Ernest Schier's review (Philadelphia *Bulletin*, December 24, 1963), it is a play in which two couples in various combinations (husband-wife, husband-wife, lovers) carry on the titular conversations which are about the problems of infidelity. Schier's exasperation is apparent in this line: "And they talk. Like how does he feel and how does she feel, and how does he feel about the way she feels and vice versa?"

characters gets a set piece), and the generalized concept appears to be more important than the characters who illustrate it. All three of them are losers, victims unable to escape the violence of the world ("That is the *killing* ground out there") to which they contribute. Randall is a young Negro with a genius IQ, a prostitute for a mother, and a hole in his heart, who uses a cape, sneakers, dark glasses, an umbrella sharpened at the end, and a language that is half hipster, half Uncle Tom as his mask, his insulation.[10] Rosie is a college girl from the Bronx with a success-oriented stepfather and a lack of good looks, in search of an abortion after her one ludicrous attempt at romance, who is against hypocrisy but wears an orange wig. Glas, who runs the candy store in which the play takes place, is the last to tell his story. He is a German Communist who, presumably to keep himself free to fight the Nazis, deserted his Jewish wife and son and, as a railway engineer, transported Jews to a concentration camp; when the Stalin-Hitler pact was signed, he discovered, too late, that his cause was hollow, escaped to America, and is now hiding behind the dirty windows of the candy store waiting for a judgment which only he can make. It is for the sake of Glas's story that the action takes place on June 1, 1962, the day that Eichmann was hanged.

The first two acts having been devoted to unmasking, the third is concerned with what cannot be done. A mock trial is held in which Glas is found guilty not only of abandoning his family and transporting Jews, but of continuing to live. Randall executes him with an empty pistol and then turns the gun on Rosie and himself. In that gesture, the play's best dramatic image, the guilt of all three and the impossibility of doing anything are brought together neatly and effectively. Hanley, of course, cannot leave it here. Rosie, suddenly aware that Randall did not know for certain that

---

[10] Although the details are different and the playwright uses the character for quite another purpose, the Sax in Lewis John Carlino's *Sarah and the Sax* (1962) suggests Randall in his defensive use of eccentric dress and a slipping hipster facade. The similarity is emphasized by the fact that Clarence Williams III, who was to play Randall six months later, appeared as the Sax at the Theatre de Lys, May 4, 1964.

the gun was unloaded, initiates a discussion of the implications of it all, and Glas is forced to spell out the fact that Randall must die violently for what he has done (by this time we know that he has killed his mother) as Glas must live without the violence which would give him release and she must do whatever she is going to do (substitute art for life, says Randall earlier) because "We choose the dark streets up which we walk. . . . And if we are guilty of the denial of life . . . who is there to save us from that . . . but ourselves?" This kind of heavy explicitness runs all through the play, explanations trampling simple presentations that have already done the job. At the beginning of the play, Glas, as store-keeper, asks, "What can I do for you?" Randall toys with the phrase, "I mean, what can you *do* for me. The possibilities are endless . . . ," but he settles for an egg cream which, since the seltzer tap is broken, Glas cannot provide. After that, the relentless discussion about the impossibility of saving others comes as ponderous afterthought, even when Rosie, who is never as cynical as she likes to think, is seen struggling not to believe in their helplessness.

Slow Dance is a difficult play to accept. Its three characters are creations that reflect contemporary concerns—the "Negro problem," guilt in relation to the Nazi death camps, the limitations of the middle-class family structure—without making valid comments on them. Instead, they are used to make and remake Hanley's point about the "killing ground." Yet, for all the underlining, there is something amorphous about the play, as though Hanley wanted to use Randall's vitality, Glas's compassion, Rosie's naivety to make a positive statement in the midst of a play with a controlling idea that is completely despairing. He admits as much to the *Times* interviewer when he says, "If, in the final moments of the play, the audience has faced the darkness, and if, at least, the thought is planted that there might be something better, that's all that it's about." The trouble is that the possibility of something positive does not exist in the action of the play. In fact, there is no unifying action. Each scene provides its own revelation, one which does not move us toward a conclusion; at best, each contributes to an intellectual point which is at variance with the emotional center of the play. For, finally, a strange thing happens in *Slow Dance on the Killing Ground*. The three characters manage somehow to break the ideational bonds that constrict them and, by the end of the play, to suggest a small community of concern which reaches out to the audience. It is this, I suspect, and not whatever the play is trying to say, that brought the favorable reviews. Hanley said in the *Times*, "They were real people to me. What they finally represent to others may be something bigger and larger and that's all to the good." That's a difficult statement to swallow, as hard to get down as his insistence that his gratuitous forum is a real candy store. Perhaps the opposite of his statement is true—that he started out with concepts and ended with almost viable characters. In any case, it is clear that *Slow Dance*, for all its shortcomings, is Hanley's most ambitious attempt at a play.

It might even be called his last attempt at a play. In 1965, *Mrs. Dally Has a Lover* and *Today Is Independence Day* were produced on Broadway under the collective title *Mrs. Dally*. According to the listing in *The Best Plays of 1965–1966*, it was supposed to be "an extensive re-working" of the earlier material, but the reviews do not give that impression. The play, indifferently received, had a limited run. Hanley has yet to indicate that he can write a play in which character and concept work together, in which the idea is embodied rather than illustrated or explicated.

MURRAY SCHISGAL

"The only way to really get yourself any kind of attention is to be produced in the New York theater, not only the attention of the rest of the United States but also the rest of the world." So Murray Schisgal told Alan S. Downer in a USIA interview (in *The American Theater Today*), taped after it was clear that *Luv* was a great commercial success. The ironic thing about the remark is that Schisgal is one of those playwrights, like Albee, who came to the American theater only after his work had been produced in Europe—England, in Schisgal's case. *Schrecks,* a bill of three one-acters—*The Typists, The Postman* (later called *The Tiger*), and *A Simple Kind of Love Story*—subtitled "An Evening of Hysteria," opened in London on December 11, 1960. The next year, London saw *Ducks and Lovers,* a full-length play involving a gypsy king who goes into advertising and his transmigrated father who gets cooked in a duck soup (or so I gather from the English reviews); it has yet to be produced in the United States. On April 18, 1963, *Luv* opened in London in a production which, according to Harold Clurman (in *The Naked Image*), never realized the possibilities in the script; it may, then, have been the particular New York production and not the fact of New York production that gave Schisgal the "attention" he speaks fondly of in the quotation above. In any case, by the time *Luv* turned up in London, Schisgal had made his American debut; *The Typists* and *The Tiger* opened off-Broadway earlier that year.

The Typists is the story of a young man and woman with the conventional dreams (of success in his case, marriage in hers) who grow old at their typewriters, doing the routine job of addressing advertising postcards. The play uses the passage of an ordinary office day (it opens with sun streaming through the window and closes "almost in complete darkness") to represent their lives. The two characters, like those in Thornton Wilder's *The Long Christmas Dinner,* age perceptibly as the day passes. In the process, the man gradually accepts that he will not become a lawyer and will not "make my bundle," that his marriage is a mess, that drink is a comfort; the woman accepts that there will be no phone calls and no one to go home to but mother, that she will always be the sibling who lost, whose sister got not only their father's love (the onyx ring) but a husband and family. The play is sprinkled with the kind of cliché that has become Schisgal's trademark and target ("We all live alone, Miss Payton; we all live alone in a cruel and lonely world"), but only occasionally, as in their mutual analysis scene in which each decides that the other wanted "love," does it become comic. The prevailing tone is sentimental, which, I assume, was Schisgal's intention—a play to balance the satire of *The Tiger*. The weakness in *The Typists* is that Schisgal lacks a quality that Wilder has, an ability to use bromidic idiom in a way that is at once funny and touching. The reason is that Schisgal is not genuinely idiomatic. His lines are overstatements (for instance, the "cruel and lonely" in the line quoted above), like those in Jules Feiffer cartoons, comments on attitudes and habits of speech rather than reproductions of them. They tend to come out aggressively comic or mushy. *The Typists*, going for mildness, ends in mush.

The *Tiger* is much more successful at the cliché game. In it a bookish postman, asserting his "primitive, animal strength," kidnaps and carries back to his basement apartment a suburban housewife who is in town for her weekly breather, a game of bridge with the girls. The central joke, so far as the action is concerned, is that the abductor throws his masculine weight around, threatening violence, demanding obedience, in a way that quickly indicates his helplessness to the audience, which waits complacently for the victim, busy at various feminine escape ruses, to realize that she is not in danger. Once this realization comes and the couple relax into conversation, Schisgal sends them wandering hand-in-hand through the land of intellectual cliché, stopping at all the proper lamentable landmarks: conformity, lack of communication, loss of identity, competitive materialism, the atomic bomb. Most of the speeches are obvious, but they become funny in the context of the kidnaping and through the earnestness and sense of discovery with which they are delivered. Schisgal manipulates the discussion to get specific comic effects, as when he has the woman keep repeating, "Nobody listens," while the man, busy talking, fails to hear her; or as in her speech on suburban routine and indifference which somehow ends in her trying to sell him a raffle ticket. Her attempt to teach him French leads— as French must in their bromidic paradise—to a lights-out sexual interlude and the promise of future trysts which will convert their basement bower into a suburban home-away-from-home: "Next time I come I'm going to give this place a good cleaning. It's a mess."

Every time one of the men in *Luv* asks Ellen a question and she snaps out the precise answer (on 1928 election returns, on Sugar Ray Robinson's record), I am reminded of the scene in *The Tiger* in which the couple have an information contest that ends in a spelling bee. It is not in its details, however, but in its general tone and intention that *Luv* resembles *The Tiger*, for the full-length comedy, like the one-acter, is an extended joke about the stereotypes that pervade our speech and thought. In an interview in *The New York Times* (November 22, 1964), Schisgal spelled out the meaning of the play so explicitly that his remarks sound almost like a critical parody:[11] "The sense of it is that the emotion of love has been perverted and misused to such an extent that it can only be defined by using another word which comes closer to what we experience, to what we think, and how we behave. . . . L-u-v is the perversion of l-o-v-e."[12] The tone of the play is set at the beginning when Milt interrupts Harry, who is about to commit suicide, and keeps him teetering on the bridge railing as he launches into a conventional long-time-no-see speech ("How have you been doing, Harry? What's been happening?").

The pattern of the play is a simple one, based on two very obvious reversals. In Act I, Milt persuades Harry to live, assuring him that love will counter the existential meaninglessness of it all,

[11] Schisgal has a problem about interviews. Perhaps because the material of his comedy is stereotype and generalizations on any subject (particularly the aesthetics of playwriting) run to cliché, he always sounds as though he is (or ought to be) joking. This is particularly noticeable in the USIA interview in which he rambles, repeats himself, mouths fatuous truths: "I am trying to keep them [the audience] on the edge of their seats and to have them participate with me in what the actors are doing. I think astonishment and awe belong properly in the theater. If I can manage an iota of either emotion, well, that's what I am striving for anyway." On the page, his jargon-ridden remarks are funny enough, but on tape, emphasized by his hesitations, they are a delight. His mutual interview with Alan Arkin (*TV Guide*, September 3, 1966), which is intentionally funny, cannot touch the USIA one for pure amusement, and it, presumably, is an accidental parody. Here lies the danger for Schisgal, not only as interviewee, but as playwright when and if he decides to write a serious play without a satiric surface.

[12] *Luv* may be a perversion of *love* to Schisgal, but it is the way *love* is spelled in Sir James Pitman's "initial teaching alphabet." According to most teachers of the method (as reported by Joseph Adcock in *The Sunday Bulletin Magazine*, November 20, 1966), children make an easy transition from i/t/a to standard English. Maybe there is a message in there for Schisgal.

and then Harry convinces Milt to live by agreeing to meet Ellen, the wife who will not give Milt the divorce he wants. At the end of Act I, Ellen leaves Milt for Harry, and in Act II, after several unsuccessful attempts to murder Harry, Milt and Ellen go off together again. Within this frame of action, the three characters perform a number of vaudeville turns, which include slapstick accidents at the bridge railing and Harry's knife-throwing trick. Some of these—particularly the second-act gags about falling into the water—look like filler, an attempt to puff out a short play that has already done all that it is going to do, but most of the routines have thematic relevance. Harry's sudden attacks of paralysis in which he "stiffens like a board and . . . topples forward," his momentary blindness, deafness, muteness provide opportunities for familiar physical and verbal gags which can be used to satirize the fashionable sense of desolation which wonders what's to move, see, hear, say in such a world. Ellen's torch song ("Love cast its shadow over my heart"), which becomes a romantic duet (Ellen and Harry) and a joyful solo (Milt at the end of Act I), is a standard parody, which kids the way popular music uses and is used by people in l-u-v.

Aside from all the business that harks back to well-worn vaudeville and revue turns, there are comic routines, like those in *The Tiger*, designed to mock contemporary attitudes and the American penchant for analyzing, defining, measuring them. First Milt and Harry and then Ellen and Harry vie to see who had the most unhappy childhood. Ellen's nonstop self-analysis covers, among other things, the plight of the intellectual woman in a society that will not let her be both an intellectual and a woman ("But why did they teach me trigonometry and biochemistry and paleontology? . . . I'll never forgive the Board of Education for that"). Ellen's performance charts are a comment on scientific sexuality and on the fondness for cataloguing information. The "How much do you love me?" cliché survives an Act I drubbing, when Harry and Ellen go through a series of laboratory tests to see if their love can withstand pain (he stomps on her foot, she punches him in the stomach) and material deprivation (he throws her mink into the river), and at the end of Act II it rides off stage with Ellen and Milt, each assuring the other that he loves "more."

What all this adds up to is a series of sketches, somewhat broader than those done by Mike Nicholas and Elaine May or the various *Second City* companies, held together by a plot that is also a joke. The trick with *Luv*, as B. Poirot-Delpech said in his review in *Le Monde* (November 14–15, 1965), is that it speaks to two audiences at once, the admirers of *Cactus Flower* and those of *The Bald Soprano*; in this play, at least, Murray Schisgal managed to write an absurdist satire that is also a successful Broadway comedy. Still, as the French critic said, it is *"un peu étiré."*

Once *Luv* was established as a hit on Broadway, Schisgal published *Fragments, Windows and Other Plays,* a collection of five one-acters. There is no indication in the volume of when he wrote these plays, all of which carry a 1965 copyright. Jax, one of the characters in *Fragments,* shares not only Harry's sense of the meaninglessness of things but also his on-again-off-again paralysis, blindness, and deafness, which makes me suspect that this one, at least, was written before *Luv;* it seems unlikely that a playwright would shift a device from a successful play to a later one-acter. Two of the plays, *Fragments* and *Reverberations* (renamed *The Basement*), had a brief off-Broadway run in the fall of 1967. *Fragments* is the more interesting of the two.[13] Three men (Jax, Max, and Baxter) share a single room, which is divided into private living areas which they do not want one another to cross. Jax spends the play lying on a cot, dictating nonsense letters to various authorities ("To the Atomic Energy Commission, Keep up your good work. Best regards"), waiting to die: "Oh, God, I'm dying, and I've done nothing, I've learned nothing, nothing, nothing, nothing." Baxter is a drunk who comes back, after a few lost days, with a knife that he bought to commit suicide. Max is the one who works, the neat one, the one who tries to believe "the world is tomorrow, with decent education, with science, with understanding," but Baxter's "Make noise" and Jax's "He's a baby"

[13] The discussion here is based on the printed plays. There were presumably revisions before the New York opening (the name of the hero of *Reverberations* was changed to Zach), but, judging by Clive Barnes' review (*The New York Times*, October 3, 1967), the changes were minimal.

belie that possibility. They keep passing Baxter's knife back and forth, suggesting suicide or threatening murder. Ann, who comes to visit them, to help them and be helped by them, turns to one after another, only to be driven away by their failure to make clear what they want from her. At the end Baxter and Max are struggling with one another, while Jax lies on his cot repeating a "When we were boys" speech that has been used a number of times before. In fact, the play is built on repetition of speeches—directly or in slight variations—presumably to suggest a pattern of recurrence. There are a number of hints (they have all been working on a novel for ten years, Max turns out to have written a Jax letter, they cannot get away from one another) to suggest that the three men are fragments of a single personality, but whether they are one or three, their situation is marked by despair. Although there are a number of jokes and a number of passages that might play funnily, *Fragments* is apparently doing seriously what *Luv*, in the character of Harry, was doing satirically.

Reverberations is a more difficult play to characterize. It appears to be a comedy about a monomaniacal researcher (a mad scientist? there is much business of inserting tubes in the orifices of a chimpanzee) whose selfless devotion (there is a fantasy sequence in which he humbly accepts an award) to truth has caused him to sacrifice his family. Both the scientist (Max) and his family (represented by his wife and brother) appear at first as figures of fun. The scene with the wife is primarily a Jewish-mother routine (eat, you should force yourself), which incidentally recapitulates their courtship (in I-said-you-said dialogue) and establishes that they are childless by his choice. The scene with the brother is straight out of a standard Jewish-family play, an attempt at emotional blackmail (father's dying, think what you owe me, don't you care what your nephews look like, Uncle Eli is dying) to get Max home again. The chief device in the play is that Max will let no one into his basement laboratory; the wife plays her scene on the stairway so that the audience sees only her legs and the brother is simply a large head peering in the barred window. There is a sudden transition toward the end of the play in which the brother, as Max nails boards across the window to shut him out, whispers that the wife cried when she saw pictures of the nephews. "He's lying, Mina. . . . Tell him he's lying," shouts Max, and her answer "clearly, deliberately cold and emphatic" is "I hate you. How I hate you." At this point, the lights fade and the chimpanzee begins to glow red in the dark. It is difficult to conceive of the play except as a grotesque comedy, but surely Schisgal intends that the accusations of the wife and brother be taken as Max's own self-accusations, reverberations, as the title says; this requires the audience to take seriously the stereotypical ideas that the play itself—by its use of cliché, by its physical tricks—appears to be mocking.

The other three plays in the collection are *Windows, Memorial Day,* and *The Old Jew.* The last of these is an extremely fakey play, ostensibly about a lonely old man who, having lost his family and his sweetheart in the concentration camps, is unable to exist in society. It consists of a monologue in which he invites his invisible neighbors to come in and then denounces them for having forgotten; as his denunciation builds, the phone rings and, in answering it, the old man is revealed as a young actor who, judging by an echo line, shares some of his character's loneliness. Similarly pat endings mar the other two plays, but they are more interesting, if only as examples of Schisgal's preoccupation with cliché. *Windows* is a play about the strangeness of being a stranger, in which a young couple, certain that they will not be accepted in their new neighborhood, are at first abused by and then—after an encounter with a group of teen-agers—invited to join the neighbors. The young people speak an adolescent variation ("we kids of this generation") on the jargonesque summing-up speeches of Ellen in *Luv.* *Memorial Day* is an antifamily play that looks for a minute as though it is going to be antiwar. It is a sketch in which a couple go to pull their son out of a dry well in which they have hidden him to keep him from going to a war that has just ended. As they manipulate the rope, their conversation reveals the standard pointless marriage and the usual contest for the son's love; what they pull up is a straw dummy in a soldier's suit.

At his best—in *The Tiger* and *Luv*—Schisgal plays a serious comic game designed to puncture the balloons of cliché which pass as speech and thought among many Americans, particularly semieducated, urban college graduates. His work, inventive as it is, is beset by two problems. The first is that he has established a tone which he cannot escape. He has been so successful in using the earnestness of his characters as a satirical device that plays less clearly defined than *Luv—Fragments*, for instance—seem like unrealized jokes rather than attempts at pain or pathos. If Schisgal is limited in the ways in which he can be serious, his work is also marred by a tendency toward comic overstatement. In a review of *Luv* that later appeared as the Introduction to the published play, Walter Kerr blamed Mike Nichols, the director, for "the easy humor of producing chamber-pots." Whether it was Nichols or Schisgal who first thought of the chamber pot that Milt finds as he rummages in the trash basket, it has found its way into the published script and has thus attached itself to Schisgal. It is certainly typical of a kind of obviousness that the playwright often falls back on, as in the ending of *Luv* when the audience-pleasing dog hangs onto Harry's pants leg, reminding us that his disillusionment began when a dog urinated on him. There is a minimal amount of humor in a peeing dog, and what there is is quite different in quality and intention from the central comic concerns of *Luv*. A similar obtrusive joke occurs at the end of *The Typists* when, after a lifetime of addressing cards, Paul finally reads the advertisement on the other side and discovers, "We've been selling knickers." In this case, the line is an apparent hangover from the English production, not even recognizable as a joke to most American audiences.

The best examples of Schisgal's inclination to overdo can be found in *The Love Song of Barney Kempinski* (1966), the combination travelogue, slapstick chase, and character comedy which the American Broadcasting Corporation used to launch their highly publicized Stage 67, a program that was supposed to bring creative writing back to television. Schisgal's problem here is that, too often, after inventing a successful joke he ruins it by trying to top it. For instance, after an extended and very funny sequence in which the hero tries to deliver a package to a yogi in a contemplative trance, there is an explosion (into nirvana presumably) which leaves the yogi floating in the air. On another occasion the hero is denounced as a thief by a clerk in the courthouse, a little character gem of outraged pettishness, and then Schisgal kills the characterization by revealing that the clerk's desk drawer is full of stolen watches. Schisgal is among the cleverest of the playwrights of the 1960's, but even his best work hints that his cleverness may be a burden as well as a blessing.

FOUR

The Negro Revolution

Bow, Mr. Blackbird, bow, Mr. Crow.
Bow, Mr. Blackbird, bow no mo'!
—FROM A CHILDREN'S RING
GAME, SOUTHERN GEORGIA

When *Sponono*, the South African play by Alan Paton and Krishna Shah, ran briefly on Broadway in April, 1964, Loften Mitchell and Langston Hughes went to see it together. Mitchell describes the occasion in *Black Drama*: "When the play ended with the good white man and the good black boy reaching for each other's hand, Langston groaned: 'Oh, these white liberals! They'd better change that ending or Malcolm will be down here shouting!' "

There is a certain amount of fakery in Mitchell's cheerful reporting of Hughes's groan, for he goes on in the same chapter to praise conventional reaching-out plays like David Westheimer's *My Sweet Charlie* (1966) and *The Zulu and the Zayda* (1965), by Howard Da Silva and Felix Leon, probably because friends of his were involved in the production of both plays. Still, the Hughes line reflects the uneasiness with which the American theater treated the Negro situation in the 1960's. Traditional "Negro" plays, whether condescendingly folksy or socially committed, became dated, and all attitudes toward the Negro, particularly that of the liberal, became suspect. The white playwrights who knew most what they were doing as playwrights used the current or historical Negro situation for artistic purposes of their own— Edward Albee's *The Death of Bessie Smith*, Robert Lowell's *The Old Glory*, William Hanley's *Slow Dance on the Killing Ground*. Other white writers, struggling with what should have been the subject matter of the decade, were content to do good or make capital. Even the Negro dramatists, of whom there were fewer produced than the popular media sometimes suggested, were never on very sure grounds about who they were and what they should be saying. They were caught between their desire to be artists ("I have never written about 'the Negro question,'" Lorraine Hansberry wrote in *The New York Times*, October 11, 1964) and their need to be black ("If I say, 'Look at that woman falling out of the window,' it is a Negro who is saying it," wrote LeRoi Jones in *Home*), and were never quite able to convince their audiences, their interviewers, themselves, and their material that the two were one. In the background, Jean Genet's *The Blacks* ran on relentlessly year after year (May 4, 1961 to September 27, 1964) at the St. Marks Playhouse, dispensing aggression (black) and guilt (white) to audiences that seemed ready for it, even though many Negroes (see *Black Drama*) were outraged at the play.

In a way, *The Blacks* is the play most relevant to the whole problem of Negro drama in the 1960's, not for what it says about Negro-white relations, but for what it says about "saying." The characters in Genet's play act out a ritual in which attitudes are presented, parodied, replaced, but all the time—somewhere outside—a real thing is supposed to be happening. Presumably something is happening right now, outside the theater, a revolution that will not be won or lost for years and not really understood for years after that, but when and if that understanding comes, it is quite likely that most of the plays in this chapter—like the post-riot apologetics of white officialdom, the ironic Biblical exhortations from Adam Clayton Powell in Bimini, the nervous sloganeering fragments that Rap Brown drops at the feet of reporters—will be seen as dramatic (and/or rhetorical) exercises that at once obscured and contributed to the changes that the society was undergoing. That is an unkind thing to say about a play, of course, but in the long run most plays become artifacts rather than works of art, reflections of their time rather than dramas for all time. Right now, however, without the comfort of long-term perspective, I will try to pick my way through the plays which deal with the Negro or with someone's idea of the Negro in America.

We might as well begin with the reaching-out plays. The assumption behind all of them is that although the roots of prejudice are deep (as we used to say on Broadway in the 1940's), rational man, placed in a situation in which he must confront another human being rather than an abstract idea, will discover that color does not matter. *My Sweet Charlie* is a perfect example of this kind of drama. Westheimer's play, based on his own novel, contrives to place a pregnant, poor-white teen-ager and an educated and articulate Negro, a civil rights worker on the run after his failure at nonviolence, in a deserted summer house together and then puts them through a number of comic or touching scenes in which he slowly becomes the understanding father she never had. Although no one questioned Westheimer's sincerity, his play seemed more good-hearted than relevant in a post-Watts America, and it lasted only a few weeks on Broadway. Perhaps its problem was not that it seemed unrealistic, but that it never went all the way and turned itself into a goodwill fantasy.

Certainly *The Zulu and the Zayda*, as false as it is saccharine, pulled in audiences for five months and then found its way into summer stock. The Dan Jacobson short story on which the play is based, "The Zulu and the Zeide," is a simple tale about a Jewish grandfather who becomes dependent on the Zulu boy who takes care of him and the old man's son who grows jealous. Da Silva and Leon have turned it into a stock Broadway liberal play, with Harold Rome songs to decorate the message. The difference between the play and its source can best be illustrated by Paulus' attitude toward his job as "Zayda sitter," to borrow a phrase from one of the play's blackout yocks. In the story, after the old man's death, Paulus has to remind the tearful Harry that he wants his savings, for the Zulu's concern for the old man was only professional, a job done with care to earn the money to bring his own family to Johannesburg. In the scene in the play in which Harry sends Paulus away, he gives him an extra month's wages, and Paulus, a Zulu variation on the poster proletarian that I wrongly assumed Da Silva had outgrown, puts the extra money on the table and leaves after looking at his employer "compassionately." The racial situation is in the background of Jacobson's story, as it is in most South African writing, but Da Silva and Leon pull it to the front and hit the social point heavily. From the opening scene, in which a policeman asks Johannes, the houseboy-narrator, for his pass, to the arrest of the Zayda and a group of Negroes after the old man forces Paulus to take him into the restricted compound, the play comments directly on the South African situation. Yet the play is not really about that; it is about the love and friendship of the Zulu and the Zayda. The whole work can be summed up in Paulus' heart-tugging "You man. Me man. I you like. You me like." Summed up in more ways than one, for the Zulu's lines, which recall the "Me Tink Me Hear Sounds in de Night" kind of line that Lorraine Hansberry sighed over in *Theatre Arts* (October, 1960), contain a built-in condescension. In fact, a play that depends for its charm on a Yiddish comedian speaking Zulu and a Negro speaking Yiddish is *Vetter-Tomische* for all that it opts for the brotherhood of man.[1]

---

[1] Sarah in Lewis John Carlino's *Sarah and the Sax* is a distaff Zayda. The language barrier here is self-imposed, the Sax's defense against the insult of charity, but Sarah penetrates it with her own loneliness, and the Negro promises to come by for chicken paprikash.

Perhaps *Golden Boy* (1964), the Charles Strouse–Lee Adams–William Gibson musical, constructed for Sammy Davis, Jr., out of Clifford Odets' 1937 play, belongs with the reaching-out plays. At least the sentimental ending[2] does. In the Gibson version, Lorna does not die with Joe in the crash of his Ferrari (in 1937, it was a Duesenberg). Instead, she appears with Joe's father and brother. When Mr. Wellington[3] says that they will bring Joe home, "where he belongs," Lorna gets the curtain line: "Oh my God, he belonged anywhere—anywhere a human being could—walk. . . ." Then she stumbles, and the two men take her hands, providing the audience with the picture of the white girl between the two Negro men, the three of them drawn together by the martyrdom of Joe, their mutual distrust erased by grief.

That ending is as misleading as it is false, for the play is not really about Negro-white relations on a personal level. It is true that some of Lorna's reluctance to accept Joe openly stems from her unwillingness to face the difficulties of intermarriage ("I haven't—the guts to—make a life—with you"), but her loyalty to Tom Moody, Joe's manager, who has an old claim on her, is retained from the original play. In any case, Gibson is mainly concerned with making a social point by adapting Odets' ideational assumptions to a new context. As Joe Bonaparte embraced the myth of American success and died in the process, so too does Joe Wellington. The musical is certainly not laying down the LeRoi Jones line, insisting that a Negro "can never honestly enter into the lunatic asylum of white America," as Jones puts it in *Home*. Joe Wellington's ambition is false because it is tied to the props and rituals of success (expensive clothes, celebrity parties) and it implies not change but escape. There is an attempt to present Joe's preoccupation with himself dramatically and musically in Act II, Scene 6, in which he sings "No More," meaning

---

[2] In the printed version. The original-cast recording (Capitol VAS 2124) ends with a reprise of "Gimme Some." Since I did not see the show, I do not know where the reprise fell. Perhaps Joe appeared at the end, like Jeanette MacDonald in *Smilin' Through*, a saccharine irony for the final curtain.

[3] The translation of Odets' Bonaparte. The name in the musical is not used as character definition, as Bonaparte is in the early scenes of the play.

that he will not be a slave to Lorna, and the chorus, singing it as a comment on the racial situation, forms a dancing united front from which Joe, in his attempt to make it alone, is excluded. The scene is better in conception than in realization, however, because Strouse's music, a pseudo-spiritual, is more lament than affirmation, and the recording suggests that it was turned into a big number for Davis, which it should not have been.

The chief dramatic problem with the book is that Gibson has dropped Joe's alternative, his violin, perhaps because the fiddling fighter who ruins his hands has become something of a joke since the original *Golden Boy* tried to use the device seriously,[4] but he has found no workable substitute to explain why Joe is unwilling to punch. Joe's hesitancy figures through much of the show, but it is not sufficiently motivated, so that the breaking of his hand at the Act I curtain is neither symbolic nor psychologically sound. There are more important problems with *Golden Boy*, however, than motivational deficiencies. *Carmen Jones* and the comments on it by Negro writers like James Baldwin (*Commentary*, January, 1955) and Lorraine Hansberry (*Theatre Arts*, October, 1960) must have haunted the men who put *Golden Boy* together. In his Afterword to the published play, Gibson says that Davis warned him to "Write colored." Actually, the Odets idiom has disappeared and has been replaced by nothing at all; perhaps, as Baldwin said of *Carmen Jones*, the Negro speech has been "liberalized, if one may so put it, out of its force and precision." In Gibson's lines, the speech is simply nondescript; in some of Lee Adams' lyrics—notably in "Don't Forget One Hundred and Twenty-seventh Street"—both words and references are embarrassing. After the success of *Bye, Bye Birdie* in suggesting a musical idiom, one might have expected more from Strouse, but the music is Broadway bland, not even qualifying as what Charles Keil (in *Urban Blues*) calls "refined or light soul."

---

[4] In an article in *The New York Times* (June 25, 1967), Sanford Allen, the Negro concert violinist, pointed out the obstacles that have kept Negroes from serious music. Perhaps there was sound sociology in Gibson's assumption that a Harlem junkman, even a solid citizen like Mr. Wellington, would not be forcing a violin into his son's hands.

In contrast to *Golden Boy* and *The Zulu and the Zayda,* in which good intentions drown in the devices of popular theater, *In White America* (1963) is at once moving and angry. A documentary play put together by Martin B. Duberman, an historian, *In White America* is the only play by a white dramatist in which the social commitment is not sentimentalized. "My starting point," Duberman says in the Preface to his play, "was the wish to describe what it has been like to be a Negro in this country (to the extent that a white man can describe it)." He has done so through the nonfictional voices of Americans, black and white, in documents that he has gathered, arranged, and stringently edited so that points are made quickly and neatly. A house servant tells Frederick Law Olmsted how well treated he is but adds, "Oh, yes, sir, I'd like it better to be free; I would dat, master." A runaway slave answers a letter from his mistress demanding his return, "you say, 'You know we raised you as we did our own children.' Woman, did you raise your *own children* for the market?" In most cases, the force of a speech is self-contained, but there are occasions in which juxtaposition heightens the effect. Hannah Tutson's account of her whipping at the hands of white men, one of whom kept demanding sex of her, is the more horrifying for being followed by Senator Ben Tillman's defense of lynching as a protection of the purity of white women menaced by the black beast.

The history of the Negro in America, as it comes through Duberman's play, is one of a continued longing and demand for freedom and the stifling of that demand for the sake of the status quo. Yet the play is a positive one, each of its two acts ending on a note of hope. Act I is an indictment of slavery, ending with Emancipation, described effectively in the words of Colonel Thomas Wentworth Higginson, who commanded the first regiment of ex-slaves in the Union army ("it seemed the choked voice of a race at last unloosed"), worked in with the singing of "America." Act II catalogues the failure of the promises that the Emancipation Proclamation implied, but it ends, after Little Rock, with the reading of the preamble to the Constitution and the singing of "Oh, freedom. . . ." In an appendix offering an alternate ending (from Lincoln's second annual message to Congress), Duberman says that he was tempted to use more recent material but that he decided to stop with Little Rock because "it was difficult to 'top' the Little Rock scene dramatically." More important, I should think, the 15-year-old girl facing the mob in Little Rock embodies the sense of excitement, of achievement, of new emancipation that was characteristic of the late 1950's. Duberman plainly wants *In White America* to end on that note, to be a kind of weapon in the 1960's, not a reflection of the ambiguity that began to touch the civil rights movement after the first flush of victory.

One of the manifestations of the changing racial situation in America in the 1960's is that Negro actors have found more and more varied roles opening to them. Thus, Ruby Dee plays Cordelia in Stratford, Connecticut, and Diana Sands turns up as Phaedra in Philadelphia; most of the leading resident companies have Negro actors, often playing roles that once would have been designated as "white." Anyone who remembers that an actor as fine as the late Leigh Whipper had very few chances to show a wide audience what he was capable of (Crooks in *Of Mice and Men*, the preacher in *The Ox-Bow Incident*) can only welcome the change. There are complications, however. It may be enlightened to ignore color (as a matter of fact, I suspect that it is insulting), but it is not very practical. I remember seeing a performance, years ago, by one of the first determinedly integrated off-Broadway groups in which a white father and an Oriental mother had a Negro son, and I was so fascinated by the genetics of it that I missed the first act altogether. Even under less ludicrous conditions, the presence of a Negro in a contemporary play cannot help carrying social implications which change the play in certain ways, suggesting attitudes that play and producer alike may be working diligently to avoid. This can be seen even in pieces of fluff, like the Richard Rodgers-Samuel Taylor musical *No Strings* (1962) and the Bill Manhoff comedy *The Owl and the Pussycat* (1964).

No Strings is a stupendously dull musical for which Samuel Taylor, who once was capable of sophistication and wit (*The*

Pleasure of His Company), wrote an Oscar Hammerstein book. In it, an American writer is rescued from the empty glitter of Europe and sent safely home to rural Maine, where he will presumably create like crazy. His rescuer is one of the most corrupt characters in contemporary drama, a virginal whore who accepts expensive gifts from a wealthy Frenchman without offering favors in return. Rodgers and Taylor, of course, do not see her this way; for them, she is the innocent American girl, bursting with life and expectation. In a note in the published play, they say that the heroine "is designed to be played by an American colored girl," but there is no reference to her color in the show except an oblique one in a song in which she celebrates "Up north of Central Park," which is evidently but never specifically Harlem. When the time comes for her to follow her man to Maine, he will not let her go, will not take her from the Paris which is as necessary to her career as fashion model as the Maine woods is to his as novelist; curtain on twin spots and a whining reprise of "The Sweetest Sounds." Although the ending is supposed to hinge on differences of personality and occupation, it looks as though Rodgers and Taylor are being liberal and hidebound at the same time in *No Strings*, offering an interracial romance but not letting it reach marriage.

The Owl and the Pussycat is a standard Broadway comedy with a pseudo-serious message (be yourself) disguised by a few funny lines and a great deal of busyness. At the end of the play Felix (the sales clerk who thinks he is a writer) and Doris (the part-time whore who thinks she is an actress) admit what they are, and that, the curtain implies, is a beginning for them. From an audience standpoint, the play is stacked in favor of Doris, for she is a functioning body with common sense, while Felix is a stumbling intellect who keeps trying to stifle his sexual instincts. In fact, the play is conventionally anti-intellectual, full of Doris's folk wisdom (". . . that's all your brains are good for. To keep people away because you're scared to death of people!") which an unwary audience is likely to take as simple truth. Doris was not written as a Negro and has been played in summer stock and in road companies by actresses of all colors—white, black, yellow. When the play opened on Broadway with Diana Sands as Doris, there was a great deal of publicity about the triumph of talent over color, but I find it somewhat disquieting. I can understand why an actress would welcome a Broadway lead, but that is not the same thing as accepting as a breakthrough the news that a Negro girl can now play a dumb whore with a heart of gold opposite a white man.[5]

In turning to Peter S. Feibleman's *Tiger Tiger Burning Bright* (1962) after discussing *No Strings* and *The Owl and the Pussycat*, I am not suggesting that they are of similar quality. Based, very distantly, on his own novel *A Place Without Twilight*, Feibleman's play is a complicated one, suggestive and demanding, finally self-defeating in its attempt to hold onto the ambiguities of its subject and at the same time to resolve them in terms that the commercial theater can accept. I placed *Tiger* here because it is a play about a Negro family, and I cannot see that they need to be colored. The central conflict in the play is between Mama, who lives in a fantasy world in which death is equated with safety and the dangerous real world is held at bay, and Cille, who embodies reality. The chief bone of contention is Clarence, the "tiger cat," trapped by his mother's fantasy, which he helps to feed (he invents a death in battle for his brother who is in prison up north). In the end, the framed telegram is smashed, as is Mama's world, and the house, now Cille's, loses Clarence and his younger brother as well. Feibleman's tendency to treat his central idea as a poetic rather than an intellectual concept, as something that must be intimated ("Today you're a shadow"), wrapped in amorphousness, suggests the southern school of Truman Capote and Carson McCullers; and much of the detail—Mama's addiction to her morning record ("Thank God for a Garden"), the delicate posturing of Adelaide, the one outsider Mama will accept—suggests that school's eccentricities. There is much talk of color, particularly the color of

[5] I doubt if casting it the other way around would do much good, but it might be interesting to see a production of the play with, say, Louis Gossett and Phyllis Newman, who has played Doris, in the leads.

twilight (which Clarence presumably is), but much of it can be seen as metaphor rather than pigment, in terms of the dream world of Mama and not as a fact in the large world that she wants to escape.

From the first page of *A Place Without Twilight*, when Dan says, "Let's pretend we ain't niggers," the novel is openly concerned with color and what it means; the trap that Mama makes and calls a shelter rests on her conviction that to be black is to be vulnerable. The play, presumably, is based on the same assumption, but it is not so much in the play as in the fact that Negro actors fill the parts on stage. Since I know the play only from the page, I was constantly aware in reading it that with a few deletions it could be performed by whites and make a perfectly valid statement about the conflict between fantasy and reality. *Tiger*, then, is either not a play about Negroes at all or else, as I suspect, it is the most sophisticated Negro play yet written by a white playwright.

In an article on the need for a Negro theater (*The New York Times*, August 14, 1966), Douglas Turner Ward commented, almost as an aside, on a forum on "What Negro Playwrights Are Saying," in which "not even panel members could cite enough plays to make the plural subject matter viable." If we add his own name to those he gives—Louis Peterson, Lorraine Hansberry, Ossie Davis, James Baldwin, LeRoi Jones—the list of Negro dramatists who have attracted attention in recent years is almost exhausted. Loften Mitchell, Adrienne Kennedy, John O. Killens come to mind, but their work is not very well known and is not easily available. Louis Peterson, whose *Take a Giant Step* (1953) marked him as a promising playwright, has written mainly for television and the movies in recent years, returning to the stage only with *Entertain a Ghost* (1962), an unsuccessful off-Broadway play described in *The Best Plays of 1961–1962* as "a play within a play" about "marital difficulties." The discussion in this chapter will stay pretty close to the remaining names on Ward's list.

Lorraine Hansberry died on January 12, 1965. Her second

play, unhappily her last, *The Sign in Sidney Brustein's Window*, closed two days earlier, after 101 performances. Miss Hansberry's husband and producer, Robert Nemiroff, told the story of the play's run in "The One Hundred and One 'Final' Performances of *Sidney Brustein*," which was published as an introduction to the play. In his account, friends of the play and its author, mostly theater people, fought a determined battle (placing ads, raising money, stirring up publicity) to keep the show running, because its admirers were convinced that it had a potential audience which, despite favorable reviews, never materialized. Nemiroff insists that the campaign was for the play's sake, but to someone on the outside, aware that the playwright was dying, the day-by-day reports seemed more like evidence of great kindness to a very sick woman. This is not intended as a criticism—the second motive seems to me as admirable as the first—but as an explanation of why it is—or was then, at least—difficult to see *The Sign in Sidney Brustein's Window* outside the emotional context of its troubled run.

In its central dramatic action, *Sidney Brustein* bears a strong resemblance to Miss Hansberry's *A Raisin in the Sun* (1959). Like Walter Lee Younger in the earlier play, Sidney passes through confusion to triumph to apparent defeat to a new commitment that is presumably less naive, less starry-eyed. Sidney, however, is no Walter Lee, no Negro working man fighting a losing battle with the American dream in a Chicago slum; Sidney, as Miss Hansberry says in the *Times* article quoted at the beginning of this chapter, is "a nervous, ulcerated, banjo-making young man in whom I see an embodiment of a certain kind of Greenwich Village intellectual." The most determined voice in a highly articulate circle, Sidney is an essentially sensitive man so bemused by the power of his intellectual insights and the neatness of his verbal summaries that he plays with and at his friends and family without quite recognizing that the name of the game is aggression. In part, his sallies ("Dear old Mav, Mother of the Philistines") are defensive, the last rattle of an activist who is suffering from what his friend Alton calls "*ostrich*-ism . . . the great sad withdrawal from the affairs of men." We see Sidney at his most typical as the play begins, musing over the failure of a nightclub he has been running, bewildered that there were not more people who wanted folk music without "hoked-up come-ons" and insisting, without hearing the contradiction in his words, "It *would* have done okay if Bruno had done a better job on the publicity."

Throughout the play, Sidney suffers from a reluctance to blame himself for anything and from the habit of seeing every person as limited by the role for which he has been cast in Sidney's life. Having exchanged the nightclub for a newspaper, he at first hesitantly, then enthusiastically joins a campaign for better government (that is the sign in his window), only to learn in the moment of triumph that the candidate he supported, his old friend Wally, is owned by the powers he is supposedly fighting. While Sidney is getting his political education, his marriage is collapsing because Iris is tired of being his wild-mountain girl, the fantasy wife in his perennial dream of an escape to the woods. Act III, Scene 1 is an intellectual orgy in which Sidney, very drunk and very sorry for himself, acts out an absurdist drama of despair with his sister-in-law Gloria, an expensive call-girl, and David, a playwright of the absurdist-despair persusasion.[6] Even here, Sidney is playing with words, but after Gloria's suicide he climbs out of the chaos, determined to go on with the fight, and Iris, still unconvinced but willing to try, joins him for a positive curtain.

I was reminded of the end of *A Raisin in the Sun*, in which Walter Lee worked his stumbling way "into his manhood." As in the earlier play, Miss Hansberry has drawn a hero more complicated than the commitment she demands of him. Not that a new

[6] This scene and the fantasy sequence (II, 1) are nonrealistic passages in an essentially realistic play. Nemiroff suggests that there is nothing unusual about Miss Hansberry's using a mixed genre, that *Raisin*, in the scene in which Walter Lee plays at being an African chieftain, is non-naturalistic. It does make a difference, however, whether a game is being played by a character or by the author. On Broadway, *Sidney Brustein* was a realistic play. The "absurdist" scene was shortened and played as the characters' game and II, 1 was cut out, although some of the lines that defined Iris' relation to her father were shifted to another scene. Nor did the Broadway production let Sidney directly address the audience, as Miss Hansberry suggests he should at several places in the script.

commitment is a falsification of Sidney's character. The energy, the courage, the sympathy, the likableness that underlie his preoccupation with his own small hurts and triumphs would almost certainly move him once again to some kind of action. The difficulty is that Miss Hansberry seems to be suggesting that Sidney has come through to a new clarity and not, as in Act I, to a simple rearrangement of his delusions. It is true that the social affirmation is tempered by a recognition of evil, but the end cannot escape being touched with hokum. That, of course, is one of Miss Hansberry's main points, for the play is an attack on an intellectual stance ("Presume no commitment, disavow all engagement, mock all great expectations," Sidney says) which equates the committed with the square. In *Sidney Brustein*, as in *Raisin*, Miss Hansberry is caught between her concept of drama as the means to a social statement and drama as an examination of character.

The double nature of Miss Hansberry's play can best be seen in the figures that surround Sidney and Iris—the Philistine sister, the call-girl sister, the homosexual playwright, the Negro radical, the accommodating liberal, the Bohemian artist. All of them are stereotypes and, at the same time, attempts to transcend stereotype. Occasionally, often for no more than a line, the attempt is successful, as when David's play opens to enthusiastic reviews. His pose, social as well as artistic, is one of cynicism, masked as existential anguish, but he comes into Sidney's apartment as a delighted little boy: "Christ, Sid—(*Pure unadulterated wonder*) *I'm famous.*" More often the transcendence is simply a reversal, as when Iris's apparently comfortable sister Mavis is revealed in Act II as a woman whose life is complicated and painful in ways that Sidney, hung-up on surfaces, never imagined. This discovery, however, is hardly necessary. Miss Hansberry wants to use Mavis to undercut the complacent self-righteousness of the Village crowd. She does so dramatically in Act I when Mavis is given a moving speech ("how smug it is in bohemia") to contrast to the flippancy of the friends gathered at Sidney's to eat and be bright; the revelations seem like an attempt to provide Mavis with bonafides, as though the power of the earlier scene would be any the less if she were in fact comfortable.

It is with Gloria, however, that the greatest problems arise. She has an extended scene with David, in which she tries to contradict all the literary conventions about prostitutes, yet she cannot escape being a sentimental figure. Her suicide, following a grandiloquent line to bring down the curtain on the corruption scene ("Sick people belong in hospitals!!!"), seems gratuitous for all that Miss Hansberry has so carefully prepared for it; whores have killed themselves, and worms have eaten them, but not on stage. On her death, unhappily, hinges Sidney's final resurrection.

Miss Hansberry is unique in this chapter, the only Negro playwright who attempts to write about a society larger than the Negro community, one defined in terms other than black-white relations. Not that she ignores this subject, for a play which touches as many bases as *Sidney Brustein* does ignores very little. Alton, the play's one Negro character, is an ex-Communist who talks a good revolution but who turns out to be as bound by his prejudices as the rest of the presumably emancipated characters in the play. Although he is instrumental in Sidney's first-act decision to turn political, his primary function in the play lies in his relationship with Gloria. When he discovers that she is a prostitute, he breaks their engagement, telling Sidney rather than her, after a long speech in which his reasons (or his rationalizations) are tied to his color, which has seemed of little importance through most of the play: "I don't want white man's leavings, Sidney." Although the speech is presumably true in one sense, it is also a reflection of wounded male vanity, as Sidney's line, "Just don't act like a fraternity boy meeting his own girl under the lamppost," implies. In his reaction, Alton is a standard character, like the union leader in *Juno and the Paycock*, whose understanding, so often verbalized, does not extend to marrying a pregnant Mary. In Alton's big scene, then, the audience is asked to respond sympathetically to his speech and at the same time recognize that he is acting the conventional villain's part (the deserter). Unfortunately, the scene does not carry the complex sense of human motivation that Miss Hansberry presumably intends; it is too great a contrivance (why did he not already know Gloria's business and where did he just now learn the news?), too obviously preparation for Gloria's suicide. A better scene about racial sensitivity is the one in which Iris and Sidney learn, in a letter from Gloria, that Alton has proposed to her. Their response to the news, an embarrassed silence that comes from their knowledge of Gloria's profession, is taken by Alton as a "would-you-want-your-sister" reaction. That uneasy moment reveals the latent suspicion likely to lie at the heart of even the solidest interracial friendship. Unfortunately the scene is effective only in retrospect, for the audience, not yet in on the secret about Gloria, can only share Alton's doubts about Sidney and Iris.

It is a simple matter to fault *The Sign in Sidney Brustein's Window*, to point out how often and in what ways Miss Hansberry has fallen short in her ambitious attempt to write a play that is at once complex and committed. It is more important—for me, at least—to admit that I am attracted to her desire to buck the pessimistic tide and to recognize that, although her ideational desire may finally have marred her play, she succeeds in a number of ways—in Sidney's idiomatic rhetoric, in many of the comic passages (Iris and the home permanent), in at least one of the big scenes (Mavis' in Act I), and in her depiction of many of the small contradictions of character. I cannot write eulogistic lines about a great loss to American theater, words as false as they are conventional, but Miss Hansberry's death does remove from the Broadway scene a dramatist whose first two plays showed a serious social and artistic imagination at work and a talent that made that work more worth criticizing than many of the plays I touch on glancingly in this volume.

In contrast to *Sidney Brustein*, Ossie Davis' *Purlie Victorious* (1961) rushes to embrace stereotype. In an essay in Herbert Hill's *Anger, and Beyond*, Davis explains that most of the race stereotypes "were invented by Negroes for the purpose of survival and social correction," disguises assumed to outsmart the white slave-owner and his descendants.[7] In his play, he hopes to reveal

---

[7] This is not an idea that has wide acceptance among Negro writers. In "Many Thousands Gone," a 1951 *Partisan Review* article reprinted in *Notes of a Native Son*, James Baldwin, speaking for white America, says that we created the prevailing Negro stereotypes—both of violence and of Uncle

"the truth of the situation out of which the stereotype grew in the first place." The play is a broad cartoon in which the titular hero, at once the preacher-lodge-president stereotype (Gitlow calls him "kingfish") and a freedom fighter, attempts to regain control of Big Bethel from Ol' Cap'n Cotchipee, pure Southern Colonel, burlesque variety. Although Purlie's tide of rhetoric, sprinkled with compounds and alliteration ("hill and dale, field and farm, truck and tractor, horse and mule, bird and bee and bush and tree"), spotted with free verse, is the main verbal force of the play, Big Bethel becomes his in the end because Charlie, the Ol' Cap'n's son, brought up as an integrationist by his mammy, makes out the deed to the church in Purlie's name. Since Charlie is a complete fool, there is an acid overtone in Davis' comment that he "is our hope in the white liberal community in the South and in the North"; since Mr. Charlie delivers the goods where Purlie's freedom-preaching only provides the afflatus, as much acid may spill on the Negro as on the white.

Davis' comic method can best be illustrated by the scene in which Purlie declines to let himself be whipped by the Ol' Cap'n or punched by the Sheriff ("Either you stand up like a man, so I can knock you down, or—"). The sequence is played as slapstick, and yet the harsh assumptions that underlie the demands on Purlie come through. Elsewhere, Davis uses more conventional Broadway gags (Lutiebelle's repeated "I know" punctuating one of Purlie's long explanations) or set comedy pieces, such as a downhome variation on the tea party scene in *Pygmalion*, in which Lutiebelle, given a single speech to prove that she is the college-educated Cousin Bee, gets carried away by the part: "I disremembers so many things out of my early pastime that mostly you are

---

Tom—to assuage our guilt and to escape the hatred that we do not want to believe Negroes feel for us. In the *Theatre Arts* article quoted earlier in this chapter, Lorraine Hansberry assumes that the whites created a Negro world easier to face than the real one: "one is always eager to believe that *somebody else* is exhilarated by 'plenty of nuttin'.'" Stanley M. Elkins, in *Slavery*, discussing the "Sambo" stereotype and the rewards and punishments accompanying such role-playing in a "closed" system of slavery, gives some support to the assumptions on which Davis works.

haze and vaguey!" *Purlie Victorious* provides a certain amount of very obvious fun and makes an equally obvious social point, but in a way it is self-defeating. Davis says in *Anger, and Beyond* that he was attempting to speak a language that would bring "my revolutionary message" to Negro audiences, but his play was performed before the mixed, largely white, Broadway audience. It is possible that even as they nodded agreement with its message and prided themselves in being part of an occasion in which Negro actors were performing the presumably hated stereotypes in a spirit of good clean fun, the whites found a certain comfort in the sterotypes themselves. *Purlie Victorious* is really not very far from *Amos 'n' Andy*.

The off-Broadway musical, *Fly Blackbird* (1962), by Clarence Jackson and James Hatch, is similar to *Purlie Victorious*, at least in its satirical numbers, such as "Mr. Big," in which Mr. Big and Mr. Boy sing about "the order that God created" in a patter number that recalls the minstrel show. The central conflict is between Sweet William, a successful song-and-dance man, a gradualist who sings "Everything Comes to Those Who Wait," and the young people, including his daughter, who follow his "Wait" number by singing "Now." The authors provide a song ("Who's the Fool?") for the dancer in which he admits "yes I shuffled—I had to," shuffled his daughter into Sarah Lawrence. Although the effect of most of Sweet William's songs is essentially satirical, he is treated more sympathetically than one might expect from a musical so obviously committed to a particular point of view; the young people win, of course, and the "Wake Up" finale sweeps in to drown his sad song, but his question is rejected, not reviled.

The chief device in most of the songs, whoever sings them, is the mocking of the clichés of racial encounter. Robert Hatch, who wrote the jacket notes for the original cast recording (Mercury OCM 2206), suggests that "The Gong Song" is an exception. A comic number in which the jailed demonstrators pass their time by singing about the oriental detective in the movies who is always accompanied by a gong, it is probably less a diversion than it seems; guying a favorite Hollywood stereotype about the oriental

is surely connected to what is going on elsewhere in *Fly Blackbird*.
Once the tone of the show is set, most of it is predictable. Only
occasionally are there surprises, as in "Lilac Tree," a duet by the
romantic leads which sounds like a standard sentimental ballad
until one listens to the words that come crawling out of the in-
nocuous tune: "there's a blackbird hidden in the tree with a sharp-
pointed beak and a broken wing."

The 1960's is the decade in which the blackbird got tired of
displaying its broken wing and began to concentrate on its sharp-
pointed beak. In 1964, with the production of James Baldwin's
Blues for Mr. Charlie and LeRoi Jones's *Dutchman,* two new
voices—beak voices—were heard in the theater. Unlike Ossie
Davis or Lorraine Hansberry (even when *A Raisin in the Sun* was
a hit), Baldwin and Jones created a stir far greater than the usual
excitement about talented new playwrights, black or white. One
reason is that they and their characters spoke in a tone of voice
that reflected the new militancy in Negro circles. Although *Blues*
was never a conventional success and ran as long as it did only
because donations kept it alive, the publicity that surrounded the
production of the Baldwin play and the solid success of *Dutchman*
suggested an important breakthrough for the Negro playwright, an
audience eager for an authentic, angry voice. By 1968, Baldwin,
who never really had "much respect for what goes on in the
American Theatre," as he said in "Notes for *Blues,*" had apparently returned to fiction, and Jones had crawled into his racial *cul-
de-sac*. It might be possible to see their withdrawal as a social
indicator, evidence that, in the theater as well as out, the adven-
turous spirit of the early 1960's has been caught in the presumed
white backlash. That, however, is to buy the 1964 "breakthrough"
at face value. Because Baldwin brought a reputation, as Negro
leader as well as novelist, into the theater and because of the
violence of Jones's statements, in and out of his plays, both men
made better newspaper copy than the usual theater initiate. Ever
since publicity created the English angry young men, who turned
out to be John Osborne in one play, I have been leery of neat

generalizations about the theater. That projected audience, eager for the voice of a serious Negro playwright, was probably a fiction or—as the fate of *Blues* indicated—a great deal smaller than the noisy discussion suggested; surely the fact that *Dutchman* is a good play had as much to do with its success as its subject matter did. Every new Negro playwright—in fact, every new serious playwright—has to be his own "breakthrough."

Blues for Mr. Charlie is a complicated play, working in several times at once and trying, through the various stories, to make a number of points, both ideational and dramatic. In the present, it deals with the trial of Lyle Britten for the murder of Richard Henry and the effect of that trial on the community in general and in particular on the Reverend Meridian Henry, Richard's father, and Parnell James, Meridian's white friend. In the immediate past, it presents Richard's return to his home town and his confrontation with Lyle. It is through these two characters that Baldwin hopes to give flesh to his concept of the fatal interrelationship of black and white in America, an idea he treated at length in *The Fire Next Time*, a characteristically moving, mystical, and muddled autobiographical essay published the year before *Blues* was produced. The central assumption of that book is that both Negroes and whites are trapped by the way Negroes are treated in this country and the preconceptions that lie behind that treatment. Until the whites give the Negroes the freedom to be what they want, which is not the same as demanding that they accept white values, neither race can escape a relationship, based on abstraction and suffused with hate, which cripples the country as a whole. This, less generally, more personally, is what Baldwin has been saying since he began writing. "They want only their proper place in the sun and the right to be left alone, like any other citizen of the republic," he wrote in "Many Thousands Gone." "What might be accepted as just good old American independence in someone else would be insufferable arrogance in me," says the hero of "Previous Condition," an early Baldwin story (*Commentary*, October, 1948), reprinted in *Going to Meet the Man*. On every occasion, in every genre, Baldwin has been saying what Cassius

Clay said so simply when he announced that he had become Mu-hammad Ali, "I don't have to be what you want me to be. I'm free to be who I want." In *Blues*, Richard gets Baldwin's message, but Lyle does not, and in his deafness lies the tragedy—in the social if not in the dramatic sense.

After the death of his mother, an accident that was apparently no accident, Richard, who sees as cowardice his father's way of coping, tried to escape the trap of his Southern town by going north. There, sickened by less well-labeled racism, he took to dope. After the failure of his escapes, Richard returns home, fresh from the cure at Lexington, a gun in his luggage and hatred as his latest medicine: "I'm going to treat everyone of them as though they were responsible for all the crimes that ever happened in the history of the world—oh, yes!" Annoyed that Lyle walks easily into Papa D's juke joint, Richard goes into Lyle's store and provokes a fight. This is an ugly scene (and one of the few in the play that has any dramatic vitality), but one that has been misunderstood. Some members of the audience, both black and white, assumed that Richard's behavior in this scene is some kind of policy statement (get Whitey) and praised or damned it on those grounds. Surely, however, Richard's "redneck" aggressiveness in Lyle's store is only a stage through which he passes before his death. Lorenzo, a character who often speaks Baldwin's sociological generalizations, says on the stand that "Richard couldn't stand white people." This, however, is only a partial truth, for Richard's discussion with Papa D just before his death and the testimony of Juanita, who loves him ("he said he wasn't going to run no more from white folks—never no more!—but was going to stay and be a man—a *man!*—right here"[8]) suggest that Richard has gone be-

[8] In these lines, and elsewhere in the play, the character suggests another Richard of Baldwin's, John's father in *Go Tell It on the Mountain*: "I just decided me one day that I was going to get to know everything them white bastards knew . . . Shit—he weren't going to beat my ass, then. And if he tried to kill me, I'd take him with me, I swear to my mother I would." He is contrasted to John's stepfather, who also hates all whites, but defensively, not as an assertion of self. The stepfather, who is based on Baldwin's own father, is an example of the collection of fathers who fill Baldwin's work, failing their sons at every turn. At the risk of sounding like the autobiographical

yond the hate of the store scene to a point in which he wants to be simply his own man, neither victim nor aggressor. Unfortunately for the play, this change in Richard grows less from the character than from the author's need to use him; insofar as it is motivated, it arises from his discovery of Juanita, which gives the whole thing too much the look of a love-of-a-good-woman salvation play. Unfortunately for Richard, his change finds no reflection in the rigidity of Lyle.

Lyle has much in common with Richard; he, too, is a victim of sorts. The play makes much of his having been a poor boy who had to scramble hard for the little he has. Closer to the Negroes than many of his townsmen, he does not fantasize about them, which does not mean that he has escaped the implications of whiteness in a Southern town. Like Richard, he wants to live his own life: "I want to be as strong as my Mama and Daddy and raise my children like they raised me." He is never able to see that he can really live only by escaping the consequences of his raising ("My Daddy told me not to *never* forget I was a white man"). A reluctant murderer, Lyle wants an apology, one that Richard cannot give. The best he can do is suggest that they disentangle themselves from one another: "Why don't you go home? And let me go home? Do we need all this shit? Can't we live without it?" There are too many years and too many lies in Lyle, however, and he cannot just walk away. At last, Richard begins to taunt him, using all the clichés of race that have made both men, and Lyle shoots him: "I had to kill him then. I'm a white man!" When Lyle is acquitted of the murder, he only imagines that he goes free, for the murder itself is an illustration of the way Lyle is trapped by color.

The trial, which fills most of the third act, is a comment on the

---

critics who annoy me so often, I would like to suggest that Richard (the father of *Mountain*) and Richard (the son of *Blues*) represent the father that Baldwin has always wanted and the man he has always wanted to be, the one who could say, as Baldwin does at the end of the *Harper's* (November, 1955) article that gave its title to *Notes of a Native Son*, "blackness and whiteness did not matter; to believe that they did was to acquiesce in one's own destruction." "Did not" or "ought not"? Both Richards die of their attempts to assert their individuality.

workings of justice in the South, enlightened enough to arrest Lyle but certain not to convict him. The Negro characters are presented with dignity and with righteous anger, the whites (except Parnell) as blatantly nasty. Although primarily an attack on white justice, no more subtle than any political cartoon, the trial scene does make a social point that reinforces the color trap as it is presented in Lyle and Richard. Baldwin splits the spectators into two groups, white and black, both of which shout remarks at the witnesses, the lawyers, the court. Each group assumes that everyone the other color is lying. In fact, everyone lies. Of course, the blacks tell only "white" lies (about the existence of Richard's gun and the pictures of his white girl friends from up north) and the whites tell "black" lies about attempts at rape. Surely Baldwin's point is that the racial situation is one in which only masks confront one another and lying is inevitable.

Whatever social point Baldwin hopes to make with his trial, he uses it as the climactic moment in the development of both Meridian and Parnell. The play, in fact, might be read as the trying of Meridian Henry. As a man, Meridian has felt shame at his failure to act when his wife was killed, particularly since his prudence, an habitual act rationalized as a protection of his family and community, turned Richard against him; on this level, Meridian asks and gets forgiveness from Richard. As a Christian, Meridian begins to doubt his own motivation. In the young people, particularly Lorenzo, there is a contempt for the church which reflects the idea that the Christian God is a white God and his church a device that gives the Negro an exalted reason to turn the other cheek. Meridian is forced to ask himself "would I have *been* such a Christian if I hadn't been born black? Maybe I *had* to become a Christian in order to live with any dignity at all.⁹ As a civil rights worker, an

---

⁹ The idea of the Negro church as a substitute for personal and public status that are denied through other means is implicit in the saints of *Go Tell It on the Mountain* and *The Amen Corner*. Baldwin made it explicit in the notes he wrote for *Amen*, in which he says of Sister Margaret, "She is in the church because her society has left her no other place to go." In *The Fire Next Time* he says that his father "really believed what white people said about him. This is one of the reasons that he became so holy."

advocate of nonviolence, Meridian is forced—by Richard's death and the freeing of Lyle—to recognize that his approach has failed, that he has not influenced his white Christian brothers, that the changes have not come. Early in the play, trying to quiet an angry Lorenzo, Juanita reminds him, "you're in church." Lorenzo answers, "Well, I wish to God I was in an arsenal." This helps establish a gun-Bible conflict which is resolved at the end when Meridian decides that, one way or another, his people will get justice, when he admits that he has Richard's gun, "In the pulpit. Under the Bible. Like the pilgrims of old."[10] Meridian's development makes an ideational point, one which is necessary as an indication that Richard's decision to free himself of the definitions of the white world does not imply withdrawal from social action; if the Lyles will not let the Richards walk away, then the Meridians, using Bible or gun or both, must win the right to walk. However important Meridian is to *Blues* in terms of ideas, he is a failure as a character, nondescript even in his dark night of the soul, partly because he is saddled with lines like the incredible curtain to Act I: "Would God—would *God*—would God I had died for thee—my son, my son!" That is not a man speaking; that is *literature.*

In the forgiveness scene, Richard calls his father "a public man," asserting that, at least since his mother's death, "You haven't been a private man at all." Parnell, the play's white liberal, is another public man. "I used to watch you roaring through this town like a St. George thirsty for dragons," Juanita says. "And nobody wants you to be St. George. We just want you to be

---

[10] Meridian's dilemma is real enough, but the symbols in which it is stated seemed too obvious until fact caught up with the play. A UPI story in the Connersville (Ind.) *News-Examiner* (June 9, 1966) paraphrased a statement by James Meredith, who had been shot down on a Mississippi road on June 8: "Meredith said he had thought of taking a weapon with him on his march but discarded the idea and took along a Bible instead. He said his first reaction was one of embarrassment. He said he realized he could have felled the man who shot him and that if it had been his [Meredith's] father who was the shooting victim, he would have been armed and would have fired back." *The New York Times* (June 8, 1966) does not mention the Bible. When Meredith resumed his march in 1967, there was no mention of guns or Bibles, at least in the accounts I read.

Parnell. But, of course, that's much harder." Parnell is instrumental in bringing Lyle to trial, but he cannot believe that Lyle, who is his friend (if a rich man can have a poor man for a friend), has killed Richard.

At the trial, reluctantly and to the satisfaction of no one, Parnell becomes "white," refuses to contradict Lyle's wife's account of what happened in the store. At this point, his assurance, born of the position he belittles as a wealthy, old-family white, dissolves; the public Parnell crumbles. At the end of the play, as the Negroes mass for a march on the court house, he comes to ask, not to tell: "Can I join you on the march, Juanita? Can I walk with you?" Her answer is the answer that Lyle could not give Richard, the ideological heart of the play: "Well, we can walk in the same direction, Parnell."

If Baldwin had been content to paint the portrait of a white liberal not wholly conscious of his own motivation and unaware of the figure he cut among Negroes who no longer want a great white father, Parnell might have turned into the most interesting character in the play. Instead, Baldwin saddles him with a sexual motivation, gives him an adolescent love for a Negro girl, never consummated and never forgotten. "Out with it, Parnell!" he says in his soliloquy. "I've wanted my hands full of them, wanted to drown them, laughing and dancing and making love—making love—wow!—and be transformed, formed, liberated out of this grey-white envelope." This ludicrous caricature (heightened on stage when Pat Hingle played the part with his hands cradling his crotch) is a variation on the myth about Negro sexuality that produced the black beast of which white Southern maidens are supposed to tremble in fear.[11] Parnell with his sexual hang-up is

---

[11] Baldwin has a way of seeing all relationships as sexual, as all his work indicates, but his Parnell is symptomatic of a kind of romanticizing which further muddies the dirty water of Negro-white relations. The new myth of Negro sexuality—used as metaphor or as sociological truth—is as silly and as ugly as the old white scare stories. I can see little difference between the speech of one of Baldwin's white "crackers" ("if you was to be raped by an orangoutang out of the jungle or a *stallion*, couldn't do you no worse than a nigger") and Richard's bragging ("Every one of them's got some piss-assed, faggoty white boy on a string somewhere . . . but when they want some *loving*,

bad enough, but Baldwin tops him by providing the play with an earth mother in Juanita, who is loved not only by Richard, but by Pete (the weakest of the demonstrators), by Meridian, by Parnell. Perhaps he hoped to embody the lover, the wife, the mother, the matriarch, and the mammy in one figure, but as the male characters, one after another, reveal their attraction to Juanita, she becomes impossibly significant.

Juanita is never a believable character, but then neither are the others, although Richard and Lyle, given less to explanation, come closest. Not that Baldwin is writing a realistic play. He is using a modified expressionism—with a symbolic set, direct address to the audience, easy movement from one time to another—which may indicate that he intends his characters to be simply attitudes. The minor figures are plainly stereotypes. The whites are "black"-comedy caricatures[12] in the scene in which they come to comfort Lyle at his arrest; the Negroes are the replacements for Aunt Jemima and Uncle Tom that Baldwin condemned in "Many

---

funky, down-home, bring-it-on-here-and-put-it-on-the-table style—"), because both are using the same myth as a defense and a comfort. If these were simply character speeches, it would make little difference, but Richard's accusation, wrapped in sociological generalization, turns up in Baldwin's own mouth in *The Fire Next Time* when he insists that the treatment of the Negro in America stems from "a civilization sexually so pathetic that the white man's masculinity depends on a denial of the masculinity of the blacks." His sentence embodies the truth about fatherless Negro homes, the destructive legacy of a slavery system which did not let families form, but it defines manhood so narrowly that the history of Negro-white conflict in this country can be reduced to Richard's cry, "Why are you always trying to cut off *my* cock?" LeRoi Jones, who often talks about race in America in economic and political terms, is capable of the same sexual *reductio*, not only in a character like Walker in *The Slave*, but in his essays ("Look at those weak fag faces on those patrolmen arresting that beautiful chick . . ." he writes in *Home*) and his poetry (as in "Hymn for Lanie Poo," in which the narrator attacks his assimilationist sister by describing her boyfriend as "a faggot music teacher who digs Tschaikovsky"). In one sense, Baldwin and Jones may simply be having fun, turning a stereotype inside out; in another, as in "Lanie Poo," in which the middle-class Negro is needled for trying to find a place in "the huge & loveless/white-anglo sun," they may be reaching for a metaphor for the societal sterility which they see in the white world and which they would have Negroes avoid. In the long run, however, the references become too routine, too easy, too persistent, and their authors begin to sound like Senator Tillman.

[12] Even as I use this phrase, I am aware that a collection of such caricatures could be assembled by a judicious cutting of news tapes.

Thousands Gone"—"well-adjusted young men and women, almost as dark, but ferociously literate, well-dressed and scrubbed, who are never laughed at, who are not likely ever to set foot in a cotton or tobacco field or in any but the most modern of kitchens." The main characters are a more complicated problem because Baldwin supplies them with a wealth of biographical data as though he intended to provide solid naturalistic motivation for them and as though that could be done simply by piling up detail. This is the method that he uses in his fiction, too, and it is no more successful there. Even in the best of the novels, *Go Tell It on the Mountain,* the center section that tells the stories of the three adult characters is excessively expositional, more like notes for a novel than experiences being undergone or recalled out of a present anguish. In "Stranger in the Village," a 1953 *Harper's* article included in *Notes of a Native Son,* Baldwin offers one of his favorite diagnoses of the Negro problem, which he calls the white problem: that Americans have always made abstractions of the Negro. This is ironic coming from a writer who consistently reduces men to abstractions in his essays and to cardboard cutouts in his novels and plays. A novelist beset by a need to explain his characters, Baldwin chose an even more unlikely genre in *Blues for Mr. Charlie,* in which analysis seldom moves aside for dramatic action.

Not that *Blues* was Baldwin's first attempt at a play. In the late 1950's, he prepared for the Actors Studio an adaptation of *Giovanni's Room,* a novel that might more happily have been turned into a soap opera. Much earlier than that—around 1953, judging by the introductory notes to the newly published Dial edition of the play—he wrote *The Amen Corner.* When it was performed at Howard University in 1955, or so LeRoi Jones reported in *Home,* an English professor "groaned" that it had "set the speech department back ten years." If there was anything in its storefront-church setting, its talk of jazz, its idiom that could have disturbed a self-conscious middle-class Negro in 1955, it seemed tepid enough when, in the wake of *Blues* and after a successful engagement in Los Angeles, it finally arrived in New York in

1965. *The Amen Corner* is a fairly standard maturation play, complicated by a conflict of ideas represented by the parents. Sister Margaret, who has raised David and built a church, is rigid and puritanical, but her strictness is a defense against her own inclinations and her church a refuge which she expects her son to share: "I know ain't no safety nowhere in this world if you don't stay close to God." Luke, the jazz-musician husband who comes home to die, has led a ruinous life, driven to it by Margaret's having withheld her love; weak as he is, he is the opposition: "Maybe I don't know the Lord like you do, but I know something else. I know how men and women can come together and change each other and make each other glad." David, who has been moving from the church piano to the club piano, drawn by his father's records, decides that he must go, but he tells his mother (and the audience) that he is no longer following his father, but finding his own way. This incident and the death of Luke signal the end of the ideational struggle, life versus antilife. Margaret preaches an uncharacteristic sermon ("To love the Lord is to love all his children—all of them, everyone!—and suffer with them and rejoice with them and never count the cost"), relinquishes her church to the unctuous trio who, in a comic subplot, have been trying to take it from her, and kneels at Luke's bedside for the final curtain. Not only the play's setting and its concern with an adolescent coming of age, but its general tone and its willingness to keep the social implications well in the background (at one point Luke does identify God with the power interests, but without painting them white) indicate that *The Amen Corner* is an old play, growing out of the concerns that produced *Go Tell It on the Mountain*. Its chief defect as a play is that there is no real contest; Baldwin, who is on the side of Luke's life-forcers, so stacks the emotional cards against Margaret that her giving in is a foregone conclusion. The best he can hope for is pathos in her capitulation.

There may be superficial similarities between Baldwin and LeRoi Jones, points at which their diagnoses of our supposedly sick society agree, but essentially they are in opposition. Baldwin's most violent antiwhite statement is a plea for the kind of recognition and action that will avoid the fire next time. In *Fire*, he describes his meeting with Elijah Muhammad. Although he understands the appeal of a religion that pictures all white men as devils, "I told Elijah . . . that I had many white friends, I would have no choice, if it came to it, but to perish with them. . . ." For Jones, Baldwin is an establishment writer, more interested in his own sensitivity than the reality of Negro experience; in an essay on Baldwin and Peter Abrahams, first published in *Kulchur* (Winter, 1963), reprinted in *Home*, Jones said "they will not even open their mouths to say anything but that they are well-dressed, educated and have feelings that are easily hurt." If someone would turn them white, he wrote, "then perhaps the rest of us can get down to the work at hand. Cutting throats!" *The Fire Next Time* contains a plea for love; Jones's work, as the later essays in *Home* indicate, is more concerned with the care and feeding of hate. It is only because *Dutchman* and *Blues* appeared within a month of each other and seemed, to some, twin symptoms that the two playwrights are bracketed together here.

Jones seems to me to have been potentially a much more exciting writer than Baldwin. Once you get past the opening of "The Screamers," half sociology, half autobiography, the frenzied march to "the honk" is funny and angry and painful. That story, which Jones included in *The Moderns*, an anthology he edited in 1963, and some of the sections of *The System of Dante's Hell*, published in 1965 but years in the making—for instance "The Heretics," the story of a northern Negro soldier down South—are more alive than most of Baldwin's fiction. Although Jones's poetry has always slipped too easily into blurred images, evocations that never evoke for me, his early work displays a sharp wit and a good sense of invective, both of which have turned hysterical in recent years. His plays, whatever their limitations, have usually begun with a workable dramatic image or, at least, a witty conceit. I use the past tense because, beginning in 1965, although he still spoke to white audiences, if only to abuse them, Jones began the withdrawal into his blackness and turned his writing into a tool and a weapon, fashioned for a black audience, designed to shut out the mixed admirers he once had. The books still come out—*The Baptism & the Toilet* in 1967—but they contain work written earlier in the decade.

LeRoi Jones ("One of those hopeless colored names creeping out of New Jersey," says Lula in *Dutchman*) is a light-skinned, middle-class, university-educated Negro from Newark who has spent most of the decade trying to escape his background. "I disappeared into the slums," says the narrator of "The Screamers," "and fell in love with violence, and invented for myself a mysterious economy of need." Jones did not disappear immediately. "Having been taught that art was 'what white men did,' " he wrote in *Home*, "I almost became one, to have a go at it." From 1958 to 1962 he and Hettie Cohen (who became Mrs. Jones) edited *Yūgen* ("the flower of the miraculous" as No. 2 defines it), which printed the work of Allen Ginsberg, Gregory Corso, William Burroughs, and—after William Carlos Williams appeared as imprimatur in No. 5—Robert Creeley, Jack Kerouac, Hubert Selby. Since the best of the writers who appeared in *Yūgen* were their own men and the worst of them merely mud-daubers, it is difficult to characterize them as a group—as Jones discovered when he wrote his introduction to *The Moderns*. Experimentation with generic form, preoccupation with the outsider in American society, bluntness of language, contempt for the writers whom they considered establishment—these are the tenuous bonds that joined them. They were less a group in the formal sense than a coterie, and the magazine became a kind of house organ in which the writers advertised one another. The interesting thing about that heady literary atmosphere is that Jones was at the center of it—"King of the East Village," as Isabel Eberstadt entitled an article on him in the *Herald Tribune* magazine *New York* (December 13, 1964). Although he was beginning to find his Negro subject matter (one of his few contributions to his own magazine was "Suppose Sorrow Was a Time Machine" in No. 2, a good piece about his grandfather), his identification was with a circle, primarily white but presumably indifferent to race. In Frank

O'Hara's "Personal Poem" (*Yūgen*, No. 6) Jones meets O'Hara for lunch at Moriarty's "and LeRoi comes in/and tells me Miles Davis was clubbed 12/times last night outside BIRDLAND by a cop." Then they go on to chatter about James and Melville.

What went wrong in that charmed circle—perhaps one post-clubbing lunch too many, perhaps old wounds reopened—is not clear, but during the 1960's Jones began to move away. Since all his work is heavily autobiographical, his poetry and his fiction (particularly *The System of Dante's Hell*) show his attempt to escape the middle-class background which makes him feel like an oppressor of his own kind. It is in *Home*, however, that his journey can be seen most clearly. A collection of essays written at random over a five-year period, the book is given a shape of its own by the chronological arrangement of the pieces. They move from "Cuba Libre" (1960), in which he can still use the pronoun "we" meaning "we Americans," to the essays of 1964 and 1965 where his identification is purely black and the prospect is destruction. "The Last Days of the American Empire (Including Some Instructions for Black People)" (1964) is a good example—a prediction of America's doom and a warning to the blacks to get in on the kill to avoid identification with the dying whites. Jack Richardson, interviewing Jones for *Esquire* (June, 1966), wrote that Jones "kept framing general, Spenglerian statements on the decline of the white man's world, its vacuity, moral shallowness and imminent departure." "By the time this book appears," Jones wrote in *Home* (1966), "I will be even blacker."

Ironically, just as *Dutchman* was opening a wider audience for Jones, his ideological transformation was carrying him into forbidden country where that audience could not follow. Not that *Dutchman* was his first play. In the first issues of *Yūgen* (1958), there was an advertisement for a Jones play, *A Good Girl Is Hard to Find*, which was being performed in Montclair, New Jersey. The Eberstadt article, written just before the opening of *The Slave* and *The Toilet*, said that six Jones plays (unidentified) had been done in off- and off-off-Broadway theaters. These must have included *Dante* (1961) and *Dutchman* and *The Baptism*, both produced earlier in 1964, but I have seen no reference to the other three plays. *Dante* is apparently the "The Eighth Ditch (Is Drama," the dialogue chapter of *The System of Dante's Hell*. In it, one Boy Scout buggers another while he talks on and on—accusation, revelation, blues, blues, blues—saying what his partner wants to hear. Late in the play, the seducer identifies the two of them specifically: "An underprivileged negro youth now in the boyscouts. You're what's known as a middleclass Negro youth, also in the boyscouts." As the shift from small to capital *n* in Negro indicates, some of Jones's devices are purely literary and have to be seen on the page. Basically, the idea is a pretty funny one for a treatment of the theme of the fraudulent counselors. The middle-class boy wants a glimpse into the deep, mysterious underworld, and the streetboy simply wants to screw him; the first boy never knows the difference. In his big speech in *Dutchman*, Clay says, "All the hip white boys scream for Bird. And Bird saying, 'Up your ass, feeble-minded ofay! Up your ass.' And they sit there talking about the tortured genius of Charlie Parker." In *Dante*, Jones is casting the middle-class Negro in the ofay role Clay describes, but literally.

Dutchman, Jones's best play, works on two levels at once. Lula and Clay are real people, confronting one another on a real subway. This comes across best in the character of Lula. The sudden breaks in her conversation, the abrupt changes of direction, the lapses into apparent disinterest, all suggest a genuine neurotic female. That characterization can encompass much of the play— her throwing the stuff out of her bag, her mad dance in the car, even the stabbing—but the post-stabbing use of the other subway riders moves the play completely out of the realistic. For *Dutchman* is also a kind of ritual, Jones's presentation through representative figures of his idea of the racial situation in America. Lula approaches Clay on the subway, flirting and accusing at once, and begins to attack him for the costume, the attitudes, the ambitions that mark him as middle-class: "Boy, those narrowshoulder clothes come from a tradition you ought to feel oppressed by." In the second act, her game turns nastier: "You ain't no nigger, you're just a dirty white man." What she wants, although she does not put it so primly, is that he take off the assimilationist mask and become her idea of the black man: "Get up and scream at these people. . . . Don't sit there dying the way they want you to die." He finally explodes, drags her back to the seat, clubs a protesting drunk, slaps her and makes his big speech, the point of which is that whites do not, cannot know anything about blacks, that all they see are the masks which hide the desire to kill. If the middle-class mask is false, it is no more false than the hippy-dip mask (as the streetboy in *Dante* might say) when it is forced on the Negro by an outsider who expects him to act in a particular way (as sex object, as jazzman, as protester). The speech ended, Lula ("I've heard enough") stabs Clay and then orders the other riders, black and white, to remove the body and get off the car. As the play ends, she is ready to advance on another Clay.

Dutchman, then, is an endless train ride (the title, I suppose, comes from *The Flying Dutchman*) in which society—the black as well as the white riders—acquiesces in a situation which creates the black desire to kill, provides the masks to stifle it, and, when those masks are insufficient, permits a murderous white reaction. At the end of the version of *Dutchman* published by Apollo Editions, an old Negro conductor comes through the car just as Lula moves in on her new prey; he tips his hat to her and greets the young man, "Hey, brother!" His words presumably reaffirm the possibility of a brotherhood of hate beneath two very different Tom masks. The alternate, presumably later version in Edward Parone's *New Theatre in America* (1965) drops the conductor (from the text, but not from the cast list), sensibly, since he is not really necessary to the central ritual of the play. It is not the ritual, however, and certainly not the ideational (emotional?) point it implies that gives the play its dramatic validity; nor is it the flickering possibility that the play might be read as something other than a racial drama, a play about the uses and abuses of masks which might be relevant in any human circumstance. It is the frightening vitality of Lula—and, to a lesser extent, of Clay—that makes *Dutchman* so effective a play.

The Baptism, Jones's most casually obscene play, is a hipster religious allegory, a play about the Second Coming, a religious-sexual exercise that is an extended, if implicit, pun on *coming.* An old woman, a homosexual, a minister, and a chorus of women celebrate a fifteen-year-old boy as the "Beautiful screw of the universe!" and, naturally, set out to crucify him. He cuts them down with his silver sword and then is carried off by a heavenly messenger ("The man sent me") dressed in standard cyclist's rig, who has to hit him with a tire iron to quiet him. The end of the world is set for the hour the bars close. The casual references to Negro personalities (Willie Mays, Rochester, Marcus Garvey as a false messiah) and the ambiguous "the man" do not seem to add up to much. *The Baptism* is no cousin to *Dutchman.* It belongs more properly with Frank O'Hara's *The General Returns from One Place to Another,* with which it was coupled when it was first produced. Not quite so corny as the Lawrence Ferlinghetti poem in *A Coney Island of the Mind* in which Christ is "the cat" who is "hep/to who made heaven/and earth," Jones's play is still an inverted equivalent to those once popular slang Bible stories, supposedly told by a gangster to his cellmates. No more than a cute idea, it still has an ostensibly serious point: that the world is not worth saving.

The next and last Jones production to command wide attention was the double bill *The Slave* and *The Toilet,* which opened a four-month off-Broadway run in December, 1964. According to Harold Clurman (in *The Naked Image*), both of these plays were written before *Dutchman; The Toilet,* first published in *Kulchur* (Spring, 1963), certainly was. "Was James Karolis a great sage??" asks the narrator of "Look for You Yesterday," one of the poems in *Preface to a Twenty Volume Suicide Note.* "Why did I let Ora Matthews beat him up/in the bathroom? Haven't I learned my lesson." These are central characters in the presumably autobiographical play, and the answer to that "why" is what makes the play more than the "psychodrama, designed for the acting out of sado-masochistic racial fantasies" that Robert Brustein called it in *Seasons of Discontent.* A group of Negro boys gather in the school toilet where Ray (known as Foots) is to fight Jimmy Karolis, a white boy who is supposed to have sent him a propositioning love letter. Jones makes some attempt to differentiate among the boys, but on the page, aside from Ray and Jimmy, only Ora, Big Shot, the meanest of the lot, the motherless bully, stands out as an individual. Foots tries to get out of the fight by pointing out that Ora has already roughed up Jimmy, but Jimmy wants to fight: "That's who I want to kill. Foots!" It becomes clear to the audience if not to the boys that it was Ray, using that name, who made the advances. When it looks as though Jimmy is winning the fight, Ora leaps on his back and begins to strangle him; the rest of the boys join in. Jimmy's last words are "I love someone you don't even know." After the boys have left Jimmy unconscious on the bathroom floor, Ray returns, crying, and cradles the hurt boy's head in his arms. Except for this unnecessary end—grandiose tear-jerking—the play is a valid dramatic comment on the malleability of human personality and the power of social pressure.

Jones is obviously using homosexuality to represent something else in this play. Acceptance in the white world, perhaps.[13] Donald, the only white boy in the play other than Jimmy, does not believe the accusation: "A letter? (*Groaning.*) Oh, Ray, come on." His use of "Ray" instead of "Foots" and his refusal to take part in the attack on Jimmy suggest that there are relationships in which the Ray identity is possible. Ray is also a good student, but, as Foots, he mocks the principal whose praise has threatened to cut him off from the world of the gang: "He said I'm a credit to my race. He said I'm smart-as-a-whip and should help him to keep all you unsavory elements in line." Jones told Cecil Smith (Los Angeles *Times Calendar*, March 21, 1965) that the play was based on a real incident and the reference in *Preface* seems to cast him as Ray. Given Jones's obsessive concern with his own identity in his work, the struggle that he defines as a pull between whiteness and blackness, the play is ironic since its final effect is to

---

[13] If so, this is an apparently innocent metaphor, not the nasty equation of white and homosexual that Jones uses elsewhere as invective.

suggest that Foots has lost by his choice. It is possible, however, to read the play in other than racial terms, as the story of a boy, lacking the courage to face his own individuality and its implications, who chooses the mindless, cheerful brutality of the group.

In *The Slave*, Walker, a Negro poet[14] who is the leader of a black insurrection, arrives, before his troops take the town, at the home of Grace, his former wife, white, who is now married to Brad, also white, who was once their professor and Walker's friend. Walker has come to do something to or about his two daughters, but he stays to kill Brad, to watch Grace die (after an explosion), and to torture her in her last moments by implying that he has killed the girls. Mostly, however, before these grisly events take place, he stays to talk, talk, talk. Out of their mutual accusation comes the revelation that Brad and Grace, both good liberals, are racists at heart and the suggestion that Walker's revolution, which he admits at one point may not be successful, is not necessarily going to improve things ("this is at best a war that will only change, ha, the complexion of tyranny . . ."). Along with the presentation of these Jonesian commonplaces, a triangle play seems to be trying to take shape, one in which Grace has turned away from Walker, driven off by the increasing virulence of his racial views, which seem to her a specific rather than a generalized attack, and one in which Walker seems motivated by conventional jealousy. The drama of the three people fails, however, because they, unlike Lula and Clay or the main characters in *The Toilet*, are never more than abstractions, perhaps because Jones (or Walker at least: "Christ, the worst thing that ever happened to the West was the psychological novel . . .") discounts psychology for racial identity. Jones calls his play a "fable." Presumably the moral is that whites and blacks must hate each other, and not even love (the marriage of Grace and Walker) or friendship (if that is

[14] The autobiographical elements in this play are strangely prophetic. Jones, like Walker, was a poet with a white wife and two daughters. Since the opening of the play he has left the wife and poetry as he once used it ("The aesthete came long after all the things that really formed me," says Walker. "It was the easiest weight to shed") and has become a self-declared black revolutionist.

what Walker and Brad had) or education (Brad as professor) or art (Walker as poet) or reason ("The way things are, being out of your mind is the only thing that qualifies you to stay alive," says Walker) can alter that "fact." A child cries at the end of the play, but an interracial wail rising out of the holocaust seems, in the light of what has gone before, to have neither dramatic nor thematic significance. It is a theatrical curtain to an untheatrical play, a combination of *The Desperate Hours* and a discussion, spiced with obscenity, which fails in plot and character and exists only for its central idea, which Jones has expressed more vividly in his essays.

In *Dutchman* and, to a lesser extent, in *The Toilet* Jones shows an impressive talent as a playwright. Several things, however, mitigate against an audience's perceiving his work in its complexity. His use of sexual encounter, particularly the bluntness of the homosexuality in *Dante* and *The Toilet*, may distract the audience —as often happens in the work of Tennessee Williams—marooning them on the surface of the play. Similarly, his use of obscenity is likely to offend or to titillate an audience and to keep them from taking that language, as Jones apparently does, as a bridge to a kind of reality or even to recognize that it has dramatic uses, as in Walker's "fuck you" speech near the beginning of *The Slave*, in which, by repeating the phrase five times in a rhythmic pattern, Jones conveys the exasperation of the character much more effectively than he does in the endless explanation with which he later saddles Walker. These limitations, however, may be those of the audience rather than the playwright. The most important of such distorting elements—the racial assumptions—are plainly the dramatist's. Insofar as the racial venom belongs to the character (to Clay, to Walker) it functions dramatically in plays more complicated than tracts. Yet Jones, in his essays and in the abusive appearances he used to make before white audiences, propounded the same ideas in the same idiom, and recognition of this lets the sentiments of Walker's invective or Clay's big speech become the whole play. For this reason, the plays induce opposite responses that are really the same; compare the Brustein comment on *The*

Toilet quoted above with Loften Mitchell's assertion in *Black Drama*: "What he said is that American society is a foul toilet, a slave society. It is as simple as that." It becomes as simple as that, and Jones feeds the process in his own remarks. "*The Toilet* is about the lives of black people," he says in his introduction to the play in *The Best Plays of 1964–1965*, although he goes on to admit that it is about other things as well. "Clay, in *Dutchman*, Ray in *The Toilet*, Walker in *The Slave*, are all victims," he says in "The Revolutionary Theatre," which has become a kind of manifesto for the new Jones. Victims they are, but for Jones to reduce them to that is to disown all that is subtle in his work.

The elegiac note that sounds lightly in the sentence above would be dismissed by Jones, whose new concept of the theater sacrifices subtlety for political effectiveness. "The liberal white man's objection to the theatre of the revolution (if he is 'hip' enough) will be on aesthetic grounds," he wrote in "The Revolutionary Theatre." According to a note accompanying the essay in *Liberator* (July, 1965), it was written in December, 1964, commissioned by *The New York Times*, which refused to print it, as did the *Village Voice*; according to Loften Mitchell, it was read at a conference on Negro drama at the New School in April, 1965. Through the frenzied rhetoric that is characteristic of Jones's later work emerges an idea of a theater that is at once negative and positive, against and for. What the theater is against is quite clear: "It is a political theatre, a weapon to help in the slaughter of these dim-witted fatbellied white guys who somehow believe that the rest of the world is here for them to slobber on." What it is for is a little more amorphous: "This should be a theatre of World Spirit." It should show all the victims that they are brothers, should create "new men, new heroes."

In the spring of 1965, Jones established the Black Arts Repertory Theatre/School in Harlem. It was designed, as its brochure said, for "the education and cultural awakening of the Black People in America": "There the black man will be taught that he is in a unique and privileged place in history and has, within the corrupted West, the opportunity to change the world." Later on, in

the interview with Jack Richardson, for instance, and in a letter to
The New York Times (March 12, 1967), protesting Bosley
Crowther's review of the movie version of *Dutchman,* he was to
describe the Negro as a separate species. During its short life, the
BART/S worked both as an educational and as a producing organization. Playing to a segregated Negro audience, it offered two
new Jones plays—*Experimental Death Unit #1* and *Jello.* According to an Associated Press story (Philadelphia *Bulletin,* November
30, 1965) about complaints on the use of antipoverty funds in
Harlem (some of the money had gone to BART/S), *Jello* is a play
that uses the characters from the old Jack Benny radio show[15] and
ends by letting Rochester kill them all.

As late as February, 1966, Lawrence P. Neal was reporting in
Liberator, in the second part of an article on Jones, that "The
Black Arts is a long way from being the organization it has promised to be. But hopes are high." The next month, after Neal was
wounded in the attempt of a splinter group in BART/S to win his
support, the police moved in and uncovered an "arms cache," as
the newspapers like to call it.[16] By this time, unidentified friends
told the *Times,* Jones had left the organization. At this point, The
Black Arts closed down.

Some of Jones's admirers have attempted to soften the public
image of The Black Arts, but Jones's own voice will not let them.
Loften Mitchell insists that the organization was a gentle one,
much misunderstood, but if so it was hardly the "incendiary pen-
cil" that Jones called for in "The Revolutionary Theatre": "So
that when the final curtain goes down brains are splattered over

---

[15] Jones has always made extensive use of pop-culture figures in his work. In
Preface to a Twenty Volume Suicide Note there are poems entitled "The Death
of Nick Charles" and "Duke Mantee" and in *The Dead Lecturer,* "A Poem for
Willie Best" and "Green Lantern's Solo." In "Look for You Yesterday" (in
Preface), a poem about the loss of growing up, the narrator identifies with the
Lone Ranger: "My silver bullets all gone/My black mask trampled in the
dust//& Tonto way off in the hills/moaning like Bessie Smith." Later, in
"Black Dada Nihilismus" (in *Lecturer*) and in "The Last Days of the American Empire" (in *Home*), Tonto has become insistently black and, as the essay
says, leaves "The Lone Ranger to his own devices, and his own kind of death."
[16] The information on this stage of BART/S history comes from three
stories in *The New York Times,* March 17, 18, and 19, 1966.

the seats and the floor, and bleeding nuns must wire SOS's to
Belgians with gold teeth." Mitchell says that Jones is pro-Negro,
not antiwhite, and even Lawrence P. Neal, writing in *Liberator*
(January, 1966), sees Jones's task as the development of "a
Black spiritual frame-of-reference based on the humanism of the
Bandung world (non-white world)." A Jones poem, "Black Art,"
in the same issue, calls for "Assassin poems, Poems that shoot/
guns" and speaks humanistically of a poem "cracking/steel
knuckles in a jewlady's mouth."

The only recent Jones play that I have had a chance to read is
Black Mass, which was printed in *Liberator* (June, 1966). It is a
dramatization of "Yacub's History," the Black Muslim legend of
creation in which Original Man is black, and whites are created
much later when Yacub, "the big-head scientist," as Malcolm X
explains,[17] "embittered toward Allah now, decided, as revenge, to
create upon the earth a devil race—a bleached-out, white race of
people." In Jones's version, three magicians are gathered to celebrate "The beauties and strength of our blackness of our black
arts." One of them, Jacoub, whose error, according to one of his
colleagues is "the substitution of thought for feeling," creates a
neutral being "who will not respond to the world of humanity." A
beast leaps on stage ("I white. White. White. White.") and grabs
one of the women, who immediately turns white (that is, into a
beast). While the magicians debate whether the beasts are teach-
able (Jacoub's view) or not, the beasts kill them and the remaining women and then pass through the audience "kissing and lick-
ing people as THEY hop eerily out, still screaming . . . 'White!
. . . White! Me . . . Me . . . Me . . . White!' " The play ends with

[17] In Chapter Ten of *The Autobiography of Malcolm X.* In this version the
creation took place over many centuries, through genetic manipulation, from
black to brown to red to yellow to white. C. Eric Lincoln, in *The Black Muslims in America*, quotes from one of Elijah Muhammad's columns: "The
human beast—the serpent, the dragon, the devil, and Satan—all mean one and
the same; the people or race known as the white or Caucasian race, sometimes
called European race." According to E. U. Essien-Udom, in *Black Nationalism*,
Yakub is "the man the Bible refers to as Adam." The myth assumes the
physical and mental inferiority of the white man and the emphasis on genetics
provides the kind of pseudo-scientific rationalization that white race purists
have too often used.

the voice of a narrator: "And so Brothers and Sisters, these beasts are still loose in the world. . . . Let us find them and slay them. . . . Let us declare the Holy War." The opening passages, redolent of pseudo-serious occultism, sound—except for the racist message—like the kind of cult plays that used to turn up in England at the end of the last century. The rest is blatant racist propaganda with the white beast of the Muslims substituted for Senator Tillman's black beast.

On January 4, 1968, Jones was sentenced to a term of two and a half to three years in the New Jersey State Penitentiary and fined $1000 for the illegal possession of two revolvers during the Newark riot of July, 1967. Although all of his recent writings reflect his militancy, it was disturbing to find them being used as evidence in court; Judge Leon W. Kapp, who apparently shares Jones's ideas about the revolutionary uses of literature, admitted that the severity of the sentence was based on a Jones poem ("Black People!" *Evergreen Review*, December, 1967), published after the riots, which the judge read in court. However dangerous Judge Kapp's use of the poem may be as precedent, it is clear in everything that Jones writes and says that the off-white poet has finally become the black revolutionary. There is more to regret here than the loss of a potentially good playwright.

In "American Theater: For Whites Only?" the Douglas Turner Ward article quoted earlier in this chapter, a Negro playwright called for a Negro theater different in intention from Jones's The Black Arts. Ward's most convincing argument was an aesthetic one. A Negro playwright, he insisted, writing for Broadway or off-Broadway, must assume a lack of knowledge in his audience, one which adversely affects his writing: "valuable time is wasted clueing in, exposition is demanded when action should be unfolding, the obvious must be overillustrated, and fantasy literalized." In a theater that is Negro in its concerns and in much of its audience and staff, a Negro playwright need not simplify at the expense of subtlety. "This is not a plea for either a segregated theater, or a separatist one," he wrote. "There's no reason why whites could not participate in a theater dedicated to exploring and illuminating that [Negro] experience if they found inspiration in the purpose." In April, 1967, when the Ford Foundation announced a grant of $434,000 to establish the Negro Ensemble Company, Ward's theater ceased to be simply a proposal. With an interracial board, consisting of Ward, Robert Hooks, the Negro actor who produced and performed in the successful Ward double bill, *Happy Ending* and *Day of Absence* (1965), and Gerald S. Krone, who was that show's business manager, the NEC, at once a theater and a school, launched its public program in January, 1968. Its first production, unfortunately, was Peter Weiss's *Song of the Lusitanian Bogey*, a piece of anticolonial *agitprop* so simplistic that Ward's argument for a subtlety-inducing Negro theater seems irrelevant.

Presumably it was Ward's success in his off-Broadway debut as a dramatist that led to the invitation to do a summer-guest lead column for *The New York Times* drama page, which led to the plan that led to the fact of the Negro Ensemble Company. That is an impressive structure to be built on so slight a foundation, for the two Ward plays are simply extended jokes. In *Happy Ending*, two domestics sit in tears, lamenting the coming divorce of the couple they work for. Their nephew, who has had two years of college, is shocked that they should care: "us here fighting for our rights like never before, changing the whole image, dumping stereotypes behind us and replacing 'em wit' new images of dignity and dimension." They calm Junie down and explain the facts of life to him, that they have been systematically robbing their bosses for years, that their food ("each steak I order for them, befo' butcher carves cow, I done reserved TWO for myself"), their furniture, his clothes, everything comes from the gravy train that will quit running when the divorce goes through. Junie joins them in mourning, until a phone call heralds a marital reconciliation. As the play ends, Junie asks Ellie to add more potatoes to Mr. Harrison's diet because Junie himself is putting on weight and to suggest that there are new styles. "There's hope, Junie," says Vi, the other aunt. "You'll make it, boy, you'll make it. . . ." Commenting on the morality of kitchen thievery in *The Fire Next Time,* James Baldwin wrote: "Negroes who were neither doltish nor servile did not feel that they were doing anything wrong when they robbed white people." Starting from that attitude, Ward constructs a wish-fulfillment fantasy in which the servant who carries home the leftovers is turned into a big-business executive. Along the way he draws an acid portrait of the whites—stupid, helpless, oversexed—and manages a good-natured put-down of that part of the civil rights movement which is concerned with the lip-service values of the middle class.

In "This Quiet Dust" (*Harper's,* April, 1965), William Styron tried to clarify some of the attitudes toward the Negro with which he grew up in the South: "Unnoticed by white people, the Negroes blend with the land and somehow melt and fade into it, so that only when one reflects upon their possible absence, some magical disappearance, does one realize how unimaginable this absence would be." That "magical disappearance" is the basis of the second Ward play, *Day of Absence.* A "reverse minstrel show done in white-face," Ward's "satirical fantasy" lets Negro actors play Southern whites in a town inexplicably bereft of its Negroes. The single joke, in repetitive variation on variation, is that the whites are helpless and the town is completely immobilized. The devices, both comic and satirical, are standard ones which might be both funny and effective if Ward did not feel the need to overuse them at every turn. The casual indifference of whites to the Negro situation can be seen in a line like John's "drive by her shanty," but it turns up again in the Mayor's "through all Nigra alleys" and his assistant's "our shack-to-shack search" and "inside their hovels." The attempt to lure the Negroes back with a sentimental reminder of a toilet brush and the Mayor's reminiscence of his mammy, whose radiant image has remained "all these many years after her unfortunate demise in the Po' folks home,"[18] lose their acidity when they are buried in too many similar jokes. One of the best

[18] A note on the venerability of this joke. In Samuel Foote's *Piety in Pattens* (1773), the Squire, shocked at the apparent ingratitude of the Butler, goes on about "all the favors I have done him": "because I scorn'd to treat him like an ordinary Servant, I have paid him no wages these five Years."

examples of the overextension of the gags comes in the scene in which the mayor, a stock blustery Southern politician, is told that the Negroes are gone. He simply refuses to hear. This is an old standard in which the one receiving the news hesitates as the line reaches him and then lets his disbelief alter or obscure the words. The trick with such a routine is that it be sustained only so long as there is life in it, but Ward's variations go on well past the point at which the gag should have been discarded. The characters in the play are understandably broad cartoons, but there is very little differentiation among them, no real attempt to treat the types as types. As a result the vignettes are not funny as character turns and, since only one joke is involved, the play quickly palls.

Although Ward is the only Negro playwright to attract much attention since the big Baldwin-Jones year,[19] Ronald Milner's *Who's Got His Own* (1966) was interesting enough to deserve some comment. It is a bath of revelation and self-revelation in which the mourners (widow, son, daughter), following the funeral, explain the dead man and themselves in terms of "the black thing," as the daughter calls it. The dead father, it turns out, feared himself rather than the whites, kept his distance to keep from exploding, but at the expense of his wife and family, who received much of the violence he could not release outside.[20] The point of the play is that "the black thing" is an inescapable part of the Negro male and that the white world has so structured his life that he cannot escape it, by burying it as the father tried to do or by letting it loose as the son does in his off-stage beating of a white friend who, thinking of his dinner on the stove, gives only polite attention to his black friend's crisis. The weakness here is that the

[19] The opening of Ed Bullins' *The Electronic Nigger and Others* (1968) at the American Place Theatre did excite enough critical interest to warrant moving the production to a regular off-Broadway theater for a brief commercial run under the more genteel title *Ed Bullins' Plays*. The program consisted of three one-acters that were Negro variations on standard genre pieces.

[20] Maxim Gorky suggested in his novel *Mother* that the same psychological-social pressure afflicted the illiterate Russian worker who could see no way to change his situation. Pelagea Vlassova, talking to Pavel about his dead father, says, "He used to beat me as if it wasn't his wife he was beating, but everybody he had a grudge against."

playwright seems not to recognize that the behavior of the white friend is quite normal, an indication of the limits of friendship, not indifference to the Negro as Negro; at least, the dramatist uses it as a social rather than a psychological fact, as a reflection of the situation rather than of the Negro boy's hypersensitivity. This flaw is a minor one, however.

The greatest difficulty with the play lies in its structure. It is essentially a series of narratives, one recited by each of the central characters, against a counterpoint of comment by one of the others from a different point of view. Although these performances are supposed to be indications that something is going on at that moment, some process that will lead to troubled hope for the two women and the horrified outbreak of the young man, the play fails to convey that sense of immediacy. The mother is always saying things like "I don't want to hear anymore" and "Do you mean to say that" but these seem less like emotional reactions than clumsy authorial devices. The long speeches might have worked better simply as arias, even more artificial than they are, with all the changes implicit. As it is, with all the deficiencies of *Who's Got His Own*, Milner shows a sense of the complexity of character that may serve him well when the struggle between him and his material—which one is using which—is finally resolved.

That struggle is in evidence in all the Negro playwrights discussed in this chapter. Its resolution depends on a great deal more than any artistic decision made by the playwright himself. When the Negro dramatists are finally able to use their experience in itself, neither defensively nor aggressively, chapters such as this one may disappear from surveys of American drama.

FIVE

Robert Lowell
and Some Others

---

*Oh, my play—my wonderful new scene. The
Muses have drained my sweet poet. A chair,
someone—a chair for Poet-Mine-Own. None
for me—not today. Just a footstool—to sit at
a great man's feet.*
—MME. ALEXANDRA IN *Mademoiselle Colombe*

Once verse became the exception rather than the rule in the theater, a critical literature of special pleading was engendered, a personal or vocational apologetics designed to lure the poet back to
the playhouse and to persuade the theater to throw open its doors
in welcome. There has always been something suspiciously mystical in the process. When Maxwell Anderson (in *Off Broadway*)
insists that poetry is "the language of emotion," necessary if
drama is to transcend journalism, when T. S. Eliot finds (in

Poetry and Drama) that there is a "peculiar range of sensibility" for which prose is inadequate, when Archibald MacLeish says (*Atlantic Monthly*, February, 1955) that prose has failed to give contemporary men "that very perception of the meaning of their acts which poetry on the stage has given in other times and places," I cannot help thinking of Novel's advice to the playwright in *The Plain-Dealer*: "Faith, to put his Play into Rithme; for Rithme, you know, often makes mystical Nonsense pass with the Criticks for Wit." One has only to read widely in the heroic dramas of Novel's age or in the minor Elizabethan and Jacobean playwrights to see that there is no special virtue in dramatic poetry.

The problem has always been an artificial one; it was not that the poet left the theater, but that the playwright simply quit writing verse. With a few flukey exceptions (Yeats, maybe), the best dramatists, like the worst, have a way of working with (if not within) the conventions of their age. Since the most imaginative as well as the most popular works of the contemporary stage have been written by prose dramatists, and since, as always, the hacks have followed the leaders, there developed—particularly in this country, where commercial managements have an instinct for survival almost as powerful as that of poets—a theatrical environment uncongenial to poets. This does not mean that poets quit writing plays, simply that they had to find their stages where they could. Whenever a poet's play broke through to Broadway—*The Cocktail Party* or *J. B.*—there was the whispered promise of a revival of verse drama which, of course, came to nothing. The off-Broadway success of William Alfred's *Hogan's Goat* and the attention paid to Robert Lowell's *The Old Glory* may have raised that whisper again in the 1960's, but it was false to the genuinely interesting development in the relation between the poet and the drama. Poets of all persuasions—some of them working in prose —have turned out plays in number and had them performed off-Broadway and off-off-Broadway, in colleges and regional theaters, in coffee shops and concert readings. The output of all this activity may not stack up favorably against the work of the men who are primarily dramatists, but it does seem to have lifted the apologetic haze. These days, a play by a poet need expect neither reverence for its attempt to lift our pedestrian theater to the heights of its bear-pit days nor contempt for its allegiance to art in a show-business world. In such an atmosphere, a playwright—even one in poetic robes—might appear.

Robert Lowell is the likeliest candidate at the moment. He came to the theater when, at Eric Bentley's request, he prepared a version of Racine's *Phèdre* for the French volume of the anthologist's *The Classic Theatre* (1961). Lowell's work as a poet, from *Lord Weary's Castle* (1946) to *Near the Ocean* (1967), treats death and dying, failure, the end of love, the loss of childhood, the impossibility of return—an endless falling away. It is understandable that he should be attracted to the story of Phaedra, destroyed by a love she could neither fulfill nor restrain; of Hippolytus and Aricia, victims of that love; and of the untriumphant return of Theseus—a play in which the drama is created, as Robert J. Nelson says (*University of Toronto Quarterly*, April, 1967), "by the cultivation of hope where there is none." Given the tendency that Lowell's work was to take, the preoccupation with power and violence evident in *Near the Ocean* and his two later plays, *The Old Glory* (1964) and *Prometheus Bound* (1967), Racine's play may have been the more appealing to him because the tragedy of love is complicated by a struggle for power, and declarations of love or of desire (Phaedra to Hippolytus, Hippolytus to Aricia) are made as political maneuvers. These thematic similarities are real enough, but it would be a mistake to overemphasize them since Lowell's *Phaedra* was, after all, a commissioned work and, for all the laments of George Steiner (*Kenyon Review*, Autumn, 1961) and Samuel Solomon (*London Magazine*, October, 1966), is relatively faithful to the themes, the characters, the dramatic structure of Racine.

Not that Lowell's *Phaedra* is a translation. It is plainly an "imitation," the word that Lowell has been using since *Lord Weary's Castle* to describe a new poem based on an original in another tongue. Although his introduction to *Imitations* indicates how much freedom he allows himself with such poems ("I have dropped lines, moved lines, moved stanzas, changed images and altered meter and intent"), his *Phaedra* is not so great a departure from Racine; he is essentially correct when he says, in his preface to the published play: "I have used every speech in the original, and almost every line is either translated or paraphrased." There is no point, here, in making a detailed examination of Lowell's inventions, his adaptations of Racine's language; his modified heroic couplet can hardly be a verbal reflection of Racine's alexandrines. Some idea of the kind of change Lowell made may, however, be useful as an example of his approach to theme and language for the stage.

His emphasis on the political aspect of the love story is greater than Racine's, at least to the extent of his adding a number of casual references to power, although, strangely, he drops the important *"malgré les complots"* of Theseus' last speech, through which Racine emphasizes the connection between the twin turmoils of passion and politics by indicating that civil unrest and its causes have died with Phaedra and Hippolytus. Lowell's bluntly phallic sexual imagery is often used where Racine has none at all, as in Phaedra's description of how she would have led Hippolytus through the maze: "my every flaming thought,/love-quickened, would have shot you through the dark,/straight as an arrow to your quaking mark." Even in a scene such as the one in which Phaedra asks Hippolytus to kill her, where Racine presumably understands the implications of her pleading for his sword, there is nothing in the French play as obvious as "I want your sword's spasmodic final inch." If such usage occasionally becomes ludicrous, Lowell can be effective, as when he brings an ironic pun to Racine's persistent disease-passion image in Theramenes' "this dying woman, who desires to die." Even better is the way he ties the two main themes together with metaphors that look forward to the destruction of Hippolytus—when Hippolytus describes his love as rushing "like formless monsters from the sea" and when Phaedra says rebellion is "like a sea-beast."

In general, Lowell's language is more vivid, more metaphorical, more specific in its detail than Racine's is; active where Racine's is passive, abrupt where Racine's is discursive. As an example of this last, consider the end of Act III, Scene 3: as the king and his party approach, Oenone says, "I see the King" and Phaedra, "I see Hippolytus!" In Racine, her exclamation is followed by three lines about what she fears, but Lowell, aware of the eloquence of understatement, drops the explanatory lines and leaves the fears implicit. Occasionally Lowell alters a line so that its dramatic meaning, its immediate use in relation to action or character, changes, as when Oenone's "*Ce reproche vous touche?*" becomes "You still hate someone," shifting the focus from Oenone's satisfaction that she has been persuasive to Phaedra's reaction to her argument. Such a change is relatively unimportant, and there are few of them in any case. Lowell is more likely to make a line peculiarly his own even while he lets it do the dramatic job that Racine has assigned it. Two examples should be enough to indicate what I mean. "*Mais quand tu récitais des faits moins glorieux,*" Hippolytus begins his catalogue of Theseus' sexual conquests, which ends with his reminding Theramenes that he did not want to listen, that "*Je te pressais souvent d'en abréger le cours.*" Lowell's Hippolytus blurts out, "Other things turned my stomach: that long list/of women, all refusing to resist," but the speech, like the one in Racine, indicates that the young man is as fascinated as he is revolted by his father's exploits. At the end of Act II, Theramenes reports, "*Cependant un bruit sourd veut que le roi respire:/ On prétend que Thésée a paru dans l'Epire.*" Lowell's Theramenes, full of the circumstantial detail that has always been characteristic of Lowell's poetry, says, "I've heard a rumor. Someone swam aboard/a ship off Epirus. He claims the King/is still alive." To my ear, American and of this century, the Lowell lines have more force.

There are weaknesses in Lowell's language, too. I wish he would avoid archaic words ("smites"); easy, conventional similes ("like water through a net"); mixed metaphors (Lowell borrows a *tigre* from Racine and then imagines Aricia harnessing it to a cart); phrases that are contradictory without being paradoxical ("famished, pampered bellies"); literary echoes from the wrong period (Theseus looks for Hawthorne's scarlet letter on Hippolytus' brow); lines that are out of order (Theseus' "Can I let you live?" comes after Phaedra has already told him that she is dying). These things aside, Lowell's *Phaedra* is an impressive play, and the fact that it is not really Racine does not bother me much since no one, including Lowell, really pretends that it is. Considering that Racine has never gone down very comfortably with Americans, Lowell's version may even do the French playwright a service by using a contemporary poet's language to indicate that there is dramatic life in the old boy yet.[1]

It is not *Phaedra*, whatever its virtues, which makes Lowell the most interesting of the poets turned playwright. It is *The Old Glory*. Although the plays that make up this trilogy have been performed separately,[2] it is a single work, its parts held together by a common theme and by the image of the flag. The culminating action of both *Endecott and the Red Cross* and *My Kinsman, Major Molineux* center on the flag, the rejection of the Red Cross of England in the first case, the choice of the Rattlesnake over the Union Jack in the second. The end of *Benito Cereno* is, implicitly, the culmination of a three-cornered struggle among the American flag, the Lion and the Castle of Spain, and the pirates' skull and crossbones, and all three—particularly the Lion and the Castle

---

[1] An incredibly awful production of the Lowell play at the Theatre of the Living Arts in Philadelphia (May, 1967) indicates that actors without ears can kill the living language and send an audience away convinced—as they probably were when they came in—that Racine is an overstuffed French antique on which no American theatergoer could possibly sit.

[2] Although the original plan for the production at the American Place Theatre called for the presentation of the complete trilogy, *Endecott and the Red Cross* was dropped before the opening. Of the other two plays, it was *Benito Cereno* that drew the critical praise and the audiences; when it re-opened at the Theatre de Lys in January, 1965, for a regular off-Broadway run, *My Kinsman, Major Molineux* was no longer on the bill. A revised and expanded version of *Endecott* was presented at the American Place in the spring of 1968. Although there is an increased emphasis on violence (Palfrey's account of the massacre of his father-in-law, the description of the death of the Indian chief and the displaying of his severed hand) in the revision, the play seems not to have been changed in any essential way. The discussion of *Endecott* in this chapter is based on the most recent (1966) published version of the play.

and the skull and crossbones—are used dramatically in several scenes. The flags in these plays are used, by the characters, as flags are in reality, as symbols of an abstraction worth fighting for (freedom) or against (authority). They have no intrinsic meaning beyond that which the characters bring to them. "There are flags and flags," says Endecott of the Red Cross hanging sloppily to the door in Merry Mount, not at all the same Red Cross that his troops carry. In *Benito Cereno*, Captain Delano sits complacently and watches as Babu uses the Lion and the Castle as a barber's napkin, in the scene borrowed directly from Melville, but he snaps out "That's treason," when Babu tells him that Atufal "used the Spanish flag for toilet paper," which may indicate that even another man's flag can be invested with meaning according to the occasion and the need.[3] However the characters see their flags, Lowell is using them as though they were interchangeable, indications that the oppressor and the oppressed, the authority and the usurper are one. "Flags of a hundred colors—" says Endecott, "They're all made of cloth."

The persistent flags and the other occasional artificial links between plays—Endecott's "England's like a full-rigged ship in a dead calm," which apparently looks ahead to *Benito Cereno*, Robin's "He seemed to hold the world/like a gold ball" which suggests the silver ball Babu smashes at the end of *Benito Cereno* —would be no more than literary niceties if the plays were not also part of a thematic unit. In his Introduction to the published play (a reprint of notes written to accompany the original cast

[3] The second instance may be intended as an indication of a certain unacknowledged prudery in Delano, a cousin to the sense of order and correctness that he so often expresses. Lowell may not intend the two reactions to work together at all, may be using the flag only in the immediate context, not aware of how strongly the shaving scene carries over. My first reaction to the "treason" line was to wonder why Delano responds so forcefully. My second was to wonder why Lowell let Babu use the "toilet paper" circumlocution. It was not the dramatic validity of the line that bothered me, since Lowell may have wanted to suggest in Babu something of the naughty boy trying to get a rise out of his elder. It was the phrase itself which sidetracked me into a consideration of historical accuracy; if we are to believe the experts who claim that Gayetty's Medicated Paper (1857) was the first toilet paper (a luxury item at 500 sheets for 50 cents), then it was not a phrase likely to be used in 1800.

recording of *Benito Cereno*: Columbia, DOL 319), Robert Brustein sees the plays as examinations of "American character,"
which has been "permeated with violence from its beginnings."
Although Lowell's choice of American subjects and American
sources, Nathaniel Hawthorne and Herman Melville, and his remarks to Stanley Kunitz (*The New York Times Book Review*,
October 4, 1964) about the relevance of the plays to contemporary America lend authority to the Brustein reading, it is far too
limiting. Although the plays obviously intend to illuminate American character (the persistent mercantile voice from Morton in
Endecott to Delano's "I am responsible to my owners"; the almost
willful naivety in Robin and Delano; the idealism, at once self-
satisfied and unseeing), Lowell uses American experience
("partly a tribute to that past and partly pure irony," he told
Kunitz), as he uses personal, family, and national history in his
poems, to make a generalization that has wider relevance.

The Old Glory is about revolution—Endecott initiates one,
Robin joins one, Delano puts one down—and the process by
which the oppressed become the oppressors; freedom, as Babu
demonstrates in his victory ritual, can be reached only by walking
across the fallen flag and kissing the skull of the former tyrant.
Baruch Hochman (*Tulane Drama Review*, Summer, 1967) says
that the plays "lament the ease, grace, dignity, opulence, and no-
bility of the order that is overthrown." In a way they do, of
course, since there is an elegiac quality in the last dance of the
Merry Mount revelers, a kind of dignity in Major Molineux'
facing the mob, a civilized intensity in Cereno's attempt to make
Delano understand the double nature of his words. Yet "lament"
is an overstatement; whatever virtues the fallen oppressors seem
to have come from what they are immediately—victims—and not
from what they were. "But what about the Roman mob?" asks
Lowell (as Juvenal) in *Near the Ocean*. "Their rule/is always
follow fortune and despise/the fallen." For theater audiences, the
opposite is true, particularly when the despising mob is in evidence (*Major Molineux*); the blunt violence of the man holding
the sword brings audience sympathy to the victim, even when the

former is called *freedom-fighter*, the latter *tyrant*. Lowell, as he told Kunitz, is at once liberal ("concerned with causes") and conservative ("knowing that liberalism can be a form of death too)". Even though much of his poetry is preoccupied with "the downward glide/and bias of existing," as he puts it in "Night Sweat" (in *For the Union Dead*), it would be a mistake to assume that the conservative in Lowell is positing virtue in the overthrown authorities in *The Old Glory*. After all, it is the obtuse Delano who sees the elegance and ease in Cereno's life, and the innocence of Merry Mount is the tool and the invention of the cynical Morton, for whom it is commercially useful. There is likely to be a hidden sting in even the most lavish praise, as in Robin's memory of Major Molineux, in which he recalls the scar "like a question mark": "He got it killing/Frenchmen." Although there are elements in *The Old Glory* that underline the irony of that title, the play is less concerned with the decline to the new glory than it is with the nature of power itself. The movement in time from play to play, with its suggestion that there is always a revolution in process, underlines the basic theme of the play—that, under whatever flag, power demands action and that the action is inevitably violent and tyrannical. This can probably best be seen by looking at the plays separately.

Endecott and the Red Cross is based on two Hawthorne stories, "The Maypole of Merry Mount" and "Endicott and the Red Cross." In combining the two into a single play, Lowell is able to use Hawthorne's two Endicotts as aspects of his main character, the ruler with the streak of softness toward the young couple in the first story and the man of action who rips up the flag in the second. The play is essentially a series of conversations, mostly expositional, in which the various points of view are defined: Thomas Morton's pragmatic religion and politics, Mr. Blackstone's Establishment Anglicanism, Elder Palfrey's murderous Puritanism,[4] Governor Endecott's uneasy authoritarianism.

---

[4] As an indication of Palfrey's intransigent zealousness, Lowell has him answer Endecott's excuse for lenience ("they are children") by quoting (or rather misquoting) stanzas 166-167 from "Damnation of the Infants" from Michael Wigglesworth's *The Day of Doom*, a poem which was not written until about thirty years after the incidents in the play are supposed to have taken place.

Where in the other two plays Lowell uses conversational bridges (Robin and Boy, Delano and Perkins) between scenes, here he uses abrupt and highly artificial breaks (gun shots, an arrow flying in from offstage, shouts) to bring one scene or discussion to an end and begin another.[5] There are moments in which the points of view clash dramatically, as in the scene in which Endecott, with Palfrey's assistance, sits in judgment on the Merry Mount revelers; he consistently tempers Palfrey's avenging justice, and, while doing so, uses the elder as target for his heavy irony. This is important not for the sake of Palfrey as a character or as a satirical object for Lowell, but because he represents one side of Endecott's own temperament,[6] and the play is about Endecott's growing awareness of the nature of power and his inability to escape its consequences. He "still breathes hell-fire," as the soldier says in the

---

Since those stanzas were once standard examples of Puritan harshness, often quoted in text books, Lowell may have assumed that their usefulness in at once defining and mocking the character was more important than historical accuracy. Certainly his use of George Peele's "Cupid's Curse" to accompany the Merry Mount dancers has thematic relevance: "All they who change old love for new,/Pray God they change for worse." Lowell's Peele, like his Wigglesworth, is not accurately quoted. Although some changes are understandable ("God" for Peele's "gods"; harsher lines in Palfrey than in Wigglesworth), I suspect that Lowell is quoting from memory or playing his imitation-game. Anyone who grew up in the academic environment of close textural reading might be tempted to find more significance in the changes than are really there. Lowell tends to be a little casual about sources. In Anthony Ostroff's *The Contemporary Poet as Artist and Critic*, commenting on "Skunk Hour," one of the poems in *Life Studies*, Lowell said, "Somewhere in my mind was a passage from Sartre or Camus about reaching some point of final darkness where the one free act is suicide."

[5] Considering the artificiality with which he shifts scenes, it is ludicrous that at one point Lowell gets Blackstone off stage by having him announce, like Aubrey Tanqueray in good Pinero fashion, "I have important letters to write." There are, fortunately, very few of these realistic-theater hangovers in *The Old Glory*.

[6] Daniel Hoffman suggests (*The Hollins Critic*, February, 1967) that Lowell borrowed Racine's technique of providing a confidant for his major figure, "who at the same time represents one side of that person's character," not only in giving Endecott his Palfrey, but Robin his younger brother and Delano his Perkins. A confidant is conventionally a willing ear into which the hero may pour his secrets, but when used most effectively, as in the relationship between Phaedra and Oenone, there is antagonism as well as trust, self-accusation externalized. Even in *Major Molineux*, where the confidant sometimes seems to dwindle to straight man, Boy nags Robin toward violence. In the other two plays, the prickly relationship between the main figure and his other image is evident.

exchange with the sergeant which Lowell uses to prepare for Endecott's entrance, but "no one seems to get punished,/not in the end, not so it hurts." A courtier who became a Puritan after the death of his wife ("I found our iron religion"), Endecott has learned to temporize again, to let "sinners slip through my fingers." He complains of the weight of his armor, the ache in his joints, the fever that has attacked him, physical manifestations of the distrust he feels for his role as "the arm of God here."

The key to his state of mind and to the play is the dream that he describes to Palfrey.[7] In the dream, he was at once Palfrey and a Papist, condemning his own people from the pulpit: "In the end my own soldiers/were dragging each other off to the fire." Having earlier called Palfrey an axe ("You are a natural divider"), he says, "I was hitting men with an axe—/it was a warped American axe; it hit askew." Finally, just before he hears and complies with the appalled elder's repeated cries to kneel, he says, "I was trying to nail them to the Red Cross." Calm again, he predicts what will happen—what has already begun to happen, as the audience knows from the opening scene—that England will try to impose on the colony a royal Governor and the established church and that he will be forced into an open break. At the end of the play he makes his promised speech ("a hollow, dishonest harangue,/half truth, half bombast—" as he predicted it would be) and performs his act (cuts the Red Cross from the staff) and his power is no longer equivocal. Its first manifestation is his order to shoot the captive Indians, to burn the Indian village and Merry Mount itself. "I will delay and wait on Providence," he says,

[7] Between the first edition of the play (1965) and the second printing of the Noonday paperback edition (1966), Lowell revised the scene in which Endecott tells his dream, cutting it and at the same time strengthening the images of violence. There is no indication in the volume itself that the play is a revision. This seems a good point to say that Farrar, Straus & Giroux should be ashamed of having made so sloppy a book of The Old Glory. Both Benito Cereno and Major Molineux were published in earlier versions, the first in Show (August, 1964), the second in Partisan Review (Fall, 1964). They were extensively revised, primarily by cutting, before they appeared in book form, but in the process the text was littered with disconcerting small errors—entrances and exits not properly identified, speakers mislabeled. Lowell's editors should have caught such inconsistencies.

echoing a line that he used earlier in the play, but circumstances have already forced him beyond the moment when he can "still delay, evade, pull strings." The tone of that speech and the rueful final bit with the flag (too self-conscious a curtain for my taste) convey not only regret, but a self-awareness impossible for Robin and Delano or for those other active revolutionists, Greenough and Babu.

My Kinsman, Major Molineux, based on the Hawthorne story of that name, takes place on the eve of the American revolution,[8] and the action is double—the movement toward the revolution itself and Robin's change from observer to participant. Lowell borrows Hawthorne's man with the face of two colors and makes him at once more specific (Colonel Greenough, the rebel leader) and more consciously symbolic ("I am an image of this city"). When we first see him his face is mottled, next it is half-mottled, half-red, and it must become all red before "I'll be well." The Clergyman, who at one point holds up a whirligig to see which way the wind is blowing, says "I have a sick parishioner/a whole sick parish! I have a notion/one of these flags will cure us." The contest between the Rattlesnake and the Union Jack is settled in the Rattlesnake's favor and—in the long scene in which the Major is mocked, killed, and stripped—the revolution is triumphant. The ambiguity of that victory is shown directly in the fact that Greenough has taken over the Major's mansion ("Freedom has given me this palace") and presumably his tyranny as well ("I am a king"). It is implicit in the Biblical hyperbole of the Clergyman's tirade against King George, for his phrases—"you've borne the blandishments of Sodom"; "now we'll strip the scarlet whore" —remind us that freedom's advocates include the homosexual and the prostitute.[9] It is presented dramatically in the scene in which

---

[8] In the earlier version of the play, Robin sees the counterfeit Indians on their way back from the Boston Tea Party. Although a precise date is not given, Hawthorne's story must have been set in the 1750's.

[9] The bizarre scene in which the barbers bring the homosexual to the prostitute, full of the most obvious kind of sex gag ("this pricks my fainting courage"; "Lay on, Macduff"), is a little difficult to understand in context. Perhaps, as the homosexual's falsetto song suggests, it is to be seen as a manifestation of "the breath of freedom" in the air. More likely, the joking summary

the mob chants their new new flag's slogan, "Don't tread on me," while they do the treading. After the Major's death, each of the principal characters speaks a personal word—sometimes a forgiving one—over his body, each ending with "all tyrants must die as this man died." The implications of that line for the successful revolution are obvious within the context of *The Old Glory* as a whole. The victim becomes the tyrant as the tyrant becomes the victim; it is power itself that creates the violence.

Robin's participation is almost accidental. He arrives in the city, like his counterpart in Hawthorne, a country boy come to make his way with the help of his influential kinsman. Lowell uses the same device Hawthorne does, sends Robin around the town asking after Major Molineux, but Lowell's Robin is met by the threat of violence, not by the laughter that pursues Hawthorne's young man. Although this change is appropriate to Lowell's revolution, it makes impossible the wonderfully dramatic finish that the Hawthorne story has, in which Robin, startled by the sight of the Major in tar-and-feathers, breaks into an involuntary laugh and thus becomes part of the general laughter which has been aimed at Molineux—and at Robin because of Molineux—throughout the story. Lowell's substitution is to have Robin unthinkingly take the Rattlesnake the Clergyman hands him even while he is moved and angered at what is being done to his kinsman, and the Boy, not quite aware of what he is doing, hands one of the crowd some dirt to throw at the Major. As though he knew that these gestures might be lost in a stage full of people, Lowell gives the Major a line (*"Et tu, Brute!"*)[10] to help the audience recognize what Robin has become. Up to that point, up to the appearance of the Major in his red cart, Robin has not understood what is going on.

The function of the Boy, as Robin's companion on his strange

that caps the occasion—"Once to every man and nation/comes the time a man's a man"—is an ironic reflection on the "manly" action of the last scene. So, in a different way, is the Boy's demand to Robin: "For God's sake stand and be a man!"

[10] Early in the play, Robin says to the Boy, "He swore he'd make my fortune,/and teach you Latin."

walk through town, is not simply to give Lowell a chance to present as speeches the naive reactions which in Hawthorne are Robin's thoughts, but also to depict that side of Robin which wants to meet bewilderment with violence ("You should have brained him with your stick"). To heighten the unreal quality of what Robin is experiencing, Lowell calls for an artificial set of five miniature houses with man-size doors, which light up as they become the center of a scene and dim out as Robin passes to the next. It is as though Lowell wanted to present visually the truth that lay behind the social and psychological description in Hawthorne's "Travelled youths, imitators of the European fine gentlemen of the period, trod jauntily along, half dancing to the fashionable tunes which they hummed, and making poor Robin ashamed of his quiet and natural gait."[11]

Lowell intends not only that Boston be strange to Robin, but that Boston be more than Boston, a mythical pocket in which the revolutionary action can become an image of violence that frees itself from—without losing its reference to—the American revolution in fact and in the schoolboy sense of it. One of his devices here is to let the Ferryman suggest Charon—a throwback to the kind of mythical references he used in *Lord Weary's Castle*[12]— but anyone attracted to consistency in dramatic images will find it

---

[11] Although I did not see the play in New York, I gather from the reviews (which generally preferred *Benito Cereno* to *Major Molineux*) that the production was highly stylized. In his "Director's Note" to the published play, Jonathan Miller says that he was thinking in terms of eighteenth-century political cartoons and *Alice in Wonderland*, which are not exactly the same thing, and that the costuming was designed with the cartoons in mind and the movement, of all but Robin and the Boy, to suggest marionettes. The photograph in the published play, obviously a pre-opening publicity still, shows half-masks on some of the characters and artificial poses of the townsmen alongside the country boys from Deerfield. Since Miller's inventiveness did more harm than good to Lowell's *Prometheus Bound* in its Yale production, I am suspicious of his literary and artistic analogues and his ability to implement them. On paper, some of the staging ideas sound very good, but the difficulty with *Major Molineux* in too great a division between Robin and Boy and the Bostoners lies in the end of the play in which, if the production is to remain faithful to the central action, the townsmen would have to become human or Robin and the Boy marionettes.

[12] Charon is in "In Memory of Arthur Winslow," in which the Charles River flows into the Acheron.

odd that although Boston is "the city of the dead" at the beginning of the play, at the end the Major has to die before he is "free to cross the river." In any case, the suggested Charon—who might not be identifiable in production—is a literary decoration, hardly necessary when one considers that the action itself will suggest the hellishness of the situation. Yet, hell is too uncomplicated an image to take in the final irony of the play, which comes in the muted last scene, after the frenzy of the rebellion dies down. The Boy has found the flintlock he came to town for, Robin carries the Major's sword, "a souvenir," and they are going back not to Deerfield but to Boston: "It's strange/to be here on our own—and free." I assume that Lowell is not being ironic in a simple minded fashion, balancing this line against what we have just seen, but is suggesting that, incredible as it may seem, the line is also true, although its truth must encompass the flintlock and the sword. That, presumably, is the reason the play ends with the repetition of the phrase "Major Molineux is dead," once from the Boy, once from Robin.

Benito Cereno is generally and rightfully considered the best of the trilogy, the one most able to fill a stage and hold an audience. There are a number of reasons why this should be true: Babu's revolution has an immediate relevance; the characters are more fully developed than those in the other plays; there is more overt action—or, at least, the dramatic violence at the end suggests that there is. I suspect, however, that the most compelling reason has to do with the theatrical vitality of the surface plot. At one level, *Benito Cereno*, like the Melville story on which it is based, is a mystery story. On the *San Domingo*, Delano finds himself in an unfamiliar and strangely disturbing environment, faced with a situation which holds a frightening secret. The audience, one step ahead of Delano (several steps if they have read their Melville), begin to pick up the clues that Don Benito throws out and become infected with conventional suspense—waiting either for the revelation of the true nature of the ship or for Delano's discovery of it. Robin's attempt to find Major Molineux is potentially the same kind of story, but the stylization in that play and the absence of antagonists intent on keeping or revealing the secret (Benito and Babu) kill the possibility of suspense. The mystery of the *San Domingo* is solved at a moment of high drama—the confrontation of Delano's pistol and Babu's hatchetmen—and the discovery leads directly into the two final theatrical scenes—the ceremony of the skull and the flags, and the slaughter of the rebels. There is, then, a conventional action to attract an audience until (or while) it moves to the more important elements in the play—the nature of the secret and the presentation of Delano.

The secret is that the obsequious Babu, the perfect servant, is the master, and the aloof Don Benito, the imperfect captain, is the slave. In their scenes with Delano, Don Benito tries obliquely to let the American captain know what his position is, and Babu, barely able to hold his tongue, throws out hint after hint, lines that are at once needles aimed at Don Benito and pats on his own back for the cleverness that lets him play with Delano. Their game (there is a nasty playfulness in Babu and even, at times, in Don Benito) is very necessary to the surface story, of course, and their lines are useful in eliciting revelatory answers from Delano, but they are also important as a reflection of the way a shift in power dictates a change in roles. The slave-master confusion that they embody recalls the victim-tyrant mixup at the end of *Major Molineux*, but the situation is complicated here by the fact that immediate practical (political) problems force them to pretend to the old, the conventional social situation. The rebellion, which is at once a mutiny on the *San Domingo* and a portent of white-Negro relations in the future ("You mustn't blame them too much . . ." says Don Benito. "We have kept them cooped up for ages"), follows the pattern of that in *Major Molineux*—butchery in the name of freedom. The frequent references to the French Revolution emphasize this reading. "It's easy to terrorize the defenseless," says Delano, when Babu teases Benito with a whip, and Babu answers, "That's what we thought when Don Aranda held the whip."

There is, then, no defense of the old rule, the mastery of Don Aranda and Don Benito, but in the immediate dramatic situation, in which Don Benito is a victim, the sympathy is likely to go to him as it does to Major Molineux or, at least, to go against his torturers. Babu's victory for freedom (whose flag is the skull and crossbones) was gained through killing, much of it out of revenge rather than necessity; Benito's description of Don Aranda's death ("He died very slowly and in torture") takes on a new horror when we discover that the fever that wracked the ship (like the disease in the Boston of *Major Molineux*) was the spirit of revolution and that it is Don Aranda's skeleton that is the figurehead for Babu's ship. The nature of that freedom, hinted in the scenes in Babu's "little entertainment," such as the one in which the sailor dips white dolls in a tar-pot and then tries to blacken his own face, is made very clear in the scene in which Don Benito and Perkins are forced to walk across the Spanish flag and kiss the skull ("the mouth of freedom"). "He was free to choose freedom," Babu says of Perkins, whose other alternative is death. The beauty of *Benito Cereno* is that the final scene, the new shift in power, makes a victim of Babu, forcing the audience, which has been hoping for the rescue of Delano, to switch sympathy again as Babu, in his scene with crown, rod, and ball, rehabilitates his revolution and almost turns the butchery back into a fight for freedom.

Delano is the central figure in the play. Despite his sense of himself as a man of the world, compared to the rigid Perkins, he is an American innocent, a compound of practical man and idealist, constantly confused by the failure of the world outside him to respond as he expects it should. After he knocks down the old Negro man in the scramble for the food his sailors bring, Delano nurses his sore hand and says, "It's always the man of good will that gets hurt." Certain of who he is ("I am Amasa Delano,/captain of the *President Adams*"), he reacts only to the surface of words, to the appearance in relationships and events. When Benito says, "A captain is a servant, almost a slave, Sir," one of his first attempts to warn Delano, the American responds with a tautology he thinks is a moral maxim: "No, a captain's a captain." Like Perkins, Delano imagines that the *San Domingo* could be put to rights with a little discipline, orderliness, seamanship. Yet the

Delano who congratulates Benito on his own arrival ("This is your lucky day") and blandly compares himself to the Good Samaritan is only the apparent Delano, the traditional comic American. Underneath he is beset by doubts and contradictions which the disorder on the ship brings to the surface. Not that he recognizes the complications even then. He vacillates between the smug self-reliance of the New Englander—

> He ought to dress himself properly and speak his mind.
> That's what we do. That's why we're strong:
> everybody trusts us.

—and a longing for the comforts of slavery, the mutual dependency that he reads into the Benito-Babu charade in which, of course, he casts himself in Benito's role. His self-doubt and his rejection of it are seen most clearly in the reiterated line, "Who could want to kill Amasa Delano?" which he repeats in the confrontation scene, a baffled reaction to the assertion, first by Atufal, then by Babu, "We want to kill you."

Although the situation in the play uncovers the subsurface Delano, the events push him into a rigidity which denies it. This can best be seen by comparing him to Perkins. As the play opens, Perkins is the untraveled New Englander, untroubled by subtleties of any kind, bluntly suspicious of anything foreign, Catholic, Negro, and Delano condescends to him grandly, parading his own worldliness, toying with paradox and ambiguity ("In a civilized country, Perkins,/ . . . /everyone disbelieves in slavery and wants slaves"). Yet Delano's speeches are full of Perkins lines, lightly masked as sophisticated remarks, such as his description of the French, "They're like the rest of the Latins,/they're hardly white people." In the course of the play, the two characters change position. Perkins lets "a little foreign dirt rub off on" him, as Delano says he should, if that means that he responds to situations directly rather than through preconceived abstractions. "I only have one life, Sir," he says when he kisses the skull, and Delano, as simple as the Perkins who opened the play, cries out, "You are no longer an American, Perkins!" The final revelation of the new

Perkins comes in his anguished cry just before Delano kills Babu, "Let him surrender. Let him surrender./We want to save someone."

Delano has by this time become the power figure on the ship, and another side of the man emerges. As a kind of after-image to Delano's complacency there is, from the beginning, the possibility of violence. The underside of his idealistic impulse to clean up the *San Domingo* can be seen shortly after he boards her when he wonders whether or not he should "take it over by force." Lowell lets the reference pass from the personal to the national as Delano tells Babu "how we shoot pirates" and comments to Perkins, "This old world needs new blood/and Yankee gunnery to hold it up." At the end of the play it gets both Yankee rifles and newly shed blood. In asserting his power, Delano must act violently; once he does, the violence becomes gratuitous, as it did with the mutineers on the ship. He shoots Babu, over the protests of both Perkins and Benito, and then empties his pistol into the body. His last line, "This is your future," is not only Delano's petulant reaction to the discomfort he has been put through, but is Lowell's recognition that Babu's "The future is with us" is ironic in a context in which the passage of power from Benito to Delano to Babu (from Europe to America to Africa and Asia) promises the same old authoritarian violence.[13]

There are two elements in *Benito Cereno*, both presumably designed to enrich the play's allusiveness, which provide difficulties, at least for the man who expects Lowell to be as meticulous as Melville. The first is the pattern of historical reference; the second, the specific contemporary analogies. Lowell substitutes "About the year 1800" for the exact date of the Melville story, 1799, an elasticity that allows him to take in public figures and events that can be used in relation to the play's themes, characters, and dramatic situation. A direct analogy is made between the mutiny on the ship and the French Revolution in the dinner scene in which the *Marseillaise* is played and Francesco, one of the

---

[13] In the earlier version of the play Delano says, "I am your future," a line that is even more effective in expressing the double sense of that last scene.

slaves, is identified as *ancien régime* even though he had an uncle who "voted for the death of the French King." At the beginning of the play, Perkins says, "Thank God our Revolution ended where the French one began," and Delano deprecates the French in lines that point toward his own position at the end of the play: "they start with a paper republic/and end with a toy soldier, like Bonaparte." Babu plays with a comparison between the two revolutions (*Major Molineux* has already suggested it dramatically if the trilogy is seen as a whole) when he says that Francesco fears the Americans and when he asks if it is true that Jefferson has set up a guillotine on the steps of the Capitol. Historical revolution is further identified with the mutiny by the name *San Domingo*, which Lowell substitutes for the original *San Dominick*, for the slave uprising under Toussaint L'Ouverture took place in Haiti (also called Santo Domingo) at the time of the French Revolution and Haiti became independent in 1804. The name change for the other ship—from *Bachelor's Delight* to *President Adams*—has less to do with the theme of violence and power than it does with Delano and Perkins. Their discussion of the election in which Adams lost to Jefferson and of the character of the two men provides an analogy for the captain and his bosun. Adams, "a nervous dry fellow," the sort who "doesn't export," suggests Perkins, and Delano thinks of himself as more like Jefferson; yet when he repeats his description of Jefferson as "a gentleman and an American," he adds, "He's not lifting a finger to free his slaves," an addition that is a signal for the rigid illiberality that Delano will display before the play is over. At one point, Delano reminds Benito that "my government blew/the bowels out of the pirates at Tripoli," so Jefferson, during whose administration the Tripolitan War took place, is identified, at least obliquely, with violence. The play then takes place shortly after Jefferson's election (1800), after the Tripolitan War (1801–1805), after Napoleon's elevation to power (1799, when he became First Consul, or 1802, when he became consul for life) and, perhaps, after Haitian independence.

At first, Lowell's changes and additions appear to add up to a total historical context, but as the date becomes more amorphous it appears that the references have allusive value only within the immediate lines and scenes in which they appear. It is also a little disturbing that Lowell moved the encounter of the two ships from the west coast of South America to "an island harbor off the coast of Trinidad," a change which adds nothing to the play. Presumably, he wanted to put the vessels in rebellious water (*San Domingo*), but he retained some of the details of the presumed voyage of the *San Dominick* in Melville's story, a voyage so incredible in the new geographical setting that even the obtuse Delano might have been unable to swallow it, and he retained Babu's demand that the ship be sailed to Africa, an odd idea with Haiti, a black and revolutionary haven, comparatively near. This kind of critical lint-picking may seem a little unnecessary, but Lowell invites it by introducing elements that he never adjusts to the work as a whole. Cavils such as these can be made only after a close reading, not while watching a play in performance, but when one admires a work—as I do *The Old Glory*—one cannot help wishing that the author had made it all of a piece.

The doubts about the contemporary references are not so *recherché*. There are places in the play in which Lowell's attitude toward American involvement in the affairs of other nations seems to break into the open, disrupt the dramatic context, and make an immediate satiric point at the expense of the total analogy. It is obvious that Delano is designed—by Melville as well as Lowell— as a representative American of sorts, a man who does mischief with the best of intentions, and that he is to be a comment on the author's time as much as a figure from his own. He can do that best, however, by acting out his own drama in his own setting. For the most part, Lowell's play works as that kind of analogy. Although the mutiny may have something in common with the black rebellion of LeRoi Jones's *The Slave* or the promised revolution on the lips of today's fiercest black nationalist, for the most part Babu's revolution is made to keep its thematic place.

There are two noticeably intrusive references in *Benito Cereno*. The first is to American aid and the implicit attitudes that accompany it. In the scene in which Delano and Perkins bring the food to the ship, they are met with turmoil, which ends in voilence, rather than the orderly gratitude they expect. The chant of the Negroes, "Feed me, Master Yankee!"; the obvious irony of Francesco's repetitive identification as "American" of the water, the pumpkin, the cider he serves at dinner; Perkins' "They think America is Santa Claus"—all these come across as statements about America today, incidentally relevant to Delano's character, rather than actions involving Delano which also have a contemporary validity. The other disturbing moment comes at the end of the play when, just as Babu thinks he has the upper hand, the hidden seamen fire into the mutineers. Lowell's stage direction says "Several Negroes, mostly women, fall." This is a fairly obvious theatrical device to suggest that it is the innocent who get hurt, but I cannot help wondering why the seamen would shoot the women before they shot the hatchetmen who might conceivably kill Delano and Perkins. If all that Lowell wants is a dramatic image to show the ease with which armed strength turns into ugly violence, how much more effective it would be for the seamen to go on shooting, as they do, and the women to fall on the third or fourth volley. I suspect, however, that what he wants to suggest—as an opponent of the war in Vietnam—is that weapons are indiscriminate about their targets,[14] a comment on napalm bombs rather than on hand weapons that can be aimed. "My theme might be summed up in this paradox," Lowell told Kunitz in the interview in the *Times Book Review*, "we Americans might save the world or blow it up; perhaps we should do neither." This is not really the theme of *The Old Glory*, unless it be read as a cautionary tale eschewing power. The stage directions for the "roar of gunfire" must have been written by the Lowell "concerned with causes," momentarily elbowing the poet aside. Although these apparent lapses into topicality do some disservice to the play as a whole,

[14] To be fair to Lowell, the original story does have such a comment, but Melville's device does not operate at the expense of tactical common sense. Delano's ship, giving chase, fires into the fleeing mutiny ship, killing captive Spaniards as well as rebelling slaves. Nor is there the chance in the original for the women to stand for innocent victims since, in Melville, they are among the cruelest of the mutineers.

Benito Cereno withstands them, as it does its other flaws, and remains a work of great force.

Since *The Old Glory* is a play written by a major American poet, perhaps a word should be said about the verse. The most revealing thing may already have been said by Robert Brustein— presumably responding to the recording of *Benito Cereno*—when he commented on the playwright's "heavily charged prose style." The absence of a fixed metrical pattern in that play and in *Endecott* (*Major Molineux* has a strong four-stress line) makes Lowell's verse, in the mouth of an actor, almost indistinguishable from prose. Only the frequent repetition, in word and line, tells the ear the verse is there. The language is particularly direct and simple in *Endecott and the Red Cross* and *My Kinsman, Major Molineux,* only occasionally slipping into alliteration ("May God guard and guide our Governor") or elaborate sound play ("Two real beers for the Deerfield boys"). The dramatic usefulness of such lines is doubtful in most instances, although one might make a case for the alliterative line above as another device to poke fun at Palfrey. There is very little incidental figurative language; much of the metaphor is central to the play and used in most cases in conjunction with its visual counterpart (flags, armor, animal masks).

The language of *Benito Cereno* is much richer than that in the other two plays. In Delano's description of the approaching *San Domingo,* for instance, the adjectives describing both the ship and the sea—*gray, creeping, cracked and rotten, decayed, battered*— help set the ominous mood of the play, and the similes—"like the beheaded French Queen's high wig"; "like a raped Versailles"— point to the mutiny that Delano takes so long to see. Sometimes Lowell seems to be playing a double game with Delano's figurative speech. "He is like some Jesuit-haunted Hapsburg king/about to leave the world and hope the world will end," he says of Benito, a speech that seems designed not simply to touch on the shift-of-power theme but to make fun of Delano's pomposity; as often happens when one of Delano's figures becomes grandiose, Perkins deflates it with a simple line, "He said he was lost in the storm."

The best verbal effects in the play grow directly out of the dramatic situation; in the face of Delano's ignorance of what is going on, the lines of Babu and Benito are purposefully loaded with double meaning and those of Delano often accidentally ironic. Since Melville's prose lines reflect the same kind of verbal nuance, it is obvious that the effective language of the play is not the result of its being in verse. The fact that the author is a poet, conscious of the possibilities of language, may have let him escape the tendency, too common on the Broadway stage, to avoid words and locutions that might offend an actor's personal inarticulateness or an audience's reluctance really to listen. That escape puts him in modern drama's best prose tradition, makes him a legitimate descendant of Ibsen, Chekhov, Shaw. "I am fascinated by the prose grip on things that somehow lets the music in," Lowell said in the Kunitz interview; it is a fascination that had already led to "91 Revere Street," the autobiographical section at the center of *Life Studies*, and would be seen again in his next play, *Prometheus Bound*.[15]

Prometheus Bound is still another Lowell "imitation," rather farther from Aeschylus than the Lowell *Phaedra* is from Racine. According to the "Author's Note" to the published play (*New York Review of Books*, July 13, 1967), he worked from a translation, the "dullest" he could find, not to be tempted to borrow a line. Lowell retains the plot of the play, the failure of friends and foes alike to persuade Prometheus to give in to Zeus, and its structure, the sequence of confrontations—scenes with Hephaestus, with Ocean, with Io, with Hermes, divided by exchanges between Prometheus and the Chorus of Seabirds, here reduced to three. Whatever Aeschylus did in his trilogy (and, I suppose, being Aeschylus, he reconciled Zeus to man and damped down the Promethean fire), the surviving play is concerned with Zeus as tyrant, the heavenly rebel who, with a successful revolution on his

---

[15] According to Stanley Kunitz, Lowell was commissioned by Lincoln Center to do an acting version of the *Oresteia* to be put on in the fall of 1965, and his *Agamemnon* was completed during the summer of that year. The trilogy has presumably not been completed. The *Agamemnon* has not been published or performed.

hands, had to adjust to his new eminence. From that source, Lowell has derived a play thematically reminiscent of *The Old Glory*, another study of the consequences of power. "He is harsh because he is new to power," Hephaestus says by way of apology for Zeus, but the play makes clear that the harshness is an occupational disease of rulers. Prometheus recalls the time when he searched ("a fool's errand") for "powers I hoped to defeat and tame and put to work," when Zeus was one of his fellow searchers, but the world they created, though "more delicate, and reasonable" was "as confused and dangerous as ever a few miles down." Although the new heaven is more ably run than the old one, the bumbling home of Cronus and the Titans, it is also more efficient in its tyranny. There is no escape from Zeus. Prometheus makes that clear with the story of his two brothers—Atlas, who "was submissive," and Typho, who "was rebellious," both of whom were punished by Zeus, the one with the world on his shoulders, the other buried beneath Mt. Etna.

Prometheus is confronted in the play by four characters, each of whom represents some kind of accommodation to Zeus. Hephaestus, the efficient workman, taking comfort in doing a job well, regretfully chains Prometheus to his rock—"a hammer in the hand of power," as Prometheus says. Ocean is a tool as well, at first masking his errand for Zeus in the rhetoric of friendship and politic wisdom; he admits, "I have grown old and carefree by teaching myself to give in." Io's acquiescence to power, made clear in her long, sensuous soliloquy, is more mindless than Ocean's self-indulgence, an attempt to achieve the placidity of cows: "They have never resisted the gods." Hermes is Zeus's bully boy, come to threaten Prometheus. None of them has gained by serving Zeus. Io, who wanted to be a cow by her own definition, has been turned into a heifer in fact and forced to wander the world, driven by a swarm of stinging flies; Hera's jealousy is the ostensible cause, but Io suspects Zeus: "I sometimes think his mischievous and uncanny mind plans and consents to everything that has been done to me." Hephaestus, who has been crippled by Zeus, warns Prometheus against rebellion ("Each step I take tells me what it is to go against Zeus"), but there is no comfort in the man (god) who works only out of fear. Ocean, too, although he holds disaster at bay for the moment, even basks in the friendship of the chief god, lives in fear and scurries away at the end of his interview with Prometheus, afraid that he may be incriminated if he stays too long on that infamous rock. Only Hermes seems at all certain of his position, but for all his sense of importance and his elaborate attempts at condescension, Prometheus' open contempt reduces him—for the audience, at least—to a pale reflection of Zeus, second-string tyranny.

Faced with four such examples, Prometheus chooses to remain obstinate, refuses to recognize an alternative in Hermes' "You must hunt with the gods, or be hunted down and torn to pieces." This is not a romantic act of defiance—one of the conventional readings of Aeschylus' play—but the final disillusion of heaven's intellectual, the brightest of the gods, who can see the possibility of evolution upward and the inevitability of decline; the painful paradox is expressed in the words describing his search for "a key, *my* key, *the* key, the one that must be there, because it can't be there." One of the Seabirds offers cold comfort: "Stubborn as you are, you know one thing. You know that intelligence is suffering." Prometheus' cry in his last speech—"I am burning in my own fire"—suggests that his greatest pain is self-inflicted, not caused by the liver-eating eagle of Zeus. Yet that fire has another meaning. It is the fire that Prometheus gave to man, which "is already rising to bury the gods." Prometheus predicts Zeus's inevitable fall, another in a line of rulers, "each the betrayer of his own father, each betrayed by his son." For a moment, shortly before Hermes appears, Prometheus fancies a return to power, an alliance with Zeus to "trick or at least delay the fire," but Zeus wants nothing from Prometheus except some information which, if he had it, still would not stop the next heavenly revolution.

The general movement of *Prometheus Bound* can be seen in its controlling image. Just before Prometheus' final speech, Power and Force appear and repeat the lines with which they open the play. The suggestion, then, is that the action is cyclical, a reflection of the pattern of tyranny-rebellion-tyranny-rebellion evident in the heavenly history of castrating sons; Hermes' description of Prometheus' punishment—the liver that is eaten only to heal and be eaten again, the crumbling of the rock and the fall which repeats itself—suggests the same kind of cycle. Yet the continuous references to falling (Prometheus in space, Zeus from power), Prometheus' "we are all beginning to slide on our thinning downward thread," Force's "Beyond here, everything is downhill"—all these suggest another direction. The two images can work together, of course, to form a downward spiral, as though the circle of violence in *The Old Glory* had been joined with the sense of decline that pervades so much of Lowell's poetry. Yet, this is a spiral that can come to an end. "Used skillfully," Prometheus says early in the play, "fire can remake, or destroy the earth." Most of what he says about men, in his description of Io's journey, emphasizes their lack of trust, their violence, their failure to differentiate between creation and destruction ("they will discover that the city they were building and improving is a quarry"—here a place of punishment). By the end of the play, he says, "Fire will be the first absolute power, and the last to rule." It might be possible, I suppose, to read that line positively, to suggest that the fire of intellect can bring to a halt the ancient patterns of violence, but I think not. As Endecott, Robin, and Delano taught us in *The Old Glory*, as Zeus shows us in this play, power leads to violence. In a thermonuclear age, the absolute power is the last to rule because it leads to final destruction. That, I assume, is what Lowell's *Prometheus Bound* is saying. If it is, there is a contradiction between the idea of a final end and the recurring pattern suggested by the reappearance of Power and Force. There are contradictions of a minor sort, as well, as in Hephaestus' first speech, in which he regrets having to imprison Prometheus "in endless winter" and, then, a few sentences later, says "Each day will bring you the fertile heat of summer." Given Lowell's habit of rewriting, *Prometheus Bound* is probably a play in process. It is already a fascinating work but hardly one to cheer the audience with a comforting vicarious defiance of the gods, for men are about to become gods in *Prometheus Bound,* and, as Prometheus says, "God is only able to kill."

In his "Author's Note," Lowell calls *Prometheus Bound* "the most undramatic" of the Greek tragedies, a series of orations that take place around a central character chained to one spot. There may be a kind of apology tucked away in that accurate description of the Greek play, for Lowell's version is very static, particularly to an American audience unused to a dramatic action so relentlessly verbal. *The Old Glory* has some of the same quality, yet that play provides for a great amount of activity on stage. I suspect that the complaints one sometimes hears about nothing happening in Lowell's plays has less to do with stage action than it does with characterization. In an interview with Frederick Seidel (in *Writers at Work,* Second Series), Lowell compared his power of creating characters in his poems with that of Robert Frost. Of the persona of "Mother Marie Therese" (in *The Mills of the Kavanaughs*), Lowell said:

> And I don't believe anybody would think my nun was quite a real person. She has a heart and she's alive, I hope, and she has a lot of color to her and drama, and has some things that Frost's characters don't, but she doesn't have their wonderful quality of life.

This could be said of the characters in Lowell's plays as well. They do not climb off the page, as do Uncle Vanya and Big Daddy and George and Martha. Even on stage, they can suggest men, down to the details of thought and gesture that make individuals, without quite becoming men.[16] In part, this is because Lowell's plays are not in the realistic tradition. Yet, I am not faulting Lowell's characters because they are not true-to-life, as the cliché has it, but because they lack theatrical validity. They are somewhat hedged in by his virtues—his intellectuality, his irony, his sense of language, his emphasis on theme, his preoccupation with the major concerns of our or any time. It may be that this deficiency will limit him as a playwright, not let him break through to a large audience where he can work on several levels at once.

---

[16] Yet an actor can create a character within Lowell's character, as Kenneth Haigh did with Prometheus at Yale and as Jack Ryland did with Perkins at the Theatre de Lys, which suggests that everything is there except the "life."

Even so, it is already clear, on the evidence of the two "imitations" and *The Old Glory*, that Lowell is one of the most impressive dramatists to turn up in the 1960's.

The other poet whose reputation as a playwright began in a production at the American Place Theatre is William Alfred, whose *Hogan's Goat* (1965) moved from its original limited engagement to a long off-Broadway run. Alfred had written an earlier play in conventional blank verse—*Agamemnon* (1953). He calls it "a tragedy, a play about the moral limits of life, and what the cost of violating them is," which is as good a way as any, I suppose, to describe a play primarily concerned with the conflict between the public and private lives of its characters and the way public acts have private consequences. One might even describe *Hogan's Goat* that way, but it is probably more useful to think of it as a *hybris* tragedy smothered by the melodrama that Alfred used "deliberately," as he told a *New Yorker* interviewer (December 18, 1965).

Hogan's Goat is set in the Brooklyn Irish community in 1890. In an action that covers four days, it tells the story of Matthew Stanton, ward leader and saloon keeper, who thinks wrongly that he is about to take the mayor's office away from Ned Quinn; in the end both men are defeated by events, the most important of which is the death of Matt's wife Kathleen. Despite Alfred's admission to having embraced melodrama, I assume that he has in mind a tragedy of pride, but the play is in conflict with itself in several ways. For one thing, Alfred keeps a good part of the information secret from the audience, so that there is no definable irony in the early sequences. He has always had a problem about when to reveal information. In *Agamemnon*, there is a scene in which Cassandra nurses a soldier who has been flogged, who never responds to her questions; at the end, another soldier explains that "they've torn out his tongue," a revelation that gives Alfred a shock finish for his scene, but at the expense of the more complicated effect he would have achieved by letting the audience, but not Cassandra, know the truth. It is not until Scene 8 in *Hogan's*

Goat that we learn that Matt was not just Ag Hogan's lover, her "goat," but her husband as well and that he is not legally married to Kathleen. The business with the little tin box and the hidden marriage certificate is used simply for manipulative effect, to forward the fairly obvious plot or to get an immediate emotional scene, which would be legitimate enough in a play going simply for suspense or tears. In *Hogan's Goat*, in which we are supposed to take seriously the conflict between the hero's sense of his self and the facts of his past life and present circumstances, it would be dramatically useful for the audience to be able to recognize the mixture of truth, self-delusion, and open lying that marks all of Matt's speeches.

There are intellectual as well as generic difficulties in *Hogan's Goat*, problems about the nature of the pride that brings Matt Stanton down. That pride and its consequences is the central theme of the play is clear from the fact that Matt operates in a context in which *pride* is the operative word. Kathleen uses it to describe herself as well as Matt; both Josie Finn and Father Coyne used it of Ned Quinn; Quinn says the dead Ag Hogan "always was too proud." Black Jack Haggerty quotes from *Measure for Measure*: "Ah, man! Proud man!/ Dressed in a little brief authority." A number of the minor characters—noticeably Josie, who, when it is too late, regrets that she never saw Ag Hogan after she had a hand in the split between Ag and Matt—undergo chastening self-discoveries that parallel Matt's fall. Even the subtheme about the need of the mob to destroy the heroes and leaders they praise is an extension of the main one: "They turn upon the strong, and pull them down,/And not from virtue, James, but vicious pride." The speaker is Ned Quinn, and one of the pullers in this case is Matt.

Matt Stanton's pride takes two different forms. The first is clear in his relationship to the people around him. He was a dirt poor and dirty immigrant who made his way up in the world by using as stepping stones those who helped him (Ned) and loved him (Ag). His pride is in part a product of his attempt to escape his past. It can be seen, retrospectively, in his rejection of Ag (and the nickname "Hogan's goat") and, in the play itself, in his denunciation of Josie, who always loved him; in the insult that he offers his supposed friends and followers in an attempt to set himself apart ("they're to learn their place and keep it./We're with them, but not of them"); in his tendency to confuse love and slavery. Just before her death, Kathleen gives a psycho-social analysis of Matt's shortcomings: "You've taken all your life without return!/You never gave yourself to a single soul/For all your noble talk." When he collapses over her body (after having pushed her down the steps), the implication is that he has been broken because he has never been sufficiently human, never able to love.

If this were all there were to it, the ending might be taken as an operatic variation on a standard Broadway cliché. There is, however, the other side to Matt's pride, his self-assertion, his faith in the individual rather than in rules and institutions. In Scene 3 he goes to a strange priest to get absolution for the dead Ag, a last attempt to gain forgiveness, which is frustrated by a narrow-minded confessor who cannot see past a man's words to his pain. "Who can absolve us but ourselves!" Matt cries. "I'll not fall to my knees for man or God." Alfred spends the rest of the play forcing him to his knees, to the moment in which he asks both man and God to "help me and forgive me." To reach for the mayoralty of Brooklyn, however, does not seem to be a very exalted act of *hybris*. Alfred punishes his hero for lacking heart, but, since Matt's speeches contain the kind of sentiments about American possibility that an upward-mobility audience might find attractive, the play ends disconcertingly by suggesting that man should be purposefully little.

Even if we give Alfred the benefit of the doubt and assume that he intends Matt's flaw to be a virtue gone wrong and even if the grandiose hokum of Kathleen's death scene be taken straight ("I was trying to make a theatre where people *felt* again," Alfred said in the *New Yorker* interview), the end is impossible for two reasons. In the first place, from what we have seen of Matt and Ned Quinn (Ned shares the fall: "I'm nobody. I'm nothing—"), it is impossible to understand why Kathleen's death should affect them when they stepped over the body of poor Ag Hogan, whom both of them loved, and went their political ways with no evidence of soul-searching. In the second, Father Coyne's curtain line ("Cry for us all while you're at it. Cry for us all!"), even if Alfred intends it to tie back into the general theme of pride, works as a bid for tears that obscures whatever has happened to Matt Stanton by reducing it to an instance of the sorrow of things. Imagine Oedipus or Hamlet being elbowed off stage by a generalization.

Alfred's verse is slightly irregular iambic pentameter, bursting with metaphor and simile. For the most part, the figures of speech, many of which are nasty invective, are used not for their thematic relevance but to establish the Irishness of the characters. Other verbal devices reflect the political milieu. Repetition, as in Ned Quinn's use of "I kept my office" to punctuate a long speech, seems less a poetic than a public-speaking device. Wilfrid Sheed, reviewing the play in *Commonweal* (January 14, 1966), praised Alfred for having captured a verbal convention ("the old grand-piano style") at once genuine and highly artificial:

> The love scenes are awful, like your Aunt Minnie singing, "I'll take you home again Kathleen," but this is absolutely intrinsic to the rhetoric; and it is balanced by plenty of inventive vituperation which is the other side of the coin.

This theatricality of language is finally self-defeating because it fails to convey the presumably genuine emotion that pushes the characters from one overstated moment to the next; in the end, everyone seems to suffer in platform style. Of course, that may be why *Hogan's Goat* was such a success; at a play in which intellectual and emotional substance has been sacrificed to flamboyance, an audience can relax into the comfort of a pseudo-experience.

It is a far cry from Lowell and Alfred to Kenneth Koch. In a review of *Thank You and Other Poems* (in *The King of the Cats*), F. W. Dupee constructs an aesthetics for Koch out of a reading of "On the Great Atlantic Rainway," the first poem in the volume: "he will flee the sunlight of approved poetic practice, staking his poetic chances on whatever wonders may turn up in the wet weather ('rainways') of *unapproved* poetic practice." Substitute *dramatic* for *poetic* and you have a rationale (if you need one) for Koch's collection *Bertha and Other Plays* (1966), although *unapproved* should not be taken to mean *untried*. Koch, who poses as a poetic brash young man, is dramatically an old-fashioned boy, for his clever little plays (the phrase is meant as description, not condescension; the plays are short and Koch is clever) are avant-garde after the fashion of the 1920's. They recall the work of the Dadaists and Surrealists in France and even more—since his idiom is American—that of Gertrude Stein and Ring Lardner. Like some of his French counterparts, he works closely with artists (Robert Rauschenberg, Jean Tinguely, Red Grooms), and, like Stein, he has had Virgil Thomson as collaborator, at least to the extent of a trumpet solo for *Bertha*.

Some of the plays are purely literary games, obviously not for production. In "The Gold Standard," one of *Six Improvisational Plays* (1965), Koch calls for the entrance of two monks who "try, without the slightest success, to explain the gold standard to each other, for four hours"; in *Without Kinship* (written in the late 1950's), the talking characters include a football, an ironing board, and two pebbles named Melvin and Charmian, who "go together and form a driveway," a development which, for some reason, reminds me of the moment in Lardner's *Clemo Uti* when "Two queels enter, overcome with water lilies." Most of the plays, however, could be performed, and several of them—*Bertha* (1959), *Pericles* (1960), *George Washington Crossing the Delaware* (1962), *The Construction of Boston* (1962), and *Guinevere* (1964)[17]—have been done in experimental productions or for brief off-Broadway runs. *Bertha*, in its second production, was one of a repertory, labeled *Theatre of the Absurd*, produced at the Cherry Lane Theatre in 1962. Koch seems not quite at home in the company of Beckett, Albee, Genet, Ionesco, Arrabal, Richardson; as absurd as his plays are, to describe them I would never use a big, big A.

[17] The dates here are production dates. According to Koch, the plays in his collection are in chronological order, which means that *Guinevere*, which was first published in *Yūgen* (No. 7) in 1961, was written before *Bertha*. *Pericles*, which was included in his *Poems* (1953), was the first of his plays.

The three most successful of his plays are *Guinevere, Bertha,* and *George Washington Crossing the Delaware.* Subtitled "The Death of the Kangaroo," *Guinevere* is made up of apparently disconnected speeches, lyric nonsense ("Pure Pins the lobster!") that one can imagine being read with effective intensity. A plot of sorts emerges. Guinevere, innocently at home among the animals, loves and is loved by the Kangaroo (Kangaroo: "Yes yes." Guinevere: "O Joy!") until the attractively evil Yellowmay comes in and "takes off all Guinevere's clothes"; the Kangaroo apparently dies of a broken heart ("O mournful existence within the matchbox") for his dead body is dragged across the empty stage at the end of the play. Presumably as a result of seeing *Guinevere* on stage, Koch brought the characters back in a less happy sequel, *The Return of Yellowmay,* and in *The Revolt of the Giant Animals,* a nine-liner with six speaking parts. He also used Yellowmay (disguised as the Arno) and the animals in *The Building of Florence.* None of these—all written shortly before the plays were published—have the verbal inventiveness of *Guinevere.*

Bertha is a mock heroic play in ten tiny scenes. Occasionally, as in Scene 6, in which the jealous queen blows up the lovers in the rose garden, the reference seems to be specific, to the aging Queen Elizabeth (Bette Davis) casting a suspicious eye at her ladies in waiting. Most of the time, it suggests any chronicle play, echoing with the continuing march of conquering armies. One of the funniest of Koch's plays, *Bertha* has point as well. Its heroine, the mad Queen of Norway, leads her nation into unwanted wars and practices a little incidental cruelty on the side, and yet, at her death, she is hailed as a "great queen."

Second Citizen: She conquered her own country many times!
Third Citizen: Norway was happy under her rule!

George Washington is a pastiche of parody, shifting targets from scene to scene. One of them is the standard history play, such as Maxwell Anderson's *Valley Forge,* in which the characters seem to be aware that they are historical figures ("There goes the greatest man who will ever live in America!" says Cornwallis of Washington). Another is the conventional war movie. This can be

seen not only in the usual common-soldier exchanges (Jack and
Jim and the shared cigarette), but in a hilarious home-front scene,
English stiff-upper-lip variation, the funnier because the familiar
content of such scenes is rendered the more obvious by being put
into language that suggests the editorial page ("when a people
fights for its freedom . . ."). The plot hinges on a dream sequence
(the movies again) in which Washington relives the cherry-tree
incident (a variant on the impatient father-indulgent mother-
whiney child scene). "I cannot tell a lie," says the child George,
"but I can run! I can flee from injustice!" He swims the river to
get away from his father, an escape which, in his father's words, is
"The ONLY WAY!" Vision accomplished, Washington wakes up
and leads his men across the Delaware, a neat trick considering
that the action is set in Alpine, New Jersey, which is across the
Hudson from Yonkers. Koch's playfulness, his semiserious gags,
his elegant nonsense are bearable only in small doses. I never
managed to get through his mock-epic, *Ko, or A Season on Earth*,
but even brevity is no assurance of quality. At its best, Koch's
work is both funny and irreverent. At its worst, it is as flat as a
bad joke delivered by a comedian who has been told that he is an
artist.

No other play-writing poets are doing exactly what Koch is, but
LeRoi Jones's *The Baptism* and Frank O'Hara's *The General
Returns from One Place to Another*, performed as a double bill in
1964, are reminiscent of his work. They do not, however, represent a body of work for either author. By the time *The Baptism*
was produced, Jones had begun to see theater as a weapon, not a
game. So far as I know, at the time of his death in 1967, O'Hara
had published only one other play, the very early *Try! Try!*
(1953). Both Jones and O'Hara have a stronger sense of unity in
their plays than Koch does; their use of parody and playfulness is
more likely to be in the service of a central dramatic image. The
O'Hara play was a happy surprise to me, since I find his earlier
play and much of his poetry unreadable.

In twenty-one short scenes, he makes a political point comically
—that General MacArthur's famous promise to return should not
have been taken as a long-term project. O'Hara's general wanders

from country to country in Southeast Asia, visiting again the sites of his military triumphs, only to find himself unwanted or unrecognized ("Art's long, and conquered people are short. That's why they don't recognize me"). Two things contribute to the play's effectiveness. One is the character of the general himself; his soliloquies as well as his public speeches are models of cliché, but done obliquely so that the bromide is recognizable through a faint aura of exoticism. The other is that O'Hara's Southeast Asia is straight off a movie lot. The mysterious Mrs. Forbes in her floppy hat ("It was so expensive buying my way out of Bandung"); Luoa-Lin Foo-Constance, the beautiful spy-cum-prostitute who sings "Moon of Manakura"; the decayed night clubs, arbored terraces, ubiquitous palm trees—all these have the stamp of Hollywood in the 1930's. In "To the Film Industry in Crisis," a name-filled, celebratory poem in *Meditations in an Emergency*, O'Hara cries out, "you, Motion Picture Industry,/ it's you I love"; that declaration, plus the fact that the play is dedicated to Warner Brothers, among others, should indicate that the film parody in *The General Returns* is, in part, only an instance of the kind of campy fun that O'Hara displays elsewhere in his poetry. Still, given the persistence of the old film image of Southeast Asia in the face of our involvement there in fact, the play conveys, very broadly, a creepy sense of unreality which sounds very like a comment on American foreign policy.

Lawrence Ferlinghetti is the only poet with a sizable body of dramatic work—two collections, *Unfair Arguments with Existence* (1963) and *Routines* (1964)—in any way comparable to Koch, but there is more method in Ferlinghetti's madness. He seems to be trying to discover a theatrical form, a "kind of Third Stream Theatre . . . between oldstyle dramas & spontaneous Action or improvisation," as he says in "Notes on *Routines*." Antonin Artaud has been an important influence on Ferlinghetti,[18]

[18] At about the time he was beginning his own theatrical experiments, Ferlinghetti translated Artaud's one play, *Le jet de sang* (*Evergreen Review*, January–February, 1963). His version is not remarkably different from and certainly not superior to the translations of Ruby Cohn (*Tulane Drama Review*, Winter, 1963) and George E. Wellwarth (in his and Michael Benedikt's *Modern French Theatre*).

one that he both admits and disowns; in the "Notes on the Plays," in *Unfair Arguments*, he says, "I don't love his madness." Although Ferlinghetti rejects the underlying concept of cruelty in Artaud's theory, he seems to be attracted to Artaud's somewhat amorphous idea of the use of theatrical image as a disintegrative force that frees the individual from a stifling society and an integrative force that cuts through to the truth of existence. Ferlinghetti, who has an incredible knack for nondefinition, hopes, in his *Routines*, to reach "pure Poetic Action not necessarily logical or rational but with, at best, that kind of inexpressible inchoate meaning that springs from wild surmises of the imagination . . ." His dramatic images are much more conscious than this quotation suggests, more logical and rational. He seems to have taken to heart Artaud's strictures against the primacy of the word and to have turned to the other theatrical elements—light, sound, movement—for the achievement of his image. The influence here is not all Artaud, of course. By way of introduction to *Ha-Ha*, one of the *Routines*, he reprints an Elliot Paul scenario from *transition* (February, 1928); this and his use of loudspeakers to represent orators in *Servants of the People*, a throwback to the phonographs of Jean Cocteau's *The Wedding on the Eiffel Tower* (1921), suggest affinities with an ancient avant-garde less austere than Artaud as theorist.

The quality that finally separates Ferlinghetti from the avant-garde and Artaud alike is that he is relentlessly didactic. Although he may think of his plays as "pure Poetic Action," they are mini-moralities, tiny sermons, cautioning by example. Anyone who sits down and reads straight through a volume of Ferlinghetti's poetry —say *A Coney Island of the Mind*—will be struck by two things; he has a remarkable talent for the inventive use of the trivia of America and a mind so conventional that, had he found the style to match it, he might have become successful on Broadway. He is in favor of love and against war; he believes in freedom and distrusts money, property, the suburbs. The plays embody such persistent commonplaces. Occasional lines like "My country, tears of thee"[19] stand out as verbal jokes with a happy hook in them, but too often Ferlinghetti settles for ponderous gags like "good old *Death Magazine!*" in *Motherlode* or pretentious social commentary, such as "this lifeboat full of flush-toilets which we call civilization" in *The Customs Collector in the Baggy Pants.* There are make-love-not-war plays, such as *The Soldiers of No Country* and *Ha-Ha;* make-love-accept-no-substitute plays, such as *Motherlode, The Customs Collector, Our Little Trip* and *His Head;* be-concerned plays, such as *Three Thousand Red Ants;* the Negro-problem-is-more-complicated-than-you-think plays, such as *The Alligation* and *The Jig Is Up* (that *is* a funny title); watch-out-for-the-establishment plays, such as *Servants of the People* and *An Evening at the Carnival.* This kind of listing is not fair, of course, since the labels obscure the fact that the plays (or routines or arguments) vary widely, in effectiveness as well as method. *The Customs Collector* is a long monologue; *The Nose of Sisyphus* is wordless. The audience is separate from the action in *The Soldiers of No Country;* in *Our Little Trip* it takes place among them (as they lie on the floor on blankets); *Servants of the People* depends for the effectiveness of its end on a preconceived audience reaction, retreat before advancing fire hoses.

Some of the images that Ferlinghetti invents or borrows—the light bulbs of diminishing sizes to represent the characters in *The Victims of Amnesia,* the pet alligator in *The Alligation,* the Statue-of-Liberty furnace in *Ha-Ha*—are potentially very effective, but he sometimes seems to distrust them and shore them up unnecessarily. In *The Alligation,* for instance, Ladybird—a nicely done Mississippi-voice bit that suggests Tennessee Williams—is caught between her pet, who wants his freedom now, and pressure from people outside, who think it is disgraceful that she lives with an

[19]Ferlinghetti liked the line so well that he used it in "Junkman's Obbligato," one of the "Oral Messages" in *A Coney Island of the Mind,* before he worked it into *The Soldiers of No Country.* The two works also share supposedly meaningful references to the environment as an "automobile graveyard or city dump." Fernando Arrabal, whose *Le Cimitière des Voitures* was published in English in 1960, as *The Automobile Graveyard,* may be the source of the first of those images.

alligator. Ferlinghetti is not content to let the situation be its own comment. He sends Blind Indian to make everything painfully obvious: "You say How, you mean How keep alligator pet . . . How not let grow, How not let free—How keep everything same!" Elsewhere, he saddles Blind Indian with standard Ferlinghetti denunciation lines: "America smoke big black cigar. America big mad movie!" Ferlinghetti's desire for a short play, at once free of conventional plot and characters and of the pure chance of improvisation, for a theatrical routine that can speak to an audience by penetrating the routines of daily life, is an admirable one. How successful he is in production I cannot say, but on the page, even at his best, he falls short of his goal because, for me at least, his schoolmasterish concern for my freedom turns his liberating vehicles into traps.

There is variety—if something less than excitement—in the recent dramatic work of more conventional poets. Their demands on the theater range from the elaborate scenic devices Peter Viereck calls for to the barest indication of props to place Howard Nemerov's words in context. Their styles range from the prose of Louis Coxe to the rhymed stanzas with which I. A. Richards varies his basic blank verse. Their settings range from the mythic (Donald Finkel) to the modern (Mark Van Doren) or—in Archibald MacLeish's new play—manage to encompass both at once.

MacLeish's *Herakles* (1967)—an earlier version was performed by the APA in their Ann Arbor season, 1965—brings Professor Hoadley, fresh from a Nobel acceptance speech attacking the "snivelling despair" of the age, and his family to Greece, where he hopes to refresh his own sense of heroic possibility. There are two human existences, according to Hoadley—one in history ("a blundering, bewildered, mortal maze/of human suffering where even God/himself must suffer with us") and one in story ("the heroic/mutinous, revolted man/who will not eat his bread in suffering"). In history, says Miss Parfit, governess to the Hoadleys' daughter, "everything *was* true *once*." In story, says Mrs. Hoadley, "nothing was ever true once: only always." This exchange comes in the second act when the family (except for the professor, who is crippled) climb up to the site of the ancient oracle and find themselves actually in the story, the homecoming of Herakles. The Greek hero (who I assume is to be played by the actor who plays Hoadley, although MacLeish never indicates that as his intention) comes on, boisterously pleased with himself: "Enemies defeated,/deeds done, bloody, mucking/world made over like a summer day." The oracle makes him understand what Megara, his wife, already knows, that blinded by his triumph he has killed his sons who went out to welcome him home. The point of the play seems to be that the Herakles myth represents man at his most heroic, fighting to perfect an imperfect universe but in the process losing the possibility of human compassion. There is a parallel story (alas, all exposition) in Hoadley's rejection of his son. At the end, Megara takes Herackles back to the bodies of their sons ("Only human/hands can bury what we have to bury") and Mrs. Hoadley goes back to her life, moving "from the one despair to the next, from the hope in/this day to the hope in that one . . ."

In the argument with her husband in the first act, Mrs. Hoadley says, "To want the world without the suffering is madness!/What would we be or know or bear/or love without the suffering to love for?" At that moment, she sounds like a straw woman set up to be knocked down by Hoadley's heroic arguments, but the play ends on a note that recalls the end of *J.B.*, the suggestion that man's comfort in the world lies in what is human in him rather than in what is divine. The straw is made flesh—thematically, at least. Dramatically, no. Herakles has a certain bumptious vitality and Megara an angry patience that might help fill a stage, but the Hoadleys, refugees from a conventional family play, are as difficult to believe as the characters in MacLeish's earlier *The Music Crept by Me upon the Waters.*

Mark Van Doren's first play, *The Last Days of Lincoln* (1958), less successful as a portrait of the man than as an ironic statement about the failure of his peace plans, has been performed here and there across the country during the 1960's. Its accept-

ance may explain the appearance of three new Van Doren plays—
Never, Never Ask His Name (1965), set in New England in
1840, and two contemporary comedies, *A Little Night Music*
(1966) and *The Weekend that Was* (1966). *Never, Never* and
Night Music share a common theme, that the truth, however painful, is better than a festering secret, and *Weekend* celebrates youth
by revealing that they still cherish "Poetry, indignation, loathing,
love,/And—most remarkable of all—fidelity." All three are written in flat, conversational iambic pentameter, and the characters,
who seem to have been conceived as individuals, manage never to
get born. Louis Coxe's *Decoration Day* (1964) uses its central
character, an aged Civil War veteran, and flashback scenes to
make a complicated point about the men who fight wars—that
they do so because they feel they have to, over the protests of their
women and in spite of the manipulations of money and power,
and that they are lost (in death or in outliving their battles) in
causes that are always defeated by time. James Schevill's recent
plays are very different from *The Bloody Tenet* (1957), the verse
drama about Roger Williams, in fact and in myth, that was his
initiation as a playwright. *American Power* (1964) is a pair of
related one-act plays, *The Space Fan* and *The Master*, that share a
common suspicion of America, an amorphousness of dramatic
line and satiric point, and an admitted family relation to the Theatre of the Absurd; *The Black President* (1965) is a treatment of
the problem of race in a white-dominated world in the modified
Brechtian fashion—songs, comic turns, brief emotional scenes—
one has come to expect of the productions of Joan Littlewood, for
whom it was first written in 1961. Except for the idea of making a
traveling salesman of Silenus, a medicine-show type dealing in
love potions and dirty books, Donald Finkel's *The Jar* (1961) is
empty. When I was a brash young man, I capped my review of
Peter Viereck's *Shame and Glory of the Intellectuals* (*Hudson
Review*, Summer, 1953) by saying that it "is enthusiastic without
order, is clever without wit, is morally indignant without real
morality or genuine dignity." Both Viereck and I are older now,
but after reading *The Tree Witch* (1961), a play in which WE,

"the adjusted moderns," choose the old aunties (life-denying materialism) over the dryad (warmth, growth, life), and finding Viereck at his old stand, selling the same old bromides in the same jazzily wrapped packages, I felt sympathetic to my old outrage; more restrained, I will simply echo the dryad's question, "Yet, what's less Greek than pedant posing pagan?" I. A. Richards' *Tomorrow Morning, Faustus!* (1962) is an apparent attempt to make a serious point about the need of contemporary man, faced with possible annihilation, to escape received categories of thinking; it is difficult, idiosyncratic, schoolmasterish, schoolboyish, and occasionally, as in Faustus's comment on Utopias ("Like going to live in a poem and finding it/A Government Regulation when you get there"), neatly amusing.

Howard Nemerov's two short Biblical plays—*Cain* (1959) and *Endor* (1961)—are among the more interesting of the recent plays by poets. There is a lightly ironic tone about *Cain* which carries it from the too broad opening (Cain's making a joke about apples) and the attractive comedy in the terrible smugness of Abel and Adam to the serious statement, embodied in Cain's act and its consequences, about the way man's attempts to change things and the complex of fear, power, and estrangement that results from those attempts turn out to be simply a continuation of the world as God conceived it. "You don't accept life as it is, that's your trouble," says Abel primly, but, as God indicates ("I was the serpent in the Garden"), "life as it is" is where man lives, accepting or not. The play ends as Adam and Eve face up to their new loss (Cain) and Eve makes a declaration of love (for a moment there, I suspected a parody of *J.B.*), a finish that Nemerov may intend as a modulation from the philosophic central section back to the quotidian, but it hangs on the play like an afterthought.

Endor uses Saul's visit to the witch to make a statement about man's need not to know the future. This is clear in the repeated images of the blind man or the man "walking a strange road at night" and in the play's action. Although Saul sees his own defeat and his commander learns that he will betray Saul and gain nothing by it, they eat and drink and, the prophecy forgotten, go out to face David's forces; only the malicious bureaucrat "Must blunder through the battlefield with my/Absurd and heavy knowledge of the end." The suggestion is that there is a difference—a qualitative one—between the man who rests unknowing in God and the one who absurdly (in the Camus sense) sees to the end of things, between the innocent one who acts and the knowing one who simply goes through the motions. The characterization in both plays is rudimentary, the simplest kind of stereotype chosen to embody an idea. This can be fun in an obvious way, as in Adam's scenes at the beginning of *Cain*, but for the most part the plays are carried by their sustaining ideas rather than by the men for whom those ideas presumably represent emotional struggles. Watching the vision in the fire in which David, indifferent to motivation, has the commander killed, the minister says: "These poets!/Real people scarcely exist for them."

Taken out of context, that line might have served as an epigraph for this whole chapter.

SIX

Saul Bellow
and Some Others

*I have written a big (and awfully good)
four-act play, by which I hope to make my
fortune.* —HENRY JAMES

Novelists, like poets, seem unable to stay out of the theater. In
their case, no one—including the novelists themselves—pretend
that they are returning drama to an ancient purity or high seriousness. In fact, the image of the novelist in the theater is a variation
on the comic professor, an innocent abroad, stumbling over his
own literary talent as he moves ineptly through a world he never
made. He is implicit in Saul Bellow's account (*The New York
Times*, September 27, 1964) of the first version of *The Last
Analysis*, which Lillian Hellman, who had suggested he write a

play, estimated "would run about eight hours without Wagnerian orchestration"; in James Baldwin's admission, in the notes to the recently published trade edition of *The Amen Corner*, that "I knew, for one thing, that very few novelists are able to write plays"; in Walter Kerr's review of Bruce Jay Friedman's *Scuba Duba* (*The New York Times*, October 22, 1967), which he found "stageworthy" and "side-splitting" enough to suggest that "we must revise the rules." Even if that bumbling figure is an obvious fake—a weapon for the theater professional, a shield for the novelist about to turn dramatist—the historical evidence (consider the plays of Thomas Wolfe and Theodore Dreiser) is hardly in the novelists' favor. Still, they come and, like the poets, find stages to give them temporary shelter—if not on Broadway, then off, if not off-Broadway, then in San Francisco, London, Boston, Nashville. In an earlier chapter, under another rubric, I have considered the dramatic work of Baldwin (pp. 125–134) and Peter S. Feibleman (pp. 116–117). The works considered below come from novelists who vary in quality and turn out to be playwrights who display the same kind of variety. The best of them, as novelist and playwright, is Saul Bellow.

As long ago as 1954, Bellow displayed an attraction to the theater. That year, he published his first and only drama criticism (in the May–June issue of *Partisan Review*) and his first one-act play, *The Wrecker* (in *New World Writing 6*). Although he opens his omnibus review as though he were going to write the conventional *Partisan* put-down ("The last play I saw, prior to this season, was *Harvey* . . ."), he finds things to admire, at least in a few off-Broadway corners. He praises Jean-Paul Sartre and Theodore Hoffman, who had directed a production of *No Exit*, for not sacrificing theater to philosophy, after offering this caveat to the reader, "I do not go to the theater in quest of ideas, but to be diverted, delighted, awed, and in search of opportunities to laugh and to cry." In part, this is a slightly schmaltzy variation on the perennial Bellow attempt to rescue art from the intellectuals,[1] but,

[1] He was still at it in his address to the 1966 P.E.N. International Congress, printed that year in the July 10 *New York Times Book Review* as "Cloister Culture."

more importantly, it is an indication of where he would go as a playwright. Not that he intended to forego ideas in the theater; instead he wanted to insure their theatricality, which, for him, as he said in the *Times* piece quoted in the first paragraph, meant choosing the "most acceptable form at this time, the farce." Less broad than his later work, *The Wrecker*, is a first step in Bellow's attempt to make a serious farceur of himself. It is an exercise in antimaterialism in which a man, living in an apartment house about to be torn down, foregoes the money he would receive if he vacated early in order to wreck the place himself; although both he and his wife hesitate momentarily over the implications of destroying the bedroom, they march off, crowbar and hatchet in hand, agreed that "the best way to preserve the marriage is to destroy the home."

Ten years later, Bellow's first full-length play came to Broadway. It lasted only three weeks, a brief run that suggests as much about Broadway (farces should act like farces) as it does about the play. *The Last Analysis*—at least, the revised version published in 1965—may never find itself among the masterpieces of modern drama (that is, it is not in a class with the best of the Bellow novels), but it is one of the most fascinating and funniest plays to turn up in the 1960's and—as the 1966 production at the Theatre of the Living Arts in Philadelphia indicated—it is superbly at home on the stage. It is the story of a clown-hero, himself an object of satire, who triumphs over more conventional satirical targets, as prime a collection of vultures as one could expect to find this side of Henry Becque. Wife, mistress, son, sister-agent, cousin-lawyer, midwife-aunt, they all descend on Bummidge, once a big-time comic, hoping that—mad though he may be—there is still a dollar to be made on him. At the end of Act I, he has his assistant staple him to the wall, his arms spread out in a crucifixion that is his protest and his joke: "Forgive them, Father, for, for . . . What comes next?" The line not only kills the possibility of the scene's becoming solemn, but it absolves the assembled family of innocence.

Bummidge, suffering from the "Pagliacci gangrene" ("Caused as all gangrene is by a failure of circulation. Cut off by self-pity.

Passivity. Fear. Masochistic rage"), given to attacks of Human-
itis[2] ("Suddenly, being human is too much for me"), has settled
into a warehouse where, with the help of a sexy girl who wants to
be treated as a brain and a ratcatcher who cannot laugh, he is
exploring his past in an attempt to isolate his troubles and those of
the world. His method (*"Existenz*-Action-Self-analysis") allows
him to analyze himself, leaping from patient's couch to analyst's
chair, donning glasses in midair, and to star in recreations of his
past which are a cross between psychodrama and standard Jewish
comedy. Most of the first act consists of *Room Service* complications, barriers he must surmount or get around in order to put on
a closed-circuit television broadcast, demonstrating the Bummidge
method to invited guests—scientists and show-business associates.
The heart of the broadcast, in more ways than one ("Personally,
the fellow just stormed my heart," says Fiddleman, the Hollywood
tycoon, who is ready to package Bummidge's discovery), is an
elaborate enactment of the cycle of birth, life, death, rebirth, a
slightly portentous production that suggests an Expressionist
parody and is not really as funny as it ought to be, probably
because it is necessary to the serious story that underlies the farce.
At the end, suffering from rebirth trauma (or pretending it),
Bummidge rejects Fiddleman's money and all his familial, emotional, and business attachments (the ratcatcher drags them off in
a great net), and sets off to buy back the Trilby Theater, the site
of his vaudeville triumphs, which he will turn into a comedy clinic
where the audience can act out its problems with Bummidge.

Any description of the play is necessarily misleading because, in
production, Bummy the clown continually upstages Bummidge the
thinker; the role is a virtuoso one—like that of Archie Rice in *The
Entertainer*—calling for a performer who can move in and around
the ideas of the play, doing low comedy bits that put them in
perspective without killing them. There is a great deal of conventional fun at the expense of psychoanalysis and of psychological

---

[2] An earlier version of the play was called *Humanitas*. Three scenes—containing some funny physical business not in the final version—were published
in *Partisan Review* (Summer, 1962).

clichés (Bummidge and his son Max, who plays his own grandfather in some scenes, do endless variations on the father-son
struggle), but it would be a mistake to take the obvious satire as
the main point of the play. The central figure is Bummidge, and he
comes across as a farce protagonist, moving at a dead run through
a menacing world—one in which ideas rather than trick chairs
give way beneath him—which he finally defeats through that mixture of innocence and malevolence that has always been the stock
in trade of great comics. Or does he? There is some difficulty
about the end of the play, about what actually is resolved. Bummidge is beset by three things: by his friends and relatives; by the
kind of existential anguish that dogged Herzog—the hero of the
novel written at the same time as *The Last Analysis*—until he
discovered that it was self-pity; by ideas, "programs, fancies, or
brainstorms" against which is played "the mind's comical struggle
for survival," as Bellow says in the "Author's Note" to the published play. There is no doubt about his defeating the comic vil-
lains; the ratcatcher's net is all the evidence we need. At that level,
the play moves to the conventional farce ending, the happy hysteria that replaces the earlier frenzy, and the audience—responding to the obvious victory—might assume that Bummidge's last
burst of rhetoric—"Onwards, to the Trilby"—indicates that he
has mastered himself and his ideational world. Bellow, in the
Times article, assumes that Bummidge "does manage to burst the
bonds of metaphor . . . to 'get off the couch,'" to have the last
analysis, and the words that are spoken just before Bummidge's
death and rebirth suggest as much:

> But suppose all we fumblers and bumblers, we cranks and creeps
> and cripples, we proud, sniffing, ragged-assed paupers of heart and
> soul, sick with every personal vice, rattled, proud, spoiled, and
> distracted—suppose we look again for the manhood we are born to
> inherit.

Yet Bummidge's last moment is more ambiguous than Herzog's
final relaxed decision to give no more messages or Henderson's
replenishing run around the airport in *Henderson, the Rain King*.
As he stands at the end of the play, arranging his toga around him,

convinced that he has passed through the brutal and the mediocre stages and is "ready for the sublime," he seems less like a man who has come through, like a mind who has survived, than like a demented king about to lead his tiny band of loyal followers back into the ideational thickets from which he has just emerged. If he gets the Trilby, surely that makes him Svengali. As Winkleman says early in the play, "Who needs another homemade intellectual?" *The Last Analysis* is a somber farce, tempered by Bummidge's triumph over his human antagonists, in which the author seems not quite willing to recognize that his hero's escape is the same old trap. It may be that Bellow avoids the harsh implications of the final scene because he is as delighted with Bummidge as a sympathetic audience would be, as convinced that a character who displays so much vitality, wit, coarse humor, and comic pain deserves to win. Thanks to Bummidge and the rogue's gallery that surrounds him, *The Last Analysis* turns out to be a very funny play which makes many sharp comments on American society and attitudes. In the last analysis, that is a great deal.

According to a note in the program for *Under the Weather* (1966), Bellow's most recent theatrical attempt, his three one-act farces were scheduled for production in Rome, under the title *C'e speranza nel sesso?* (*Is There Any Hope for Sex?*). This is a more appropriate title than the punning *Under the Weather*, which was possible only because the program identified the three plays in terms of the weather against which the action is played; in one case—*Orange Soufflé*—the weather is completely irrelevant. Although the plays have more to do with sex than they have with weather, it might be more sensible to think of them simply as *The Bellow Plays*, the title of the London production, which preceded by five months the disastrous New York opening. Broadway was even less receptive to *Under the Weather* than it was to *The Last Analysis*.

Out from Under is the story of a widower, Harry Faufill, who chooses the night of his engagement party to protest the encroachment of commercialism and materialism (a Chevrolet agency has moved into his block) by letting the air out of a tire on a car

parked in front of his house. For a moment, particularly in the
lines of Flora, the fiancée, it looks as though Bellow is making fun
of conventional Broadway psychology, but the play comes to
Flora's conclusion: that Harry is a reluctant bridegroom. It goes
beyond that, however, by suggesting not only that Harry, the
talker, will marry Flora, the doer, but that he is lucky to get her.
"There's never been such an age of privilege for women," says
Harry, pontificating to a friend on the phone, while outside—alas,
unseen by the audience—Flora, fighting a blizzard, is trying to
change the tire so the police will not arrest her intended. Harry is
a standard Bellow character, an unwilling victim given to herz-
soggy bleats, but Flora is more interesting; big, bubbly, not too
bright, she is the Jewish mother as sex object, a would-be wife
who faces the future with determined vivaciousness, touched ever
so lightly with loss. In a nostalgic moment right after her entrance,
she remembers Harry as a high school cheerleader, and, flushed by
the occasion and a little drink, she goes into a cheer by way of
demonstration:

> Baby in the high-chair
> Who put him there
> Pa, Ma zis-boom-bah
> Richfield, Richfield, rah-rah-rah!

She leaps on the last "rah" and comes down to say, "Now Rich-
field is all colored," and, then, after a pause, "We should have
stayed together."

A similar comic pathos—at times almost sentimental—colors
the broad farce of the other two plays: *A Wen,* in which a Nobel
scientist tries and presumably succeeds in reliving the purity of the
moment in which he first played "Show" with a girl on the block,
by convincing her—now the wife of a Detroit chiropodist—to let
him see again the birthmark that lies near her sex; and *Orange
Soufflé,* in which a retired whore tries and fails to impress on her
one customer, an eighty-eight-year-old millionaire, that she has
social talents and graces other than the ones that have brought
him to her each month for years. "I never can get your long
underwear to lie flat under your stockings," she says as she dresses

him, and he answers, "My mother had the same problem." One of the chief jokes in *A Wen* is that the scientist, another Bellow intellectual in search of innocence, is given to making speeches, but, as with Harry, as with Hilda in *Orange Soufflé*, as with Bummidge, the joke is in the need to talk, to explain, to justify and not in the content of the lines, which, as often as not, is a mixture of conscious cliché and oblique truth. Describing a time when he fell down in the street and refused to get up because he did not want to disturb a mathematical thought, the scientist says, "You see the occasion seemed grotesque, but it was redeemed by an ecstasy, by devotion to pure truth, by the ennoblement of reason." In those words lies the point of *A Wen*—slapstick ending and all—and, I assume, of the bulk of Bellow's work.

Mark Harris' *Friedman & Son* (1962) is another intellectual Jewish comedy, more didactic and finally less intriguing than those of Saul Bellow. The plot is a simple one. Schimmel, a businessman with a thick skin and an uneasy grasp of factual truth, goes first to A. B. Ferguson, a writer, to convince him that he should hold a testimonial dinner for his father, Solomon Friedman; then to Friedman to sell him a dinner for the son. In the last act, he brings the two together, after a separation of four and a half years, in a meeting in which they propose a celebration (a pair of pants made by the tailor grandfather as the American flag, an Arab girl as the Statue of Liberty) so outrageous that Schimmel excuses himself, leaving them to the pleasure of their discovery—which the audience made early in the first act—that the son and the father are very much the same. A conventional play, as I have described it, Harris breaks with "the old realism . . . the accepted conveniences of plot," as he says in the essay published with the play, at least to the extent of a fantasy device by which, as the dinners are discussed, the figures who will take part appear in spots, going through their routines or, occasionally, quarreling with the principal characters. Hardly the departure that Harris' comments imply, the device does give him a little more freedom in conveying information and ideas that are, however, not beyond the scope of conventional realism.

The father's legal battle with the political establishment over a piece of real estate and the son's quarrel with the literary establishment turn out to be the same fight, and they use the same vocabulary: *stinker, conspiracy.* The father resents that a company called "Federated—something—Synagogues" (even Schimmel, who was part of it, cannot remember the name) tried to force him to sell his land for a parking lot, because "A parking lot is not a synagogue, a synagogue is not a parking lot, in one you pray, in the other you park." The son resents that his publisher wanted him to manufacture a salable item, a modern *Abie's Irish Rose,* concocted of his own marriage and local-color trips to Israel and Ireland: "In tone be topical, be direct, be simple, don't confuse your reader, don't linger over words, words don't matter . . ." Friedman's reaction: "That sentence he shouldn't have said." Although both father and son could have made money on their deals, both rejected them because they were mislabeled.

The play, finally, is about words, about the way in which they are misused, worn as disguises, twisted to mask corruption, and about how the Friedmans and their sons, true believers in the word (the gift dictionary serves as the direct connection between father and son, a tie even though the son no longer uses it), can cut through the pretenses to the truth inside. They can do so, the play says, as long as they remain immigrants, for the grandfather's scissors are used throughout the play, cutting speeches, contracts, Schimmel's card. The political implications are made clear through the use of President John Kennedy, identified as Ferguson's classmate at Harvard and, like him, in danger of forgetting the immigrant past from which he is descended. Ferguson plays with the line from Kennedy's Inaugural Address, "Remember that, in the past, those who foolishly sought power by riding the back of the tiger ended up inside." At the end, the Mayor, conjured up for one of the dinner sequences, speaks lines that are presumably Ferguson's, "In Irish there's an old expression: Get off the tiger, be an immigrant again. Don't join stinkers in conspiracies." In the accompanying essay, Harris says, "Assimilation was not impossible but undesirable" and assumes that this is what Robert Frost meant when he told Kennedy, "Be an Irishman."

Interestingly enough, what Harris has done with Friedman and his son (and with the off-stage Kennedy) is to revive a stock figure of nineteenth-century American drama, the Yankee character who, although he speaks a comic dialect, uses the real meaning of words to explode pretensions and unmask chicanery; now, however, it is the immigrant and his remembering sons and grandsons who have taken over the role. In the introductory essay, which is largely autobiographical, Harris makes clear that *Friedman & Son* grew out of a number of pressures working on him: his almost reluctant attempt to rediscover his father after the man's death; his suspicion that his Jewishness might, after all, not be that obvious in his work ("Nobody happens to be Jewish, Pop," says Ferguson. "Jewish is a condition of existence"); his struggles with television, with Broadway, even with *The New York Times Book Review*, which made him wonder how much he was giving in as a writer, and to whom. Although the theme of the play is an interesting one and there are occasionally attractive lines (Schimmel's "Go ahead, make me a character in your newest immortal work"), the play is too obvious, too relentless in making its point again and again. *Friedman & Son* is finally more interesting as a comment on Mark Harris than as a work in its own right.

The hero of Bruce Jay Friedman's *Scuba Duba*[3] (1967) has a Jewish mother rather than a Jewish father, but she is only a possessive voice on the phone and a cardboard cutout that moves around the stage on a track while the son talks to her. She is a device and nothing more. Like everything else in the play, she is used to elicit an easy if slightly embarrassed laugh which assures the audience that it is sophisticated enough to go beyond the conventional liberal responses to sexual, national, and racial labels. It is, among other things, a race play that calls a "spade" a

---

[3] In an editor's note on contributors (*The Saturday Evening Post*, April 22, 1967), Friedman was identified as the author of "several plays." Only one of them—*23 Pat O'Brien Movies*—was produced before *Scuba Duba*. Based on a Friedman short story of the same name, published in his collection *Far from the City of Class* (1963), it was produced in 1966 by the American Place Theatre on a double bill with May Swenson's *The Floor*, under the collective title *Doubles and Opposites*. The story—and presumably the play—is a tepid macabre comedy in which a policeman, trying to talk a would-be suicide from a ledge, is himself convinced to jump; the title derives from the fact that the suicide keeps expecting their dialogue to follow the standard pattern of all the movies he knows in which similar scenes have occurred.

"spade," but as a joke. Friedman's hero is one of the boy-men familiar to the readers of his fiction, an advertising man named Harold Wonder, isolated in a chateau in the south of France, far from the comfort of Queens, who thinks he has lost his wife to a Negro scuba diver. Harold is inept in most situations, a natural-born dependent (calling his mother and a psychiatrist friend), taking comfort in rhetoric, in abuse (this provides the racial *frisson*), in fantasy.

In his first novel, *Stern* (1962), Friedman used this kind of character at the center of a very funny, occasionally frightening comedy which was effective because the hero's ambivalence toward himself, as a Jew and as a man, came through the laughter as a painful truth. By the time Friedman came to his second novel, *A Mother's Kisses* (1964), all that was best in his first book—his sense of the comic distance between a man and his desired image of himself—had become a joke and an excuse for extraneous gags. *Scuba Duba* adds only the opportunity to let those jokes walk the stage. The plot—what there is of it—consists of Wonder's attempt to get through the night after his wife leaves him. This gives Friedman the excuse to introduce a series of comic turns that are about as relevant to the play's presumed subject as are the peripheral caricatures in *A Mother's Kisses*. When morning comes, Harold discovers that his wife has been carried off by a poetry-writing Negro in a good tweed jacket who, despite an apparently psychosomatic cough, is too much a man for Harold to oppose, and not by the scuba diver, all fashionable black put-down, whose disguise suggests that he might have been boy enough for Harold to have had a chance. By this time it is difficult to tell who is laughing at whom, but surely Friedman intends a little pathos in the last glimpse of Harold, as the stage darkens around him, still shouting his boy's defiance after the departed wife. There are genuinely funny lines in *Scuba Duba*, but as a whole the play is the dramatic equivalent of an *Esquire* cover—a wink at substance, a nod toward wit, and a wholehearted embrace of the gross and the obvious. It was, of course, one of the resounding commercial successes of the 1967–68 season.

There is another boy-man in Jules Feiffer's *Crawling Arnold*

(1961), a one-act play in which the 35-year-old hero after the birth of his brother has taken to crawling. As the play ends, during an air-raid drill, with his parents lying on their bellies on the basement floor, having been shut out of the shelter by the Negro maid ("Let the white imperialists wipe each other out"), Arnold begins to seduce the social worker who has been brought in to cope with him, admitting that he crawls because it makes him more attractive. Since Jules Feiffer is not a novelist—*Harry, the Rat with Women,* notwithstanding—perhaps he should not be considered in this chapter. Still, like the novelists under consideration, he brings a reputation to the theater, and writes plays that are reflections of his nontheatrical work. Commenting on the London production of Feiffer's only full-length play, *Little Murders* (1967), which was better received there than in New York, Martin Esslin (*The New York Times,* June 23, 1967) called it "essentially a three-dimensional Feiffer strip cartoon." The same thing might be said for *Crawling Arnold,* except that Feiffer's cartoons are ordinarily more to the point. His central device, the regressive-aggressive crawl, is an amusing one, but, as the description above indicates, the play is random in its satire. Add that it includes jokes about television, *Reader's Digest,* and "Dear Abby," and *Crawling Arnold* is about as satirical as a Johnny Carson monologue.

Joseph Heller's *We Bombed in New Haven* (1967) is much more serious in its satirical intent, but it too is a play more impressive in conception than in fact. It is essentially a pacifist fantasy—like his novel, *Catch-22* (1961)—which uses the broadest farce to demonstrate the ludicrousness of war and pathos to suggest its horror. The most interesting thing about *Bombed* is its attempt to use the fact of dramatic production as a propaganda mechanism. The action of the play is supposed to exist at two levels of reality at once. The audience is constantly reminded that it is in a theater, that the actors—who use their own names and talk about their real credits—are putting on a play about a bombing squadron, operating out of New Haven (hence, the cute title), in a perennial war which has become simply a businesslike destruction of targets—Minnesota, for instance, which is scheduled for a strike in the second act. At the same time, we are asked to believe that the war is real, that the character Corporal Sinclair and the actor who plays him are one, and that the death of Sinclair over Constantinople is the death of the actor. The point of all this is that the audience and Captain Starkey (the character who most represents the audience for Heller) and the actor who plays Starkey are all responsible for the war, because they do their jobs unquestioningly and take comfort in the fact that the war is not real, is only something that happens in the theater or in the pages of a newspaper. When, in the last act, the actor who plays Sergeant Henderson tries to escape his role, because Henderson is scheduled to die in the take-off, and is killed on stage, Starkey, with Henderson's blood down the front of his flight jacket, still retreats from the truth, escapes into his job and his role. Although Heller's point is a tenable one—that individual responsibility can be ignored but not escaped—his ingenuity is finally self-defeating. There, at curtain call, are the presumably dead actors, and we are thrown back on the comfortable reminder which the play had been designed to bypass—that it is, after all, only a play.

Not that that is ever in doubt. What I have been describing is an idealized *We Bombed in New Haven*. If I wanted to be excessively subtle about the whole thing, I could suggest that the obviousness of the material Heller puts on stage is evidence of his artistic canniness, an attempt to make some kind of distinction between his antiwar play and the standard variety. In fact, I assume that he thinks Act I is funny and Act II is moving, but, unless one comes to the theater convinced that Heller is always funny and antiwar sentiments inevitably moving, it is difficult to agree with him. The first act is full of close-order-drill and soldier-horseplay jokes, running gags such as how can we bomb Constantinople off the map since, now that it's Istanbul, it isn't on the map anyway, and yocks about how bad the Red Cross girl's coffee is. The actress who plays that role is forced to be dumb-blonde cute through most of the play, delivering pointless lines in her own name as well as that of the character. One example should take care of *Bombed* as a comedy. The girl comes on stage complaining that she never gets any funny lines, not even sure-fire swear words, then stops, strikes a pose and says, in the voice of a Broadway comedy ingenue, "Son of a bitch." Enter Starkey, asking what's to complain and pointing out that the audience just laughed. In fact, when I saw the play, the audience was stone silent.

The serious second act is in its way as trying as the funny first. Although wars are horrible and it is the young who are destroyed by them, it is almost impossible to put that fact on stage. Instead, there is a vocabulary of pacifist playwriting, as artificially senti-mental as that of other forms of popular melodrama, which suc-ceeds only in jerking tears, in indulging the audience that it wants to make indignant. "You had nineteen years, Pop," says the Cap-tain's son at the end of the last act, blaming him for not having stopped the war, and on lines like that *We Bombed in New Haven* becomes the kind of antiwar play it has been pretending not to be.

Next to Bellow, the most interesting of the novelist-playwrights is John Hawkes, who works a dramatic vein very different from that of the authors discussed above. His four short plays, pub-lished in 1966, grew out of a year (1964–65) spent at the Actor's Workshop in San Francisco under a Ford Foundation grant. Hawkes works largely by nuance, suggesting more than he defines, hoping, I suppose, to infect the audience with a sense of uneasi-ness or dis-ease (with and without the hyphen). The world of his plays, like that of his novels, is one of matter-of-fact grotesque-ness in which blood and lust are staples ("Blood and ecstasy, that's the ticket," says Bingo in *The Wax Museum*) and innocence is forever menaced—mainly by its own innate corruption. At one pole—*The Questions*—his work suggests Harold Pinter; at the other—*The Wax Museum*—it suggests Grand Guignol, devised for a theater that has not got around to buying its bloodmaking machine. The action is minimal; the play, in Hawkes, is largely verbal. In one of the few long reviews of the published plays (*New York Review of Books*, July 31, 1967), Nigel Dennis, a play-wright who works in an intellectual farce style which makes him nearer neighbor to Bellow than to Hawkes, assumes that Hawkes does not know what he is doing, although he occasionally does it attractively, and that the plays constantly suggest more than they deliver. His attack on Hawkes is pointed and circumstantial, and, although I suspect that what he takes for limitations are the plays' virtues, his is an understandable reaction to the plays. Whatever else Hawkes is doing, he is not feeding conventional responses.

The best of the plays is *The Questions*, which was presented in a remarkably effective production on NBC's *Experiment in Television* in April, 1967. In a setting that "might be courtroom, doctor's office, sun parlor, or the pure space of psychic activity,"[4] a man questions a young girl about a triangle which began when she was a girl of fourteen and which involved her father (Papa), her mother (Mama) and a perennial guest (Adrian). The nature of that relationship seems to hang on four events (or nonevents) —the hour that Mama spent in Adrian's room, after she brought him home, bloodied, from a fall from a horse, while a perhaps unconcerned Papa made scones for tea; the tryst in the garden which turned out, to the spying girl's disgust, to be Papa and Mama; Mama's telling Papa's recurring dream of her, fully dressed but with only a brassiere on top; the foxhunt in which Papa, who did not ride, and Adrian struggled in a pit, sharing in the kill. The audience is never given a true account of these events, if such a thing is possible, because the play is concerned not with the triangle, but with the struggle that lies in the questions. The girl is protective toward Papa, seeing the triangle as innocent—until she is pushed into admitting other possibilities— and the man, for all his initial objectivity, seems intent on getting the girl to accept Papa's disgrace and his guilt. Since the play keeps hinting that the man is Papa (the questioning takes place beneath a ceiling fan like the one Papa brought from his Charleston home; the man falls easily into Papa's role in a number of the attempts to reconstruct what happened; she says, "You sound like

---

[4] It is my fondest wish for Hawkes that he avoid such slightly pretentious abstractions—like identifying the teenager in *The Innocent Party* as "a mythic force"—and leave it to the critics to decorate his nuances with noumenal names.

Papa in a bad mood"), the story is apparently either the man's attempt to get confirmation for the self-disgust he feels or—given the apparently innocent ambiguity in some of the girl's defenses— his attempt to still her disappointment in him by forcing her to defend him against his apparent self-destructiveness.

It is unnecessary to be as precise about the possibilities as I have in this description, for the play's effectiveness—rather like that of Pinter's *The Homecoming*—depends upon an obvious struggle, all the more compelling for not being concretely defined. Hawkes's language in this work is fascinating; seldom ornate, practically descriptive, it remains dry, spare, and yet evocative. Some of its subtlety comes from cleverly manipulated repetition. "So maybe you were just trying to get a rise out of him," says the man, commenting on the girl's having told Papa about Mama's revealing his dream; eleven speeches later she says, "Anyhow, I didn't get a rise out of him, which proves the point," a remark that proves no point that she has been making, in fact that brings the audience back from the moment being discussed to the questioning itself, to an accusation implied in the girl's words. The comic possibilities of the language can be illustrated by the girl's apparently straightforward description of her mother, "Except for her jokes and horsemanship and feeling for Papa and the celibacy business, she might have been a nun," which does not become completely ludicrous because our laughter gets backed up against the speaker's strange thought processes.

The other three plays are not so interesting. *The Innocent Party*, less art than aura, is the story of an adolescent girl who is seduced by or seduces her aunt against the background of a family quarrel in which the girl's parents alternate between welcoming the aunt after a long absence and accusing her of having abandoned them. In the first scene, Jane explains to her aunt that she comes to the dry, debris-filled swimming pool every morning at dawn and finds it momentarily full of water in which she looks at herself; in the final scene, the next day's dawn, she stands at the pool edge and tries "to see our faces in the water." The movement from the singular to the plural, from the seeing to the attempt suggests an initiation for Jane which has erased the difference between her and the adults, between her naturalness and their artificiality, between her promise and their loss. *The Wax Museum* is a macabre item in which an attendant at such an exhibition awakens unacknowledged desire in a coldly proper Canadian girl and, changing places with her, departs with her flesh-and-blood (a dangerous adjective in talking about Hawkes) fiancé and leaves her caressing George, the wax Mountie. "I'll crouch here forever if I have to, Papa," says Edward in *The Undertaker,* as he sits outside the bathroom door waiting for his father, the undertaker of the title, to kill himself. Since Edward is in his forties, again acting out something that happened when he was twelve, the line is an accurate one, the whole play an illustration of the father's description of death as "jumping off a tandem bicycle": "And somebody's always left, Edward." According to Herbert Blau, who wrote the introduction to the Hawkes plays, the author once described *The Undertaker* as a "farcical melodrama," a generic term which suggests—perhaps without intending to—a certain lightness of intent. In fact, *The Undertaker* and *The Wax Museum,* both of which should play well, come across simply as clever pieces, teasing the serious subjects which underlie them. *The Questions,* by comparison, is a work of dramatic substance.

For an author who uses dialogue so tellingly in his novels and stories, James Purdy is strangely inept in his two plays, published in *Children Is All* (1962). His work affects me the way Hawkes's plays affect Nigel Dennis, except that there are not even flamboyant and inventive moments—as there certainly are in the fiction—to distract me from the sense that nothing is going on. *Cracks,* which was performed off-Broadway in 1963 on a bill with Ellen Violett adaptations of four Purdy stories, is an amorphous play in which an old woman, through a dream or a visitation, is assured that, despite pain, life goes on; this is apparently comfort for the kind of fear the child displays in his desire to have closed the "cracks" through which "the zephyrs of death" blow. *Children Is All* is a longer play in which Edna Cartwright waits for the return of her convict son, but she can only recognize him by an act—cradling his head in her lap as he dies—while she calls him stranger. Much of Purdy's best work deals with the way men remain close strangers to one another, but his plays use that favorite theme without illuminating it; there is more dramatic invention in *Malcolm* and the short stories than there is in either of the plays.

A far cry from the Bellow *shtick* and the Hawkes nuance is Jesse Hill Ford's *The Conversion of Buster Drumwright*, written first as a television script (CBS Television Workshop, 1960), later expanded into a play which Donald Davidson, in his preface to the volume containing both scripts (1964), admits is "a little faultily diffuse at some points." That is an understatement, one that befits a man who gave advice on the transfer to the stage. The Bystander, in the TV version, calls Buster "about the meanest killer Tennessee ever had," a description which later becomes "the most notorious killer in the history of Tennessee." Nine words for seven and less idiomatic, that speech might stand for the faults of the stage version, which pads out its simple story with much unnecessary expositional material about the characters involved. *Conversion*, in its first form, is a neat if slightly corny variation on the old chestnut in which the con man comes to believe his own line. Ocie Hedgepath, whose sister was one of Buster's victims, comes home after fifteen years of bumming, determined to make it up to the family by avenging her death. Since Buster is guarded by a determined deputy sheriff straight out of a standard Western, Ocie can get to him only by pretending to be a preacher intent on saving the convicted murderer's soul. Using a hobodlerized retelling of the story of St. Paul ("They got him on vagrancy and throwed him in the tank"), Ocie converts Buster, but when the time comes to drown him in his baptismal water, Ocie cannot go through with it. The sentimental fadeout finds Buster still wanting the "Preacher" on hand when the hanging takes place and Ocie assuring him, "I'll be there."

The stage version goes past this scene, takes us to the murder of

Ocie by one of his brothers, and the comfort that Buster finds in Ocie's—and Paul's—courage. Ford goes to some trouble in the longer version to place the story in a context of violence and corruption (the Bystander tells with some relish how he shot an innocent man while Buster was being arrested; the real preacher approves of the Hedgepath desire for vengeance; the off-stage sheriff puts his nephew at the jail door to keep his political image untarnished), but the irony produced by such additions is as obvious as the story itself. If, as Davidson suggests, Ford was making a serious attempt to deal with a particular society and with the Christian implications of his double conversion, he failed. Even a quite ordinary Ford story, such as "The Highwayman" (*Paris Review*, Summer, 1966), in which the leading character is apparently feeble-minded, suggests that human beings are complicated and subtle creatures, not—as in *The Conversion of Buster Drumwright*—figures motivated simply by the dramatist's need for a neat reversal.

Although his idiom is very different from Ford's, Hugh Wheeler is another novelist whose plays are conventional stories masked by a deceptive look. In his case, the fact is not surprising, because his work as a novelist has been in the detective story, a form that tends toward surface variations on a basic crime-and-detection plot. With Richard Wilson Webb, Wheeler is the author of the novels published under the names Q. Patrick, Patrick Quentin, and Jonathan Stagge. Not that he writes mystery stories for the stage. His plays—or at least the two with which he made his theatrical debut in 1961—are sentimental comedies, strangely acid in tone. Since *Look: We've Come Through*, his second play, is so neat an example of the standard play in disguise, perhaps it would be better to begin with it. It is the story of a girl (at once bright and shy) and a boy (at once sensitive and shy), each superior to his surroundings, each with a crush on someone glamorous, who finally realize that their friendship is love. "Wow! What you know?" says Bobby after the obligatory pre-curtain kiss. "Live and learn, don't you?" The difference is that the boy is a homosexual (not a hustler, he insists, although he has a once-a-week regular friend) and the girl, hopped on D. H. Lawrence, loses her virginity to an actor who is just killing time until he meets his wife and agent for a contract talk at Sardi's. Wheeler's trick—and it may be one that works against him—is that, despite the pseudo-sophisticated dressing, he presents his couple as conventional naive adolescents. The other characters are also innocents of a sort. The actor is a kind of lost little boy; the wife is bumptiously intent on being sophisticated; the agent comes on clever, as though he had been watching high-society comedies on the late show ("One forgets how amusing unamusing people can be"). Presented comically at first, these characters seem increasingly nasty as the play goes on; the final kiss is the conventional rosy ending, but edged in black.

Wheeler's strange way with characters can be seen at better advantage in *Big Fish, Little Fish*, the first of his plays. It is the portrait of a school of little fish, disrupted when a big fish swims through and tempts the leader to bigger and better ponds. William Baker, a plodder in a small job in a textbook house, is the center of a band of losers—a suburban grandmother who has been his mistress for nineteen years, an art teacher with an undeclared homosexual love for him, a drunken ex-publisher with a tongue so venomous that no one else will give him house room. A successful novelist, who passed them on the way up, suggests Baker for a fancy editing job which would mean moving to Europe, disrupting the routine that sustains them, but the job turns out to be a fraud (the publisher uses Baker until the desired big name is free to take over) and what is left of the old group closes around Baker with affection and love and the happy knowledge that he will go on smothering with them in their vacuum. There is much free-flowing bitchiness in the play, most of it self-protective, and all the characters—big fish and little fish alike—are presented satirically. In the case of Baker and his friends the satire is edged with pathos. After all, the play is a strangely unpleasant variation on the old standard in which the bluebird of happiness turns up in one's own backyard, although in this case the bird may be a vulture.

It is the ambiguous quality in Wheeler's characters that makes his plays interesting, at least momentarily, but in the end this seems less like a serious concept of character than the result of a conflict between the dramatist's satirical impulse and his attraction to standard popular forms. Not harsh enough for black comedy, not vacuous enough for ordinary comedy, the Wheeler characters have not been very welcome on Broadway. *Big Fish, Little Fish* did manage to stay for three months, but *Look: We've Come Through* lasted less than a week. Since 1961, Wheeler has taken refuge in adaptation and his old stock in trade, mystery and murder, but with little luck. *We Have Always Lived in the Castle* (1966), his dramatization of Shirley Jackson's novel, ran for only nine performances, and *Rich Little Rich Girl* (1964), based on a play by Miguel Mihura and Alvaro deLaiglesia, died on the way to New York. Not that one need mourn those plays. Wheeler's dramatic talent is worth paying attention to only when he is concerned with those funny-sad characters of his who, artistically at least, have not yet come through.

One of the ways that novelists move into the theater is by adapting their own novels into plays. Since Hawkes's *The Undertaker* grows out of the father's suicide in *Second Skin*, it might be called an adaptation, but not in the conventional sense. It is not a play that uses the same material and strives for some of the same effects as those of a novel, plainly identified—by title for one thing—with the play it has whelped. J. P. Donleavy's plays, better known in England than in his own country,[5] are examples of works which depend heavily on the novels on which they are based. *The Ginger Man* (1959) is a skeletonized version of the novel (1955), using much of the dialogue from the original and often putting the narrator's words into the hero's mouth, an understandable transfer since, in the novel, the hero and the narrator are one. Sebastian Dangerfield, a not-so-young American ostensibly studying law in Dublin, cadges, begs, pawns his way through a life in

---

[5] Only one of his plays has been performed in New York—*The Ginger Man*, which finally reached off-Broadway in 1963. *A Singular Man* was tested, as the play merchants say, during the summer of 1967, tryouts that did not lead to a New York production.

which he gives all his energy to protecting his sensitive self from a world which somehow refuses to make everything "Free and easy. Easy and free—it's the way things ought to be. . . ." Like Kingsley Amis' Lucky Jim, Sebastian has a repertoire of sounds, funny faces, and fantasy plots which protect him from real or imagined demands; like John Osborne's Jimmy Porter, his self-pity manifests itself in the nastiest kind of abuse, aimed at those closest to him. The play retains this character, softening him a little and at the same time making him less complicated, primarily because there is nothing in the dramatic language that can equal the narration in which the sudden shifts in person suggest that Sebastian is constantly reacting and at the same time watching to see what effect he is creating. In reducing his characters to just four— Sebastian, his wife, one of his other women, and one of his friends —Donleavy makes the resemblance between Sebastian and Jimmy Porter the more obvious, because the four characters play much the same roles here as the four principals in *Look Back in Anger*. The whole London section of the novel has been cut away, the account of Sebastian's incipient financial success which fails to bring him peace; it becomes clear, in the last chapter, that it is mortality that has been after him all along, not landlords and bartenders and wives. The play ends with Sebastian, shorn of wife, lover, and friend, about to set sail for London; Donleavy tries to retain the impetus of the final pages of the novel by giving Sebastian a long curtain speech, ending with the novel's image of the horses racing to death. This escalation of petty annoyance into existential anguish is difficult enough in the novel, but it is impossible in the play, for there the death and funeral lines are not backed up by narrative insistence.

A *Singular Man* (1964) is a less happy adaptation of a less interesting novel (1963). The hero of the novel, another Sebastian, this time called George Smith, is a successful businessman of an unidentified variety, constantly menaced by invisible opponents, society in general, and inanimate objects that will not behave. He takes comfort (or heightens his distress) with a variety of women but gives his best attention to the mausoleum he is building. Although the play retains references to George's defensiveness (the mausoleum, the steel door to his apartment, the letters and phone calls which he parries), there is no sense of urgency at all, no indication that George has his back to any metaphysical wall. Aside from an opening scene,[6] which establishes that George, like Sebastian, is a noise maker (he uses his "Beep" in only one other scene), the play is a series of short encounters with three of his women: his wife, his secretary, and his main sex objective. Although some of the scenes (the bed scene with the wife, the rifle scene with the secretary, the scene with the secretary's mother) contain the possibility of good comedy, at once grotesque and pathetic, they come across as shorthand summaries of their equivalents in the novel. This effect is heightened by the fact that the play's dialogue is written in jagged, often fragmentary sentences, which must be difficult to speak and to listen to, a literary mannerism taken directly from the novel, where it quickly became a self-defeating device. As George's friend says in the first scene, "This has kind of gone on too long to be comic." Or serious either, alas.

Fairy Tales of New York (1960) appeared between the adaptations of the two novels. Donleavy gives each of the four acts a name, which is appropriate since they are, in fact, separate plays, held together by the central character and a satiric approach to the attitudes and jargon of a success-oriented society. Cornelius Christian, like Sebastian, is an American who studied abroad without getting a degree, but there is little point in talking about him in terms of biography; like George Smith, he is an abstraction. He is a malevolent innocent incapable of acting according to the rules. "But he says you're a threat to the United States," says O'Rourke. "You think that's true, Cornelius?" Cornelius' answer: "Yes." In "Helen," in two scenes, Cornelius brings the body of his English wife through customs and then to a funeral parlor where he is offered a job. "The Interview" is little more than its title suggests, a parody talk with a personnel man in which the interviewer gets

---

[6] This scene comes not from the novel but from a short story "One for Yes," which was published in *Meet My Maker the Mad Molecule.*

sucked into Cornelius' oddly shifting thoughts. In "The Knock-out," which takes place in the boxing room of a club, O'Rourke, who is quoting the Admiral in the lines above, persuades Cornelius to take a dive in a match with the Admiral, to build up the older man's ego, and Cornelius is knocked out in fact. In "Peach Shoes," Cornelius distresses his date by wearing the titular shoes to a restaurant where no one will serve them. After he leaves, the waiters quarrel over her and, when she does not respond, remove, bit by bit, table setting, cloth, table, chair, leaving her alone, on her knees, crying. Cornelius returns, in formal dress but barefoot with diamonds on his toes, and is served immediately. When the girl tries to apologize, he is forgiving: "That's all right. You see, the color of this [his foot] too is peach."

Fairy Tales is more interesting than the other two plays, partly because they are pale copies of works that have more vitality and substance as novels. Not that *Fairy Tales* is original. Three of the plays are based on material that appears in *Meet My Maker the Mad Molecule*, stories or sketches that I assume predated the dramatic versions, although the collection of short fiction was not published until 1964. "A Fairy Tale of New York," which is not only the source of "Helen," but of the larger play's title and the name of the principal character, appeared in *Atlantic* in January, 1961. It and "In My Peach Shoes," which reads like an outline for "Peach Shoes," show obvious borrowings; the connection between "My Painful Jaw" and "The Knockout" is more tenuous. In none of the *Fairy Tales*, however, does the original material hover over the adaptation, insisting on unflattering comparisons. The play exists in its own right. As such, it is imaginative, at least in concep-tion, in two of its cautionary anecdotes—the boxing match and the restaurant sequence. Oddly enough, neither of these is as sharply realized as my brief description suggests. "The Interview," despite its conventional subject, is the most effective of the four "acts."

"I was also trying to put more into this play than I had into the novel," wrote Norman Mailer in the Introduction to *The Deer Park* (1967), his play version of his 1955 novel, but—as with

Donleavy—the adaptation is little more than an outline, a series of scenes that borrow their substance from the fact of the novel standing somewhere off-stage. The play, like the novel, which it follows very closely, uses the professional fraudulence of Hollywood and the commercial artificiality of Desert D'Or, the resort setting for the action, as background—more metaphorical than factual in the play—against which a number of interconnected stories are presented. The central figure in the play is Charles Francis Eitel, whose artistic and political struggle—a question of manhood—is seen obliquely through his affair with Elena. He fails, presumably, because he goes back to work in Hollywood, which means a double sell-out: the recantation—a ritual testifying —of his refusal to talk before a Congressional committee on subversive activity; and the sacrifice of his script to the producer who wants to make a conventional candy-wrapper of it ("Something with angels' voices in the background. Only not full of shit . . ."). The affair with Elena dwindles into a marriage in which she plays the conventional bored wife to his cheating husband. "Sergius," he cries out as he dies, "what does one ever do with one's life?"

That is the question with which the play is concerned. In his opening monologue, Sergius, who, as in the novel, acts as narrator, identifies the inhabitants of Desert D'Or, the characters we are about to see, as dead men who imagine they are alive. "Of course, some of them may guess that if they are a little better than is expected of them, they can return to your side of the footlights." The line is obviously not intended as a compliment to the audience, a great many of whom must share "death" with the Mailer characters, but as a theatrical metaphor with which the author can suggest the possibility of being "a little better," a hope that Eitel has for Sergius and his son. Eitel's real son, the child mentioned at the end of the play, is not important in the action, but the struggle centers on two surrogate sons, both of whom represent elements of Eitel's own personality—Sergius and Marion. As a character, Marion is given plenty of motivation for his desire to see Eitel sell out, which may mean that he wants the opposite. As an ex-lover of Marion's mother, Eitel is a father who has failed Marion; as a man who chooses to remain male, Eitel is a lover who refuses Marion. Since one of Mailer's stage directions endows Marion with "an angelic smile of pure evil," his manipulations may be diabolic (he is very much at home in Desert D'Or, which Sergius calls Hell), but he is really only the devil in Eitel who, from the beginning of the play, has been tempting him to a spiritual wrestling match that he must lose.

The part of Marion has been greatly expanded from the novel, but that of Sergius—Eitel's angel—has been diminished. As in the novel, he is a young man, a pilot back from the wars, suffering from what his bombs have done to people, using drink and an affair with a movie star as a narcotic. At the end of the play, Sergius tells us that Eitel's "spirit passed on to me," which is apparently an inheritance of love. At one point, Eitel is identified with love (warmth) and Marion with sex (rhythm), but Mailer, in his Introduction, in which he identifies sex and love as his theme, says that "there is a no man's land between sex and love, and it alters in the night." Still, in "A Note on the Production," he tells us that, at the end of the play, Sergius "is full of love . . . the sort of love which comes not so unexpectedly from understanding the lives of others and forgiving them." This is an assertion, however, that is hardly verifiable within the play, despite Sergius' final positive statements about "the poor odd dialogues which give hope to us noble humans for more than one night." The relationship between Sergius and Eitel, so important to the novel, does not exist in the play. Sergius is pushed so far to the side that he disappears after Act I, Change 14 (Mailer calls his brief scenes "changes") and does not turn up again until Act II, Change 19, thirty-eight "changes" later, and what we see of him—his narrative speeches, his scenes with Lulu Meyers—suggests that he is a big, dumb, drinking Irishman and not a soul in torment.

My discussion of the play may imply a clearer ideational line and a greater artistic achievement than exist in the play. Anatole Broyard, in his review of *Why Are We in Vietnam?* (*The New York Times Book Review*, September 17, 1967), says that Mailer "experiences ideas instead of thinking them, his messages are not always clear, but they are almost always interesting enough to repay the effort." The "almost" is the trap in that sentence. *The Deer Park* has some virtues, primarily comic ones (the one-liners of the studio head, the producer's reworking of Eitel's story), but it finally fails as a play because Mailer is neither content to work in abstractions (however nonrealistic his play's form) nor able to create the characters that he otherwise needs. This weakness may be the result of his conscious attempt to avoid conventional plot, to write, as he says in the Introduction, a play that "went from explosion to explosion . . . from one moment of intensity or reality (which is to say a moment which feels more real than other moments) to the next—a play which went at full throttle all the way." Without the "dramatic scaffolding, connective tissue" that he cuts away, an audience comes to the scenes lacking the emotional freight that the characters presumably carry, and although they will not find it difficult "to fill the spaces" (there is exposition enough), the scenes are likely to remain dull and flat. "Was it possible that it was only boring, comic, and sensational?" Mailer asks in the Introduction—his response to the reviews—and his answer, after a look at what is playing in New York, is an inevitable *no*. Yet Sergius seems to have a better sense of the play than his creator does, even though Mailer put into his mouth the invitation to the audience to listen in on "conversations about movies, money and love." Too many of the explosions are pure disquisition, not interesting enough in its own right and, because of the problems in characterization, not dramatically compelling as argument in which ideas become weapons. "If 'The Deer Park' doesn't prove to be one of the four or five most exciting plays to open in New York since the Second World War," Mailer told Lewis Funke (*The New York Times*, October 10, 1966), "I will consider it an unhappy failure." It didn't, and it is.

Ray Bradbury is no Donleavy, no Mailer. He is an efficient professional who uses popular fiction, particularly science fiction, as a vehicle for old-fashioned and rather attractive humanistic ideas. He came to the theater in the 1960's, however, as a kind of crusader. He began quietly enough with the publication of a volume of short plays, *The Anthem Sprinters and Other Antics,* all derived from material growing out of his months-long visit to Ireland when he was doing the screenplay for John Huston's *Moby Dick* (1956). Convinced that "This vast audience of hungry and half-rootless children needs proclamations and declarations, new ideals to tell them what their age should mean to them," as he wrote in a contribution to *The Best Plays of 1964–1965,* he launched a theater of his own in 1964 when he presented the first installment of *The World of Ray Bradbury* at the Coronet Theatre in Los Angeles. It consisted of three short plays, *The Veldt, The Pedestrian,* and *To the Chicago Abyss.* A second group of plays— *The Wonderful Ice Cream Suit, A Device Out of Time,* and *The Day It Rained Forever*—opened in March, 1965. In October of that year, the Bradbury revolution moved east; the first group of plays arrived off-Broadway and stayed for five days. Since then, there has been quiet on the Bradbury dramatic front.

The Pedestrian and *The Day It Rained Forever,* both based on short stories written in the 1950's, can serve as examples of his work. The first, set in 1990, describes a world of forced conformity and mechanization in which the pedestrian is a kind of subversive. While the rest of the world is closeted with television, he walks the deserted city until he is arrested by a passengerless police car and carried off "To the Psychiatric Center for Research on Regressive Tendencies." To make a play of the story, Bradbury adds a second, rather reluctant pedestrian. How a man so outside his society as Bradbury's hero could have reached another person, particularly one so fearful, is never clear. Plainly the second man is only a device to make conversation possible, a way of turning a neat story into a not so neat play. In *The Day,* three old men, living in a desert hotel, wait for the one day of rain a year and, when it passes without a drop, they despair until an old woman, a music teacher who has been in search of applause, happens by and repays their hospitality by playing her harp. The music becomes the longed-for rain, and their applause comes in return. The play is essentially the same as the story except that Bradbury calls for a host of sound effects—harp, rain, firecrackers, applause—when surely mime and music would be nearer the sense of the story. In both instances, what on the page seems simple and direct becomes at once flashy and shallow when one thinks of live actors moving through the fable. Bradbury's tendency to overwrite, which slides by in a casual reading of a story, assaults the ear when Mead, in *The Pedestrian*, says, "The leaves run on the sidewalk and nibble your feet like a pack of mice." Although he intends an attack on "the old, the familiar, the safe, and the 'in' Absurd Play," his own work is not all that new, strange, and dangerous, and the best of the Absurdists could show him the difference between a dramatic image and a fictional one, a dramatic line and a literary one.

This is a lesson that all play-writing novelists must learn. Some of them—as this chapter indicates—have begun to do so.

SEVEN

Transformations
and Other Changes

How many "coming men" has one
known! Where on earth do they all go
to?   —AGNES IN *The Notorious*
                        Mrs. Ebbsmith

"Miss Ellen Stewart happens once in a lifetime," wrote Leonard
Melfi in the Introduction to *Encounters*, a collection of six of his
one-act plays, "and I am so very glad that it was during my
lifetime." This sentence is typical of the testimonials young playwrights offer to one or another of the off-off-Broadway establish-
ments, of which Miss Stewart's Café La Mama Experimental
Theatre Club is probably the most publicized. According to
Michael Smith, in his Introduction to *Eight Plays from Off-Off-*

Broadway, the off-off-Broadway label was coined by Jerry Tall-mer, then drama critic on *The Village Voice,* a few weeks after the phenomenon was born in a production, of all things, of Alfred Jarry's *King Ubu,* September 27, 1960, at Take 3, a Greenwich Village coffeehouse. This date and this production, arbitrarily chosen, as Smith admits, can serve as well as any (later theater historians can establish a true chronology) as the initiatory moment for what is likely to seem, in retrospect, one of the most important developments in American theater in the 1960's. It was born out of a dissatisfaction with and a distrust of off-Broadway production, which by the end of the 1950's had become as much an economic as an artistic enterprise, a miniature copy of uptown show business.

As soon as one begins to talk about off-off-Broadway as though it had "Nice dimensions, nice proportions," as Clov said about his kitchen in *Endgame,* it begins to sound too neatly definable. Any production of any play, but preferably a new one, in a coffee-house, a loft, a church, acted and directed by amateurs or would-be professionals or professionals working without pay, might be called an off-off-Broadway production. Not that off-off-Broad-way has remained comfortably chaotic over the last seven years. It has created its own Establishment, good, gray shoestring opera-tions that have managed somehow to continue producing long enough for their names to become known to people—readers of *The New York Times,* say—who have never ventured to see one of their shows: Caffe Cino, which opened as a coffeehouse in 1958 and began in 1961 to offer a regular program of plays; La Mama, established in imitation of Cino, which became even better known, probably because Miss Stewart makes such good copy,[1] and which eventually launched the La Mama Repertory, which carries the off-off-Broadway playwrights to European audiences; the Judson Poets' Theatre, started in 1961 at the Judson Me-morial Church, Washington Square; Theatre Genesis, begun in

[1] Josh Greenfeld's "Their Hearts Belong to La Mama" (*The New York Times Magazine,* July 9, 1967) is a good example of how difficult it is for writers to keep from becoming sentimental as they tell the story of Ellen Stewart and her struggle to keep La Mama alive.

1964 at the St. Mark's Church in-the-Bouwerie on Second Avenue; the Open Theatre, founded by Joseph Chaikin in 1963, primarily as an actors' workshop. Although presumably each of these outfits has a personality of its own, at least in the eyes of its founder (Ralph Cook says, in *Eight Plays from Off-Off-Broadway*, that "Theatre Genesis has defined itself in terms of a deeply subjective kind of realism and . . . conspicuous heterosexuality"), the best known off-off-Broadway playwrights, directors, and actors move easily back and forth among them.

Audiences are small and coterie; productions are ordinarily limited to no more than a few weeks, sometimes a few performances. Most of the off-off-Broadway reputations, particularly for out-of-town visitors like me, depend on hearsay. Even its most determined advocates, however, admit that much that goes on there is very bad. Josh Greenfeld quotes Joseph LeSeur, another *Village Voice* critic, who has come to accept the "hit-or-miss quality of La Mama's work" but who wishes "the odds were a little more in the theatergoer's favor." When the work of a much praised off-off-Broadway playwright surfaces, as happened when Paul Foster's *Balls* (1964) played at the Cherry Lane in a New Playwrights' Series or when his *The Recluse* (1964) was done on National Educational Television, it is likely to seem—to one who is not part of the club—an unfortunate advertisement for an area of theatrical activity in which the freedom to experiment, even to fail, is presumably producing new American playwrights. Yet that is precisely what off-off-Broadway is about. In an article in *The New York Times Magazine* (December 5, 1965), Elenore Lester reported that in the first half of this decade there had been 400 new plays by 200 new playwrights performed off-off-Broadway. According to Greenfeld, La Mama alone in its first six years produced 200 plays by 100 playwrights. In the face of such numbers, quality, as the history of drama has taught us, is a doubtful ingredient. The selection methods of some of the producers contribute to the doubt. "I decide on everything that comes into the room," Joseph Cino wrote in the note on Caffe Cino in *Eight Plays from Off-Off-Broadway*; he does so, he added, "by intuition much more than by reading scripts." Ellen Stewart told Greenfeld that "if a script *beeps* to me when I'm reading it, we do it." Miss Stewart's *beep* sounds like a mass-production variation on that bell that rang for Alice B. Toklas whenever she met a genius, but Miss Toklas' bell did not need to ring once every two weeks, as Miss Stewart's must if she is to adhere to La Mama's announced schedule. Since production decisions tend to be idiosyncratic, whoever makes them, after however sustained a critical (and/or commercial) analysis, and since 400 new plays, under the best of circumstances, can be expected to produce only a handful of good ones, the real point in dwelling on numbers is to emphasize that off-off-Broadway is less an achievement than an opportunity.

During the 1960's, a young playwright has had a better chance of being produced than at any time since the end of World War II, for no longer is a hearing confused with Broadway production. Not only are there the off-off-Broadway outlets described above and the conventional off-Broadway producers, who are not all artistic deadheads as the coffeehouse enthusiasts insist (they did introduce many of the playwrights discussed in earlier chapters), but there are organizations operating in the disputed territory between the two. Edward Albee, Richard Barr, and Clinton Wilder, who have produced together and separately off and on Broadway, developed a theatrical farm-team system, a Playwrights Unit which provided for full production of the plays of young dramatists, presented for a performance or two to invited audiences, some of which (most notably, LeRoi Jones's *Dutchman*) were then moved into regular off-Broadway production. The American Place Theatre, which performs in St. Clement's Church on West 46th Street, presents both a studio program for works in progress and a season of new plays to subscribers. Way off-Broadway there are increasing opportunities for new playwrights in regional and university theaters, productions which are no longer considered, as they once were, polite ways of burying playwrights. There are foundation-financed operations such as the Eugene O'Neill Memorial Theatre Foundation in Waterford, Connecticut, and the Office for Advanced Drama Research at the University of Minnesota.[2] This last, created through a Rockefeller grant, provides an opportunity for a number of playwrights to see their works in production, either by university or other groups in the Minneapolis-St. Paul area.

One result of the O.A.D.R. program is that its director, Arthur H. Ballet, has edited four volumes of what he calls *Playwrights for Tomorrow*. Some are interesting, some are dull, some good, some impossible, but their very presence in published collections is symptomatic. Aside from Ballet's volumes and the two collections John Gassner made of pre-Brustein Yale playwrights, there have been at least three collections of new playwrights within the last two years: Edward Parone's *New Theatre in America* (the Albee-Barr-Wilder playwrights), Robert Corrigan's *New American Plays*, and *Eight Plays from Off-Off-Broadway*, edited by Nick Orzel and Michael Smith. Even more unusual, within the same period, leading commercial publishers have issued volumes of plays containing the work of individual dramatists—Lanford Wilson (two volumes), Megan Terry, Ronald Ribman, Jean-Claude van Itallie, Sam Shepard, Leonard Melfi, Rosalyn Drexler, Rochelle Owens. Of these, only van Itallie has achieved the kind of commercial success which used to precede publication.

It would be almost impossible and probably pointless to give an extensive analysis of the works of the younger (or at least most

[2] There is even a kind of senior-citizens organization to further production away from Broadway. The American Playwrights Theater, which operates out of Ohio State University, is a kind of agency which offers its members (any university or community theater which pays the annual subscription fee) a chance to produce carefully chosen new plays. So far such playwrights as Robert Anderson, Barrie Stavis, Arnold Sundgaard, Jerome Weidman, James Yaffe, and George Sklar have been offered, although in some cases the work had to be withdrawn when there were not enough takers. I have seen none of the plays in question, but I have read Anderson's *The Days Between*, a soap opera about a writer's artistic and marital problems, and *Ivory Tower*, by Weidman and Yaffe, an over-psychologized attempt to use the Ezra Pound case to make a comment on the vulnerability of the idealist in the real world. If these are fair samples, the organization is not doing American drama much of a service. Most of the impossible plays that turn up in the regional and off-off-Broadway showcases I have been talking about are today's bad playwriting, not yesterday's.

recently arrived) playwrights on the American scene. I will limit myself in this chapter to a consideration of those whose talent most impresses me or whose work seems most representative.

If I were to pick one out of the great number of names that keep turning up on theatrical scratch sheets, hopefuls expected to win, place, or show in the great-American-playwright sweep-stakes, I would choose that of Ronald Ribman. I would hedge my bet, however, for I am a critic and a reporter, not a prophet, and the history of American drama is littered with great expectations. On the basis of two of his three plays,[3] however, Ribman is—for me, at least—the most exciting of the new playwrights.

Harry, Noon and Night (1965) is a strange comedy about a loser, "a failure clown," as Harry says about Moko, whom he saw and cried over years before in a circus back in Columbus, Ohio. "The kind that everything goes wrong for." Behind the strange exterior of the play is the material for a conventional psychologi-cal drama, the story of a young man perpetually in the shadow of an older, aggressive brother. The play takes place in Munich, to which Harry has retreated (after having been kicked out of an art school in Florence) and where he has found shelter of a sort with Immanuel, who shares his oblique approach to the world. Archer, the older brother, has come to take him home, and the play is an account of how Harry manages not to let himself go.

So neat a description of the action gives no indication of what the play is like. It opens on an interview between Harry (posing as a reporter) and a young soldier in the occupation army (it is 1955), a ludicrous scene in which both the soldier and Harry fondle a prostitute who sits with them while Harry confuses the soldier with a stream of questions about obvious things (what are chevrons?) and hints of an arcane superstructure within the army. At the end of the scene, Harry sends the soldier into the other

[3] I am not counting *The Final War of Olly Winter* (1967), the Ribman play that was presented by CBS Playhouse as a television original. I know the script only from a tape recording made from the television production, too in-complete a sense of it to let me comment in any detail on what seemed, at one hearing, to be a well-intentioned pacifist play, conventional in sentiment, imaginative only in some of its detail.

room to bring back the "guy picking his nose." The soldier cannot see a nose-picker, but Harry keeps insisting, piling detail on detail ("Now he's patting his little brother on the head. . . . Pretty soon he'll whop the kid for smoking. That's the way he operates. Move in close, smiling, and then, whop with his snotty hands"), finally bringing the curtain down on a hysterical, "Him! Him!" It is not until Scene Two, when Archer surreptitiously picks his nose when Immanuel is off-stage, that we recognize retrospectively that the first act contains Harry's attraction to, distrust of, and fearful longing for the protective and destructive presence of his brother.

In the second scene, Immanuel unhinges Archer even more effectively than Harry has the soldier in the first. He moves from the seducer to the diseased sufferer, from the peddler of relics (his own toenails) to the efficient cleaner of fish, changing roles that keep the practical Archer off balance, on the defensive. At the end of the scene, Archer reluctantly uses the toilet (he does not approve of the fact that the door has no lock), only to discover that it will not flush. "Anything can be straightened! You could straighten out the whole world if you wanted to," he says as he tries to straighten the float-ball rod. He then goes on to connect his remarks with Harry, who was never able to get into the Air Force because, unlike the Congressional-Medal-winning Archer, he got airsick: "You throw up in a plane, you clean it up and keep going." Finally the toilet flushes, only to overflow on Archer's feet. As he rushes off to the station, Immanuel shouts after him, "It's Harry's toilet! His! His!" a pronominal curtain that not only balances the end of the first scene but insists that in Harry's world, Archer too is a failure. "You do not see things as they are," Immanuel tells Archer, and later Harry says, "I got a blue guitar, you know. I see things as they are."

Although Ribman uses the appropriate Wallace Stevens quotation for an epigraph, the play does not suggest superiority—only difference—in Harry's vision. In the last scene, it becomes clear that what Immanuel did to Archer is a routine familiar to Harry and that he probably stayed out of the apartment to give his friend the opportunity to perform their shared fantasy. In this scene,

Harry insists that he is leaving for Paradise ("It's summer all the time in Ohio"), but his search for his belongings, his attempt to prove that a clown is always a clown (he rolls Immanuel in a mattress and tries to make him drink from a glass without using his hands), and his quarrel with the neighbors downstairs, which leads to his arrest, keep him from meeting his brother at the train station. As he is taken down the stairs, he cries, "Archer! Archer!" and Immanuel, alone on stage, still trapped in the mattress, gives the last pronoun line: "Me, Harry. What about me? Me!" Both Harry and Immanuel come through as victim and victimizer, a point that Ribman presumably wants to make through the German setting, through Harry's use of clown in relation both to the Nazis ("we will put on the clown moustaches") and to their victims ("the Dachau circus"). *Harry, Noon and Night* is a difficult play, at once funny and gross on the surface, unnecessarily complicated in some of its references, tenuous and sometimes contradictory in its connections, but it is an ambitious and fascinating attempt to use black comedy to transform a potentially conventional character and situation into a statement about human beings that transcends the specific.

Although *The Journey of the Fifth Horse* (1966) grows out of *The Diary of a Superfluous Man*, it is far more than an adaptation of the Turgenev story. Apparently working from the ironic note at the end of the story, the matter-of-fact statement that the manuscript was rejected by the publisher's reader, Ribman invents the reader (Zoditch) and tells his story along with that of Chulkaturin, showing two superfluous men, two fifth horses, one of whom does not want to recognize the other. The fifth horse, in Turgenev, is an extra horse harnessed to a four-in-hand, one that is not only useless but is attached to the others in such a way that he cannot help hurting himself; in Ribman, in which Chulkaturin's diary description is put into the mouth of his lawyer, the same combination of pain and pointlessness is indicated. The story of Chulkaturin's abortive courtship of Liza—her romance with the Captain, her marriage to the old family friend—is essentially Turgenev's plot, although Ribman comes down even more heavily on the essential separateness of the diarist, both in that story and in the scenes in which we see him with his lawyer, his doctor, his housekeeper.

Aside from the opening scene, set in the publisher's office, the entire action takes place in Zoditch's rooming house—scenes that actually happen, those that he imagines (in which he is performer) and those that come out of the manuscript. Paralleling the rejection and death of Chulkaturin is the double rejection—the real and the fantasy—of Zoditch. As he reads the manuscript, he peoples the story with characters from his own life. The publisher's daughter, whom he imagined he might win, thus becoming master, stands in for Liza; his cheeky assistant becomes the Captain; and the printer, who did accompany the daughter to the publisher's funeral and seems destined for the promotion Zoditch will not get, becomes Liza's husband-to-be. Like Chulkaturin, Zoditch sees love where there is none, not only in his fantasy conquest of the publisher's daughter, but also in his assumption that his widowed landlady wants to marry him. Responding to the scene in the diary in which Chulkaturin watches Liza burst into tears and assumes that she is his, Zoditch mutters, "You cannot make weddings out of tears! There is nothing written down here to make weddings from!" Ironically, just before that scene, Zoditch has done some fanciful marriage-making of his own, imagining himself pursued by the landlady because she—about to ask him for a raise in rent—has sent him extra coal and kerosene. As the play progresses, all of Zoditch's exasperated exclamations over the manuscript become comments on himself, although it is not until the end that the connection becomes clear enough to him to make him want to disown it. "This is a story of lies! . . . I reject this manuscript. I reject you," and finally, throwing the manuscript away, "I am the one that is loved. There is no other ending."

Some of the incidental comedy in the Chulkaturin scenes seems clumsy and unnecessary (a bit about the sex of a bullfinch), and the voice that opens and closes the play with the description of a monkey that reaches from his cage and tries to hold a passerby comes across as literary icing, but on the whole *The Journey of*

the Fifth Horse is effectively theatrical in its manipulation of the
dual roles and dramatic in its creation of a constant tension between the live Zoditch and the dead Chulkaturin. The play is full
of indications of how alike these two dissimilar men are. The most
impressive comes in the ball scene in which Chulkaturin becomes
irrationally angry at the Captain, a scene that draws its intensity
from the fact that it recalls Zoditch at the beginning of the play,
uncontrollably angry at the manuscript, abusing the handwriting
and the lack of punctuation, building to "a vacuum, a wasteland, a
desert, a void, a . . . ," sputtering off into incoherence. It is
Zoditch that gives depth to the dramatization of Chulkaturin's
story and vitality to Ribman's play.

The *Ceremony of Innocence* (1967) is a less interesting play
that the earlier two. Set in eleventh-century England, it uses flashback sequences to explain why Ethelred will not come out of
seclusion to defend his kingdom against Danish invasion. His desire for peace in England has been frustrated by the direct opposition of the fire-eaters, including his murderous, honor-mouthing
son, who finally provokes his own death; his attempt to use that
uncertain peace to bring prosperity and the civilizing arts to all his
people has been undermined by the delaying tactics of his presumed supporters, who do not want to risk their special privilege
for the general welfare. "The time is never better," says Ethelred,
rejecting the argument of his most loyal adviser, who suggests
putting aside his dreams for a more appropriate time. "We are
ever in a war, out of a war, preparing for a war, finishing a war."
The Ceremony of Innocence is almost an illustration of the Yeats
lines that provide the title—the opening section of "The Second
Coming," which serves Ribman as epigraph—but in the play there
is no rough beast slouching its way toward Bethlehem to be born.
Underlying the political surface is a personal story, almost a sexual one, which is little more than suggested in a few scenes; yet the
play implies that the murder of Thulja, the Danish princess who is
hostage to England, is, for Ethelred, the loss of more than an
image of the world he fails to create. The characters, however, are
no more than animated attitudes, put into action to prove a point

in each scene, occasionally the same point too often. The play uses its historical setting to make an intelligent, if forlorn, comment on our own time, but it does not flesh out its intelligence with dramatic and theatrical vitality as the two earlier plays did.

Jean-Claude van Itallie is plainly the most successful of the new playwrights. His *America Hurrah* (1966) ran off-Broadway for more than a year and has been produced all over the world. Success aside, van Itallie—much more than Ribman, whose work is far too idiosyncratic—is typical of the new playwrights. He joined the Open Theatre shortly after it was organized in 1963 and, as he told a *New York Times* interviewer (November 27, 1966), learned "how you could build a play—working with actors —you could build it from the inside out." It is obvious that his plays, like those of Megan Terry, reflect particular acting exercises and theories of characterization in use at the Open Theatre. His similarity to other playwrights—Lanford Wilson, for instance— who have not had his particular workshop experience suggests a larger family resemblance off-off-Broadway than that imposed by a special writing situation.

America Hurrah is made up of three short plays, two of which were produced off-off-Broadway in 1965 under other titles. *Interview* was called *Pavane* at that time, and *Motel* bore the title later given to the plays as a group; the third play, *TV*, was first presented as part of *America Hurrah*. What the three plays have in common is an attitude toward our society which can best be seen in van Itallie's description of them in the *Times* interview as "about aspects of being alive right here and now in America today —with all the implications that has, including the war in Vietnam and the advertising on the subways and everything else." There may finally be something self-defeating about the amorphousness of van Itallie's statement, about a satirical stance that seems to find all targets the same size, but there is purposive inclusiveness in that "everything else" ("the whole socio-moral-educational-economic-psychological structure," as van Itallie said in a *New York Times* article, September 17, 1967, in which he expalined why an artist must be political). *America Hurrah*, like the work of many of the younger playwrights, attacks a presumed societal malaise in which everything from napalm to plastic flowers is considered symptomatic. The theater is a part of that "out of whack" structure, as van Itallie admitted, and presumably *America Hurrah* in becoming successful became part of the decadence it set out to attack. That possibility, however, is a matter for van Itallie to worry about in future plays.

Motel, the most unusual of the three plays, was written before van Itallie joined the Open Theatre. "A Masque for Three Dolls," as its subtitle says, it consists of a mechanical recitation of the comforts of the motel (and of the society it reflects) which goes on and on while two gigantic doll figures act out a sex-and-violence ritual in which they smash the furniture, rip up the bedclothes, cover the walls with obscenities, and mutilate the motelkeeper. Toward the end of the motelkeeper's recorded monologue, which mixes bromidic generalizations with a catalogue of the material delights she offers, she begins to talk about the "Shelter motel" she is planning ("Everything to be placed under the ground"), a death-image description which becomes another catalogue, drowned out at last by screaming sirens and rock and roll music that grows louder and louder. The destroyers, the play suggests, are the creation of the destroyed. Presumably, the final effect is to be horrifying, but, in production, there was a kind of grotesque grace about the dolls—for instance, when the girl doll curtsied so cunningly after adding dribbles to the giant penis she had chalked on the wall—which made the play attractive in a way that defeated its satirical effectiveness. It almost turned into a likable sick joke.

The three "real life" characters in *TV*, a girl and two men, a triangle of sorts, work at a control console in a television viewing room where their day is acted out alongside the television shows that they sometimes ignore, sometimes become absorbed in, but can never escape. The television programs are presented by actors on stage, sometimes in pantomime (when the sound is turned down), and emphasized by stills—variations of the business on stage—flashed on a screen that hangs above the playing area. From the beginning, there are parallels between the "real" and the television action; for instance, the heroine of a Western protests the hero's leaving ("Oh, Bill") while the older of the two men, who is having an affair with the girl, explains in a phone call to his wife that he cannot get home for dinner. Sometimes these are no more than cute side-by-sides—most of them not particularly apparent to me when I first saw the play in production. It is in the total context of the play that the parallelism has dramatic relevance. As the play progresses, the television performers enlarge their playing area; finally, during the last show ("My Favorite Teen-ager"), they take over the whole stage. A witless story of a girl who does not want to go on a date because the wrong boy has asked her, this final television show is played against the viewing-room triangle. The lines begin to be the same on and off screen, and the play ends with the television characters grouped around the "real" people, reacting with imitation canned laughter to the lines that have now become pure situation comedy. This imaginative use of television parody is tempered in part by the quality of that parody itself. There are very good bits—for instance, the frighteningly bland talk show in which an unctuously sincere lady interviewer questions a green beret who has opted out of the war in Vietnam. She punctuates his troubled speech—"every day I saw things that would make you sick. Heads broken, babies smashed against walls"—with a complacent "I know," and then edges into a platitude ("War is horrible") and a race toward the final commercial. This is an exception, however. For the most part, the parody is quite conventional, not remarkably different from the self-congratulatory kidding that comedy specials frequently aim at the medium itself.

The same kind of pop-culture playing (in fact, some of the same routines) can be seen in other van Itallie plays—*It's Almost Like Being* (1965), a parody wartime movie musical, and *Where Is de Queen?* (1966), a play about a man's dream world, which is inhabited in part by television evocations. I suspect that van Itallie's parody material is partly a product of an Open Theatre exercise described by Joseph Chaikin in an interview in *Tulane Drama*

Review (Winter, 1964); called "perfect people," the exercise allows the actor to work with Madison Avenue images to help him "understand the stage as a weapon." In introducing *It's Almost Like Being* when it was published in *Tulane Drama Review* (Summer, 1965), Richard Schechner, in a note that was almost like being no comment at all, used a comparison with pop art to imply that the play was something more than a clever variation on a familiar joke. It isn't. Satirical groups such as *The Second City* and *The Establishment* have come up with sharper routines than most of those van Itallie creates. It is only his dramatic use of parody, the overlapping areas of reality (or artificiality), that makes *TV* an interesting play. To be fair to him, his stage directions indicate that this is what he is really interested in in the script, but it is difficult for an audience, continually bombarded by jokes at television's expense, not to respond to the parody itself and to use the indifference of that response as a judgment on the play.

There is little doubt that the third play in *America Hurrah* (the first in order of production; I have been discussing them in reverse) is in part the product of an Open Theatre exercise called the "transformation." The best description of this device, which Open Theatre borrowed from the Second City Workshop, can be found in Peter Feldman's director's notes to Megan Terry's *Keep Tightly Closed in a Cool Dry Place* (in *Viet Rock and Other Plays*). "It is an improvisation in which the established realities or 'given circumstances' (the Method phrase) of the scene change several times during the course of the action." The performer then, with no formal transition, becomes a new character or the same character in a new situation or at another time. This is not simply a way of developing facility in the actor; to the Open Theatre, it is a way of questioning the conventional idea of reality. A character is defined not by the social and psychological influences on his past, but by his visible acts. A play constructed out of this exercise becomes—as van Itallie's *Interview* indicates—a shifting group portrait, built of bits of action and quick character sketches.

Van Itallie's play, in which eight performers (four men and

four women) fill the changing roles, begins as a multiple job interview and then spreads its combination of impersonality and questioning widely enough to indicate that everyone needs help and
that no one—certainly not the priests, the psychoanalysts, the
politicians—can give it. As the original title suggests—although
the piece is certainly not a *pavane*—the total effect of the play, in
which movement and music thread through a pattern of miniature
scenes, should be that of an ensemble moving in a performance
that has thematic unity, not a group of characters acting out a
story. The difficulty with *Interview* is that its hastily glimpsed
characters and the scenes they play are stereotypical, the stuff of
pop culture treated nonsatirically. "We aren't afraid of ideas and
means that are naïve and primitive," Chaikin said in the interview
quoted above, but his declaration is not unambiguously positive.
The danger implicit in the "transformation" device and the sim-
plistic idea of character that accompanies it is that it can lead to a
work which allows for impressive ensemble playing but which
offers an audience only newly dressed commonplaces. Perhaps,
after all, Broadway and off-off-Broadway are sisters under the
skin.

These limitations are much more obvious in the work of Megan
Terry, a much less imaginative playwright than van Itallie. Except
for *Ex-Miss Copper Queen on a Set of Pills* (1965), a sentimental
character comedy, all of Miss Terry's work is developed in terms
of Open Theatre transformations. There are two basic plays—
those, like van Itallie's *Interview,* in which the performers assume
ever-changing roles, and those in which the transformations work
out of a dramatic context rather than a playing situation. The
former include *Calm Down Mother* (1965), a play in which three
actresses presumably present woman in all her variety, and *Viet
Rock* (1966), Miss Terry's best-known play; the latter include
The Gloaming, Oh My Darling,[4] a play about two old women in a
nursing home, an extension of one of the bits in *Calm Down*

---

[4] Miss Terry and her publisher, Simon and Schuster, show a reluctance to
give dates. I assume that all the plays mentioned here not identified with a
date are from late 1965 or 1966. The collection was published in 1967.

Mother, and *Keep Tightly Closed in a Cool Dry Place* (1965). Still a third kind of transformation is that in which the performers rather than the characters change. It is used in the Senate committee scene at the end of Act I of *Viet Rock,* and in *Comings and Goings,* a collection of stock male-female scenes, played by a reserve of performers who are sent into action, often in midscene, by arbitrary decision or the use of chance methods.

There is little point in a detailed discussion of Miss Terry's work; some consideration of *Viet Rock* and *Keep Tightly Closed* should give an indication of what she is up to. I am at a disadvantage in talking about *Viet Rock* because I have not seen it on stage and, as Miss Terry says in her production notes, "the visual images here are more important than the words." It is a pacifist play with its major emphasis on the sense of human loss in the war. This can be seen—on the page, at least—in two of those important visual images. At the beginning of the play, the actors are lying in a circle on the floor, forming "a giant flower or a small target." The flower becomes a target and ends in a huddle of dead bodies, "a tangled circle . . . the reverse of the beautiful circle of the opening." From what I read of the New York performance, this double image was not very clear to the audience (Walter Kerr saw the opening flower as "a kind of Busby Berkeley human circle"—*The New York Times,* November 27, 1966), perhaps because the material that filled the play-long break between images prepared them for nothing so subtle. The sketches are conventionally pacifist—broad parody of predictable types (Senators, superpatriots); sex-violence juxtapositions that let the author play with concepts of manhood; crudely worded and heavily sentimental tugs at the heart ("Please God, he's only nineteen,/He has only six more months to go"). Miss Terry says that the scenes were played "with an attitude of light irony" which might undercut some of their obviousness, but the tearjerker strain is too omnipresent in her work ("Oh my God! Oh my God! She's still holding on to her purse," says the drunk lady of the dead mother after the wreck in *Comings and Goings*) for me to believe that she intended such scenes to be taken other than at face value. At the end of the play, the dead arise, and the actors pass through the auditorium, each stopping to touch a member of the audience. "They must communicate the wonder and gift of being actually alive together with the audience at that moment," says the stage direction. "The gesture is patronizing and presumptuous," wrote Walter Kerr.

Keep Tightly Closed places three men in a cell together and lets them act out shifting relationships in their own characters or through transformation scenes which, according to Peter Feldman, in his director's notes, "are based on improvisations done in our workshops for the past three years." These include movie bits—the torturing of a noble Indian, an historical-epic death scene—treated comically or sentimentally and sometimes both at once. The characters in the cell are a lawyer who paid to have his wife murdered, the young man who did the job very sloppily, and the go-between. What seems to be going on in the play is that in the earlier sequences there is a pattern of two against one (always shifting), based on the unlikely possibility that one of them can be forced to take the blame; and then, at the end, they are a group, a father and his two sons, and finally parts of a single machine. They become a machine at other points in the script—a visual image like the flower in *Viet Rock*—but the significance of the image (the mechanization of the human? the possibility of unity?) escapes me. This is not surprising, since the comments by the author and two of the play's directors, Feldman and Sidney S. Walter (an Open Theatre alumnus who did it in Minneapolis), indicate that no one is very sure what the work is about. My suspicion is that, like so much of Miss Terry's work, it is for the actors rather than the audience. If the central movement of the script is the one I find there—from divisiveness to unity—that too may be no more than a lesson for the actors: how to get a genuine ensemble production.

Miss Terry's work is interesting only in the abstract, as an indication of one of the ways in which actors and playwrights may work together. All that she has done so far is to repeat the banalities of popular drama and the movies in juxtapositions that make very obvious points or no point at all. She does add an insistent homosexual tone to the mix, but I doubt that that is of any value. Her three actresses in *Calm Down Mother* are given an overt caressing scene (a hair-combing bit), and the two old ladies in *The Gloaming*, remembering when they were sixteen, kiss one another, imagining boys. The three actors in *Keep Tightly Closed* have direct homosexual scenes and transvestite bits in which one becomes the dead wife. The tough sergeant in *Viet Rock* persists in calling his recruits "girlies" or "ladies," long after the usage has any meaning as a realistic training device. None of this is done with the tone of chi-chi camp—tiresome enough in its own right— that one gets in a play like Rosalyn Drexler's *Home Movies* (1964). At one point in *The Gloaming*, Mrs. Tweed remembers riding in the snowy Maine countryside on a horse with her doctor father, a recollection which elicits Mrs. Watermelon's "That's what I mean, just one sentimental perversion after another."

Although Sam Shepard is not as closely identified with the Open Theatre as Megan Terry and Jean-Claude van Itallie, he has worked with the group, and his plays reflect a similar dependence on transformation. Except for *Melodrama Play*, the most recent of his published *Five Plays*,[5] which has something approximating a conventional plot, his plays are all constructed in the same fashion. He puts a number of not very well differentiated characters into a situation in which an undefined something seems to be going on and lets them talk, either in long monologues or in exchanges that tend toward single-sentence lines. It is possible to find meaning, in the traditional sense, in his works, to assume that the bookcase chore in *Fourteen Hundred Thousand* is a lifetime task, unwillingly undertaken; that *Icarus's Mother* is about the bomb; that *Melodrama Play* is incidentally concerned with making satirical points about the pop-music industry. Yet the communication of ideas is not Shepard's concern. Of *La Turista* (1967), he told a *New York Times* interviewer (March 5, 1967), "I mean it

[5] Shepard and Bobbs-Merrill share the shyness about dates of Miss Terry and Simon and Schuster, but I assume that all the plays in his 1967 collection date from 1965 and 1966.

to be a theatrical event, that's all." In explaining that Shepard's images "do not relate to the spectator by reflecting outside reality (they are not psychological or political)," Michael Smith, in his director's notes to *Icarus's Mother*, says, "It's always hard to tell what, if anything, Sam's plays are 'about.'" In the director's notes to *Red Cross*, Jacques Levy says, "Sam is more interested in *doing* something to audiences than in saying something to them."

Red Cross, probably the most interesting of the plays, provides a good introduction to Shepard's work. It takes place in a cabin in which everything is white. As it opens, Jim and Carol are in conversation, and she goes into a long monologue describing an imagined skiing accident in which she is totally destroyed. After she leaves, the Maid enters, and she and Jim discuss his crabs, which he proposes to cure by switching beds with Carol. Then there is a long sequence in which he tries to teach the Maid to swim, viciously pushing her beyond her capacity until she gets cramps and drowns (over his protests: "Will you please cut it out?"). She finally turns into some kind of fish, sitting on the edge of the frozen lake waiting for summer to come. Carol returns and announces that she is being eaten by bugs. As Jim turns to look at her, a stream of blood running down his forehead becomes visible to the audience. "What happened!" she asks. "When?" he replies.

The structural balance of the play is clear enough. The enacted drowning is a counterpart of the described skiing accident. The visible blood on Jim's head picks up a verbal image at the end of Carol's monologue: "All you'll see is this little red splotch of blood and a whole blanket of white snow." Shepard's directors tend to talk of his work in terms of the metaphors that he uses, but the metaphors, even when they are obviously connected, as in *Red Cross*, do not add up to anything specific. This play conveys a sense of menace, but it does so in a strangely distant fashion. Unlike Pinter, whose situations at once attract and repel audiences, commanding empathy and refusing information, Shepard simply presents images which tease, which are neither intellectually nor emotionally satisfying.

If disorientation is an Open Theatre desideratum, as Peter Feldman suggests in *Viet Rock and Other Plays*, Shepard should be the ideal Open Theatre playwright. I suspect, however, that his method is his own and that its effectiveness is limited. *Red Cross* is the only Shepard play I have seen, but I came away from a reading of *Five Plays* fascinated by some of the images—the bookcase business at the beginning of *Fourteen Hundred Thousand,* the drowning sequence in *Red Cross,* the beating of Drake in *Melodrama Play*—but only indifferently aware of the general movement of the plays as whole works. Often bored, sometimes annoyed at the verbal excess, I was also left with a feeling that there was a more interesting imagination stumblingly at work in Shepard than in either van Itallie or Miss Terry. Since Shepard is only in his twenties, the possibilities are heartening.

Michael Smith and Maria Irene Fornés are other playwrights who have worked with Open Theatre, but there is as yet no evidence of the kind of influence indicated for the three dramatists discussed above. The only Smith play I have read is *I Like It* (1963), which antedates the Open Theatre. It is a mother-son play all of which takes place in bed, with her dominant in the first scene, him in the second; except for the opening gag—we are several speeches into the play before we realize who they are—there is not much to it. Miss Fornés, whose *The Office* (1966) closed before its scheduled Broadway opening, has published two plays, *Tango Palace* and *The Successful Life of Three,* which were done as a double bill in 1965 at the Firehouse Theatre in Minneapolis, part of the O.A.D.R. project. The first is a tiresome two-character struggle (three scenes: master-pupil, parent-child, lover-lover), apparently intending some kind of general comment on the ambivalence of existence, the attraction of that which repels, which Miss Fornés, whose preface to the play is full of ponderous statements about the conflict betwen art and the search for meaning, would prefer us not to understand too quickly. *Successful Life,* which is subtitled "A Skit for Vaudeville," is a funny piece in many scenes in which Three (a plump, middle-aged man) does all the things a hero should while He (a handsome young man) stands around wondering why a good-looking, bright guy like him is not making out.

The work of Lewis John Carlino contains reminders that the transformation is not all that new as a playwriting device. As long ago as 1957, in *The Brick and the Rose,* a cityscape play in which a boy is destroyed by an environment that is more brick than rose, Carlino wrote forty-six characters to be played by ten performers. It was not until *Telemachus* (1963) that he put a name—"A Collage for Sounds and Voices"—on the form. The device is much older than that, of course, a borrowing from radio, but Carlino presumably got it from Dylan Thomas, whose *Under Milk Wood* (1953) showed the possibilities of the form for a staged reading. The opening of *Telemachus,* in fact, is a direct steal from *Under Milk Wood,* one that suffers greatly by comparison. "Downsville Town. Pre-dawn silent. Silent in the compromise of sleep. Dreamdumb. Downsville Town, trembling along its orbit to the vortex sun that waits somewhere beyond the nocolor and the night-cadenzas of snores and grunts and sighs," begins The Prophet, Carlino's narrator, and how one aches for Thomas' "It is Spring, moonless night in the small town, starless and bible-black. . . ." Even Downsville is not as funny as Thomas' Llareggub (*bugger all* backwards). Nor is there any point to Carlino's opening since his play is not, as Thomas' is, a portrait of a small town. It is a highly conventional—if many-voiced—play in which a young man goes to Hollywood, almost consents to its corruption (he sleeps with anyone, man or woman, who may help him sell a story to a studio), comes to know that his script is "one, big, romantic cliché" but that its idea (life can be beautiful) is true. "Maybe I can *be* the story," he says and returns to the girl and the bastard son he left behind. This is a simple bluebird-of-happiness story, although it is masked by the Dylantante opening and the mythic search for the father (Carlino admits a debt to Joyce) implicit in the title.

It was *Cages,* even more than *Telemachus,* which made Carlino the young hopeful of 1963. That double bill—*Snowangel* and *Epiphany*—and a later one, *Doubletalk* (1964)—consisting of *Sarah and the Sax* (1962) and *The Dirty Old Man*—give a better indication of the kind of play Carlino is comfortable with. Less pretentious than his "collages," these one-acters are simple gimmick plays, glossy and clever and finally quite empty. In *Snow-angel*, a man comes to a whore, demanding that she reenact his meeting with his lost love, and ends by playing out her one real romance. In *Epiphany*, an ornithologist who has discovered how to turn himself into a rooster is determined to use that knowledge to assert his masculinity, finally to dominate the wife who consistently outpoints him in games and implies that he is homosexual; when the metamorphosis takes place, he tries to crow and lays an egg. The plays are full of invention, scenes that performers can have fun with—the museum meeting in *Snowangel*, the game of Simon Says in *Epiphany*, the use of the saxophone as defensive weapon in *Sarah and the Sax*—but the total effect is dispiriting. The plays remain theatrical games, which would be all right if it were not for the whisper of serious subject matter that reminds us how shallow Carlino is. Even the whisper was gone from *The Exercise* (1968), Carlino's Broadway debut, but there was no successful gamesmanship to fill the emptiness.

In *This Is the Rill Speaking* (1965), Lanford Wilson wrote a "collage" play which, following Thomas' example, he called simply "a play for voices." It *is* a portrait of a small town, very Thorton Wilder in tone, in which Willy dreams of becoming a writer of a work in which "the *wonders* of Nature" would talk (hence the play's title) and "make people *really notice*"; this is that piece, but the voices are human, each so familiar, so bromidic that without emphasis no one—Willy included—would *really notice*. In some of his other plays, the performer who plays multiple roles seems to be operating in a manner much closer to the transformation as Megan Terry uses it in *Calm Down Mother*. In *Wandering* (1966), a short play which Wilson calls "a turn," two of the three characters make abrupt switches to become a gallery of accusers (friends, relatives) of the central character's refusal to conform. In *The Madness of Lady Bright* (1964), Boy and Girl fill changing roles in scenes with the leading character or complementing his monologue. Not that this device is Lady Bright's claim to fame. The play is an exception to the practice of short runs off-off-Broadway, having played 168 performances at the Caffe Cino and then, on a double bill with Wilson's *Ludlow Fair*

(1965), a brief commercial run off-Broadway. It is, if anything, an acting tour de force about "a screaming preening queen, rapidly losing a long-kept 'beauty,'" but it is such a collection of loneliness clichés that it is difficult to imagine a performance impressive enough to keep it from being a bore.

Although there are similarities between *This Is the Rill Speaking* and *Lady Bright* in the use of performers, *Rill* is much closer in style to Wilson's full-length plays, *Balm in Gilead* (1964) and *The Rimers of Eldritch* (1966). Both are large-cast plays with most of the characters on stage all the time. The scenes, which are often no more than brief exchanges, blend into one another and conversations overlap; the action is stopped occasionally and played again (in the trial in *Rimers*, Nelly is sworn in three times) or is repeated exactly later in the play. The basic intention, presumably, is to present an environment, a community, although both plays have simple, old-fashioned plots—presented somewhat indirectly—on which to hang the character decoration. Except for the overlaps and the repetitions and a certain amount of playing around with the set (the customers in *Balm* move all the props at one point, turning the coffee shop around), the plays are very like Elmer Rice's *Street Scene*. *Rimers*, like *Rill*, takes place in a small town (an almost abandoned coal town), but here the amiable banalities have become vicious. What we discover in the course of the play is that Skelly Mannor, the town eccentric (hermit and peeping tom), everyone's butt, was killed trying to save young, crippled Eva Jackson from assault by apparently clean-living Robert Conklin. The acquittal of the woman who shot him is the victory of propriety over truth, for the one person who defends him, the owner of a diner, is disbelieved because the town does not approve of her taking a young lover in her lonely, middle-aged widowhood. It is not Nelly standing trial, the Preacher says, but "the soul and responsibility of our very community." He means their having allowed Skelly to wander free in the first place, but Wilson intends the line more generally, and the glimpses into the lives of the characters make his obvious point.

Balm is set in *Lady Bright* country, an all-night coffee shop on

Upper Broadway, peopled by addicts, pushers, hustlers, prostitutes. The central character is Joe, a hustler who tries to turn
pusher, a young man who imagines that he is superior to his
surroundings. "You see me standing around," he says early in the
play, "you'd think I was just as stupid as the next guy." That line,
and the spotlight on him, should be indication enough that he will
not make it to the end of the play. In Act I, he has the hint of a
romance with Darlene, a not very bright young girl about to turn
professional; given the play's setting, they simply go to bed together, but functionally, in the face of the conventional plot, their
love scene is the key moment which saves (happy ending) or fails
to save (pathetic ending) the young man on the edge of disaster
(see all the 1930's prison movies). Pathetic in this case, for in Act
II, Joe, who has not really been able to push the stuff, is killed by
the supplier (named Chuckles, of course) who assumes that Joe
has been holding out on him. Toward the end of the play, the
exchanges that opened it are repeated, presumably to suggest that
the scene goes on, although there is no destination, and that the
disappearance of Joe, or of any of them, provides a hole that is
filled immediately by the nervous activity of the crowd. The implications of the action, however, are not the same as its effects. The
play comes across as a saccharine portrait of the subculture of
Needle Park, which Wilson describes as though he were Victor
Hugo talking about the beggars of Paris: "Their language, their
actions, their reading of morality is individual but strict." Here
and in all his work, Lanford Wilson dresses standard theater
stereotypes in the kind of mannerisms that passed for truth in the
heyday of dramatic regionalism. That is why *Street Scene* is a
usable analogy.

Leonard Melfi, like Wilson, is an off-off-Broadway veteran
whose work seems more conventional than experimental. He, too,
resembles Carlino, but not the Carlino of the "collage." Most of
Melfi's one-acters are simple character confrontations that depend on surprise to get through to the curtain. In *Halloween*
(1966), for instance, a mock ladies' man (actually a virginal
cripple) and a happy, faithful wife (actually a woman unable to

hold the love of a husband with a wandering eye) meet and—
after the putting on and taking off of Halloween masks—embrace.
Birdbath (1965) is an even fakier play, for, unlike *Halloween*, it
pulls a switch instead of unveiling a carefully prepared surprise. A
young poet, temporarily a cashier in a midtown restaurant, somewhat reluctantly asks into his apartment one of his fellow workers,
a nervous girl, apparently a virgin who tremblingly wishes that she
were not. After they do a deal of drinking, which relaxes her and
lets him swim in self-pity, we are ready for the denouement. What
Melfi has prepared for is one of two schmaltzers: either the initiation of the innocent, or the poet's last minute decision not to
violate that innocence. In either instance, the poet would conventionally find himself. Instead, as he approaches her, she whips out
a blood-stained kitchen knife to defend herself, and, lo and be-
hold, we discover that she has murdered her mother that very
morning. He puts her to bed and then writes a poem about how
sad dead birds are, what with their wings and all, and—since she
has never had one in her whole life and since it is that day—he
brings down the curtain with, "I've just written you . . . a valen-
tine."

Less characteristic of Melfi's work, but more interesting, is
Times Square (1967), which seems to be trying to treat the "celebrated block on West Forty-second Street between Broadway and
Eighth Avenue in Manhattan" and its denizens in terms of a double image, of fantasy and of fact. The seven characters suggest the
types of that street (a hustler, a con man, a slummer), but they
are costumed outlandishly, like children playing a game. In fact,
that is one of the effects Melfi intends, for he directs that they
"speak and behave and react as though they were children: . . .
never weary . . . but sometimes, somehow, woefully uncertain."
Insofar as they come across as lost children whose dream world is
threatened by reality ("Leave the garden alone," is Mr. Fascination's word to those who want to change, to clean up the Times
Square area), Melfi is being as sentimental about his characters as
Wilson is about their uptown equivalents. The unusual thing about
the play is the particular balm in this Gilead, the way in which

Melfi uses the movies. He directs that the two sides of the auditorium be hung with signs representing the movie houses that line that block of 42nd Street, and the play opens with three of the characters talking about what is playing (mostly gangster or monster films) and passing out tickets to the audience. The movies and the attitudes involved in them are treated with satirical affection, as in Laura Jean's monologue in which she describes how she and Mr. Fascination will get married and make "the sweetest-tasting syrup imaginable": "We'll keep a crystal vase near our pink and blue pillows, and after we wish and then after we kiss, we'll lower our faces to the very brim . . . and then we'll let the syrup flow from our eyes into the gentle crystal vase." The movies are also used structurally in what happens—not directly, but through the traditional Hollywood happy ending's being taken as a fact of fantasy. "How do you bring the dead back to life?" asks Mr. Fascination after Marigold Sobbing has been shot; they tell him to kiss her, which he does, and she revives.

The play, however, is not simply a comic fantasy; the language keeps turning it back to the factual 42nd Street. As Mr. Fascination carries Marigold out at the end of the play, she is telling again the story of how she saved the people trapped in the airplane, following Captain Prince Charming's direction, by kissing the golden button that released the escape ladder. The reiterated "kiss it," like the "stop *sucking* at us like that" in Mr. Fascination's monologue about the seven of them as peppermint sticks, brings us back to the sexual delicatessen of Times Square and reminds us that the movie houses, the dream palaces are the resting places, the cruising stations, the base of operations for the hustlers and prostitutes. *Times Square* is a joke and a game and a piece of penny candy with a soft center, but its use of movies is more inventive than that of any of the other young dramatists, most of whom play around with the content of films but not with the juxtaposition of content and context.

The real or apparent similarities among dramatists that made possible the groupings earlier in this chapter are not usable for the plays and playwrights considered below. They are a disparate group; all that they have in common is that there was something —a scene, a character, an idea, some dialogue—about each of their plays that made me want to suggest that they are worth paying attention to. Terrence McNally's *And Things that Go Bump in the Night* (1964) and Lawrence Osgood's *The Rook* (1964) are exceptions, in that the virtue of their plays lies not in an agreeable part here and there but in the work as a whole. The McNally play (I am speaking of the published version, not the one that flopped on Broadway) is still another destruction parable in which a bizarre family group attempt to save themselves from *It*, the nameless fear outside their basement sanctuary, by rejecting the no longer workable virtues of Grandfa ("Was. I was choking on that word. The time is. I am") and the wavering, self-pitying, jargonesque commitment of their victim ("Shakespeare, Florence . . . someone in the park. That's what I believe in"). Ruby and her two children choose evil and attempt to survive through the ritual sacrifice of a new victim invited into the sanctuary each evening, but their choice is no solution. *It* comes in the end. McNally's achievement is that he manages to convey the pain of his characters despite their nastiness, which is often very funny.

The Rook is a small power struggle, comic in some of its detail, in which chess provides both the setting (a game at two in the morning in Washington Square) and the analogy. Edna (Queen) attempts to protect her husband Alf (King) from the attack of her son-in-law Rico (Rook), often by using her daughter Adele (Pawn) as a weapon. The end is somewhat ambiguous. Although Rico wins the chess game, the last scene, in which Edna comforts Alf, suggests that she is still protecting him and that Rico has not won the larger game within the family. The chess analogy, although Osgood uses it well, would severely limit his play if it were not that the battle between Edna and Rico has dramatic validity in its own right, immediately perceivable even to one who does not know his king from his castle. Osgood's *Pigeons* (1963) has some of the fascination of *The Rook* as one watches the shifting relationships among the three women, but the ending, in which the most powerful of the three forces the other two to imitate pigeons and then joins them in their dance, reduces the play to an amusing trick. It is as though Osgood watched a group of pigeons bobbing and trilling together, decided they looked like ladies, and converted the image into a play; unlike *The Rook*, in which chess helps reveal the characters, *Pigeons* has little to say about either ladies or birds.

The characterization of the titular heroine of William Snyder's *The Days and Nights of Beebee Fenstermaker* (1962), particularly in the first act, in which she arrives, chirpingly expectant, in New York City, gives the play a quality that is superior to its obvious theme (dreams fade) and its sentimental ending. There is some interesting comic writing in Oliver Hailey's *Hey You, Light Man!* (1963), notably in Lula Roca's account of how she lost her children to the bears, but it is far too extended a treatment of the old illusion-reality theme in the traditional theater context. There are a few moments in Lee Kalcheim's *. . . And the Boy Who Came to Leave* (1965) in which the characters display themselves by a funny or a painful game (a poetry-reading scene in which Jonathan recites while Sidney puts in the "Bitter bitter bitter bitter," and the stage fills with smoke from burning sausages) which are better than the play itself, a disappointing descendant of *The Wild Duck*. In the one-act *Match Play* (1964), Kalcheim is more obviously in control, but that story of a grown-up spoiled brat, frustrated by his draft board, his father, and the girl he wants to seduce, is too slick to command much attention; its use of golf seems almost gratuitous compared to the use of chess in *The Rook*. John White's *Veronica* (1965) is an intellectual farce in which an escapist burglar teaches a pair of song writers that the commonplaces of fashionable despair are as much clichés as the boy-girl-June-moon of their trade and thus breaks the block that has kept them from writing; its strength lies not in its message, but in the fact that it is funny.

A generalization on which to end this chapter? Almost impossible and probably misleading, but let it be this. A great many of the

young playwrights, particularly those working outside the traditional commercial theater, are moving away from subtleties of
characterization and idea and going for their effects to shifting
images and a direct use of obvious sentiment. As the plays of the
1950's reflected the then prevalent acting style, born in the Actors
Studio, polished in television, so the new plays derive techniques
from the current emphasis on ensemble playing and the actor's
exercises that further it. It will be at least ten years before we
know how new or old-fashioned these plays and playwrights are.

Finally, a phenomenological postscript. Barbara Garson's *Mac-
Bird!* (1966) is more interesting as a sign of the times than as a
play. An anti-Establishment tract, it borrows the plot from *Mac-
beth* and a pastiche of Shakespeare quotes to draw a venomous
cartoon in which the leading figures, representing Johnson and
John and Robert Kennedy, all motivated by lust for power, share
a common desire to impose American mastery ("The Pox Amer-
icana") on the world. More crude than funny, verbally inept in
most of its parody, its chief claim to fame is that, in letting Mac-
Bird kill John Ken O'Dunc, it manages to suggest that Johnson
murdered Kennedy. Although Mrs. Garson cheerfully adopted
Dwight Macdonald's assumption (*New York Review of Books,*
December 1, 1966) that it was the borrowed plot that forced the
murder on her—this despite the fact that she dropped Banquo and
added the Players from *Hamlet*—her remarks to an interviewer
from the Washington *Post* (November 27, 1966) probably represent a more characteristic attitude: "I really think I've got Johnson right *even if he didn't do it*" (Italics mine). The success of
MacBird! lay less with its literary (it was a best seller before it
reached the stage in 1967) and dramatic worth than with the
accidental conjunction of a number of audiences: the young,
whose distrust of adults was particularly strong toward those in
power; those opponents of the war in Vietnam whose distaste for
Johnson was so strong that any weapon seemed attractive; the
intellectuals who felt the need to support or attack the enthusiastic

if bewildering advocacy of critics like Macdonald and Robert Brustein; and, most of all, the curious, who were drawn to it by the yards of free publicity ground out by reporters, for whom it was news, and reviewers and columnists forced, by assignment or inclination, to embrace it, denounce it, or at least mention it.

EIGHT

The Other Theater

The mission of the Cabal, if it has one, is
so to ennoble function that even eating and
excreting will be raised to the rank of arts.
    —BALTHAZAR IN *Justine*

In an early scene in Bob Merrill's *Henry, Sweet Henry* (1967),
the adolescent villainess and date broker assures the girls that she
can still wangle them invitations to the Knickerbocker Greys Happening; all that means, she explains with a shrug, is the annual
dance. When two dozen members of the National Episcopal Student Committee and the Episcopal Peace Fellowship staged a
demonstration, spiced with entertainment and an agape feast, at
the general convention of the Episcopal Church in Seattle, showing their support for the Presiding Bishop, the Right Reverend

John E. Hines, *The New York Times* (September 24, 1967) described it as a "religious 'happening,' the first to be staged at a major church assembly in this country." *Away We Go*, the 1967 summer replacement for Jackie Gleason's television show, had a regular feature called "A Happening," which turned out to be a vaguely mod label for a standard comedy sketch. To advertise the new L&M Golden Hundred, a disparate group (a yogi, a skin diver, an investment broker, some picnickers) were gathered around a park fountain, each busy in his own way and always with cigarettes at hand, in a commercial that called itself "A Happening." On radio station WIBG in Philadelphia, one of those nauseous voices that exist only on disc-jockey shows bawled out, "This is a happening," and then records were played as they are all day in any case. Tisha Fein, the twenty-one-year-old co-owner of The Psychedelic Conspiracy, a store on Los Angeles' Sunset Strip, told C. D. B. Bryan (*The New York Times Magazine*, July 2, 1967), "Oh, yes, well people over 30 come into this store and ask what it is. I tell them it's a happening." With the term having been appropriated by the mass media, the pop-culture merchandisers, the advertisers, if not by the teen-agers to whom they cater, *happening* has become a vague term which implies spontaneity, youthfulness, permissible chaos, fashionable *now*-ness. This constant din makes it difficult to talk about the Happening as a theater or art form.

There are other difficulties. Until *Nine Evenings: Theatre and Engineering*, a collateral relative of the Happening, played at New York's 25th Street Armory in October, 1966, Happenings were usually performed for small—often invited—audiences. The coterie nature of the activity can be seen not only in the names that keep turning up in descriptions of Happenings, in which one night's director becomes the next night's performer, but in remarks like that of Susan Sontag (in *Against Interpretation*); "in the audiences one sees mostly the same faces again and again." Since the pieces were designed for a few performances at most,[1]

---

[1] Allan Kaprow, in *Assemblage, Environments & Happenings*, indicates that it was the impermanence of the Happening that made it so attractive to artists who had already been drawn to perishable substances ("like toilet paper or bread") as the materials for their constructions. He suggests that Happenings

they could not draw audiences over a period of time, as a play with a run can, and since there were no published texts (in fact, no texts at all in the conventional sense), very few people were qualified to comment on them. This situation has changed within the last few years with the publication of a number of works, in part descriptive, in part theoretical, which give some sense of what the form is about; the published scripts are not particularly useful for they are simple notations by which the activity is controlled or working notes of the artist for a piece whose final script was never written down. Since my own experience of the Happening is severely limited (to an occasional Environment and an evening at the Armory), this chapter is dependent for its material, if not for its opinions, on Michael Kirby's *Happenings* (1965); Al Hansen's somewhat gushy *A Primer of Happenings and Time/Space Art* (1965); the issue of the *Tulane Drama Review* (Winter, 1965) devoted to the new theater, of which Michael Kirby was guest co-editor;[2] Claes Oldenburg's *Store Days* (1967); and Allan Kaprow's *Assemblage, Environments & Happenings* (1967). Many of the ideas in these books are derivative; they provide more detailed treatment of theories put forward when the movement was in its youthful heyday, by Allan Kaprow in *Art News* (May, 1961) and Harriet Janis and Rudi Blesh in the chapter "Environments and Happenings" in *Collage* (1962), a book that is stronger on reporting than interpretation.[3]

There is a necessary caveat for anyone approaching this new abundance of material. Most of it has been written by artists directly involved in the production of the pieces concerned, and the general impression one gets is that there is a vitality, a richness, a wit, an intensity in these productions which may not have

---

should be performed no more than once unless their scenarios are so designed that the repeated performance will not resemble the original one.

[2] Elsewhere in the chapter, this issue of the magazine will be identified simply as *TDR*.

[3] Susan Sontag's "Happenings: An Art of Radical Juxtaposition," which is good on the antecedents of the form, might be considered such a seminal essay if it had been published in 1962, the date assigned to it in *Against Interpretation*. Since it did not appear until the January, 1965, edition of *The Second Coming*, it belongs with the later works.

been there at all, which may be an after-the-fact creation called up by a committed description. By way of corrective, consider an incidental remark of Richard Schechner, a convert to the Happening, in an interview with John Cage in *TDR*: "The thing that bothered me about the Happenings I've seen is that they were obviously rehearsed but badly done." It is worth wondering if Miss Sontag's remarks on audience involvement as "the dramatic spine of the Happening" is an admission that she was bored when she was not attacked. La Monte Young's "What little of the audience still remained . . ." (in his comment on Dennis Johnson's *Avalanche* #1 in *TDR*) is an implicit audience put-down, but it may have been that the audience boredom was the result of vapidity in the work or clumsiness in the production such as that which sent me out of the Armory after twenty minutes of John Cage's *Variations* VII.

The interesting thing about the new theater is that it is not a revolution from within. It is a separate operation, an artistic endeavor less concerned with cleansing the conventional theater than with finding its own aesthetics. "They're a form of museum," John Cage said of "those theatre people" in the *TDR* interview. ". . . we should just be grateful to them for doing what they're doing and not bother them." Even so, he manages to work up a deal of outrage at Alan Schneider and George Grizzard and their concern "with the *Hamlet* situation," as though the new-theater artists were not as self-congratulatory as ordinary theater practitioners are. Insofar as the Happening is a revolutionary form, it is an implicit attack on the conventional theater, and a few of its advocates, like Dick Higgins in *Postface* (1964), can be genuinely vituperous. Still, it is probably more sensible to put aside, for the moment, the ways in which the "other" theater impinges on the conventional one and try to get some sense of what the Happening is. *TDR* indicates the variety to be found in the new theater and makes quite clear that dancers and musicians are as busy with the new form as painters and sculptors are. Still, the Happening, in its most publicized (and best documented) form, is the creation of the artists. For that reason, it may be best to begin with art and its audience.

I have no intention of turning myself into an art-appreciation lecturer, exploring the painterly problems of line, color, and composition. An understanding of art in those terms says less about the line between art and the theater, so finely walked by the Happening, than does a recognition of a pervasive response to painting and sculpture which even abstract art could not kill. Unless a man's artistic response has completely stifled his human response,[4] he will want to know what is going on in a painting—dramatically. For this reason, museum-goers find figures in abstract paintings ("Very like a whale"), a philistine pastime not far removed from the accepted critical theory about action painting—that the art lay in the doing, not the done; the dramatic content of a Jackson Pollock painting, then, became the act of painting itself, an off-stage (off-canvas) drama implicit in the great swirls of dribbled paint. How much more obvious this response is with pictures that contain figures, which tell stories or give the viewer a chance to invent his own; a narrative picture, in which the figures (performers) stand against a background (a set) seen through a frame (a proscenium arch), is a kind of frozen theater. The figures, blessed (or damned) with permanence, are caught forever on a single gesture ("For ever wilt thou love, and she be fair!"), but the experience is an active one insofar as the viewer invents a dramatic context of which he becomes a part. The most obvious example can be found in children, who have a way of wanting to climb into pictures; the most vivid in Antonin Artaud, whose description of Lucas van den Leyden's *The Daughters of Lot* (in *The Theater and Its Double*) is the recreation of an intense metaphysical drama enacted at the Louvre, more his invention than van den Leyden's. Perhaps in an age of spectators, only children and madmen enact such dramas, but I suspect not. It would be difficult to find a more self-conscious performer than myself—a perfect model of an observer—and yet I have been involved for

---

[4] To artists and art critics: I know, I know, artistic response *is* a human response, a sharpened sense of perception.

years in a drama peopled with figures from Thomas Eakins' paintings.

Some artists, of course, connive in this kind of game; it is the whole point of *trompe l'oeil* painting. Take a venerable example—Charles Willson Peale's *Staircase Group* (1795). In that painting, Peale has placed two of his sons on a stairway (unpainted wood so vivid that you can almost feel it in your fingers' ends) and called them back before they could climb out of sight. One—full figure—has paused in the act of taking a step, turning his head to see what his father (or I) want of him. The other, farther up the stairs, is looking around the edge of the picture, one finger lightly touching that edge as though it were a door frame. The painting is so arresting that generations of viewers have expected the boys to step back into the room or thought to follow them up the stairs. The Philadelphia Museum of Art has recently and unnecessarily heightened the effect by lowering the picture almost to the floor, framing it with simple wooden strips that suggest a door casing and building an actual wooden step that leads into the picture.

Among contemporary artists, Michelangelo Pistoletto has gone Peale and the *trompe l'oeil* painters one better by fastening life-size figures, derived from photographs, to a mirror-like steel surface which actually lets the spectator see himself in a dramatic scene—one of a crowd of demonstrators or an interested eavesdropper standing behind a nude woman talking on the phone. Sculptors, too, invite this kind of dramatic situation. George Segal's life-size figures inhabit recognizable environments. His staircase group—*Couple at the Staircase* (1964)—is inviting in the way Peale's is, but his has actual depth rather than the trick of perspective. It would seem quite natural to step past his kissing couple, open one of the real mailboxes on the wall, and, one's hand full of bills, start up the real stairway. To take that step—when the piece was shown at the Sculpture of the Sixties show at the Philadelphia Museum of Art—one would have had to climb over one of those fancy ropes that museums use in furniture wings as a polite way of saying "Keep Out"; as a result, Segal's sculpture was more a drama watched than participated in. Perhaps his plaster figures are too fragile to share the stage with clumsy humans. Not so, Marisol's wooden figures. When her cocktail party (*The Party,* 1965–66) was shown, one could wander among the figures, a guest among guests.

A number of artists, in recent years, have been expecting more than observation from their viewers, but not necessarily the kind of conventional dramatic response that I have been describing above. The hit of the Sculpture of the Sixties show—at least with the children and with the adults who went to the museum to be amused—was Lucas Samaras' *Corridor* (1967). Popularly known as the "mirror house," it invited people to remove their shoes and wander through. It consisted of three rooms, angled off one another, so that the exit was never visible from the entrance. The opening at either end—one of which was much smaller than the other—could serve as entrance, but the effect depended on which way one went; the corridor either opened out to let one expand or the mirrors pushed in, forcing one to crouch his way into the museum outside. During the brief walk-through, one was accompanied (or assaulted) by distorted images of oneself. Samaras' piece is simply an exaggerated example of the kind of art work which demands that the observer establish with it a sensory relationship beyond the visual, one which depends less on the content of the piece than on its shape and material. This is not a new idea, of course. Public statuary, whatever the intention of the sculptor, has always been forced into an active space relationship with the people who come in contact with it, as Charlie Chaplin testified in *City Lights* in the scene in which the unveiling revealed him asleep in the statue's lap. In a park near my house there is a statue of Little Nell standing at the feet of Charles Dickens, who sits in a chair placed on a high pedestal; the polished spots—hand holds and stepping places—indicate that children who probably never cried over *The Old Curiosity Shop* have found a way of climbing Nell's frame to reach the unreachable Dickens pinnacle. The small hippopatamus in a mother-child group at the Philadelphia Zoo has taken to wearing a cloth saddle in the summer to keep from burning the legs of small children, who understand instinctively that statues are to be touched not just seen.

Lucas Samaras, who did for museum-goers what amusement-park fun houses have done for their patrons for years, has been a regular performer in Happenings, particularly those of Claes Oldenburg. The connection is an obvious one, for Happenings ("the strange, perishable, impossible 'collages of action'" as Janis and Blesh call them) are the result of the attempts of a number of artists to do something for (or to) their audiences and with their material that would help erase the line between art and life, at least remove the formal barrier of the art show in which the gallery or the museum asks art work and spectator each to stay in his place. According to the neat pocket history of Happenings, paintings climbed off the wall, enveloped the spectator, set him to work and, lo, the Happening was born. By the end of World War II, the collage, which had been a revolutionary form before the first world war, was a respectable art form, a way of letting the painting edge its way into space and yet stay in its frame, on its wall. In the 1950's, the collage exploded into the assemblage or the "combine" as Robert Rauschenberg called his creations, such as the highly publicized *Monogram* (1959), which had a stuffed goat prominent among its materials. That photogenic goat attracted attention, but he was no more than a sign, a reminder that rubber tires and bedsprings, undainty junk of all kinds, had replaced the bits of newspaper and torn photographs that once graced collages. Assemblages escaped frames, finally escaped walls. They learned to hang from the ceiling, to sit on the floor, finally to become the room itself, to be an Environment.

Although there are historical precursors of the Environment, both acknowledged (Clarence Schmidt's wonderful mountaintop near Woodstock, New York, the photographs of which are the most exciting thing in *Assemblage, Environments & Happenings*) and unacknowledged (the restoration at Williamsburg, Virginia), the form, according to Janis and Blesh, had its contemporary rebirth in 1956 when Allan Kaprow, distressed that his art show looked like an art show, hid his paintings behind peep holes, obscured them with blinking lights, buried them in an Environment, *Penny Arcade*. The most famous of the Environments is probably Claes Oldenburg's *The Store* (1961), set up in a store building on Second Street in New York. "The static object is shown by me as one of a number of related objects," he said in a statement in *Happenings*, "in a particular 'real' place—itself an object." By this time, the Environment had been cued for action. In his statement in *Happenings*, Kaprow says:

> I immediately saw that every visitor to the Environment was part of it. I had not really thought of it before. And so I gave him occupations like moving something, turning switches on—just a few things. Increasingly during 1957 and 1958, this suggested a more "scored" responsibility for that visitor. I offered him more and more to do, until there developed the Happening.

In 1959, Kaprow's *18 Happenings in 6 Parts* was performed at the Reuben Gallery in New York. Shortly after that the constructed Environment began to disappear; the Happening moved outside, or into a found environment; sometimes it became ambulatory, spread over an extended area.

Since Kaprow is the artist most consistently identified with Happenings, partly because the name derived from his work[5] and partly because he has devoted himself almost exclusively to the new form, his development as an artist (assemblage to Environment to Happening) makes a convenient paradigm for the development of the art form itself. Kaprow, of course, sees the history of the Happening this way, as the title of his book indicates. Michael Kirby is less convinced. In his introduction to *Happenings*, he lists a number of actual or possible influences on the Happening which emphasize the theatrical aspect of the form, which keep it from being seen simply as an animated Environ-

[5] He first used the word when he published "Something to take place: a happening" in *Anthologist*, XXX (1959), 5–16. A number of the activities suggested in that script were used later that year in *18 Happenings*. Everyone involved with Happenings, including Kaprow, apologizes for that name. None of the other terminology—either conventional (*play, theater piece*) or unconventional (Oldenburg's Ray Gun Theater, Ken Dewey's Action Theatre, Carolee Schneemann's Kinetic Theatre)—has risen to the generic as *Happening* has. Michael Kirby, in using that name for his book, not only recognizes a pervasive usage but helps to harden it. The most recent, post-McLuhan contender is "mixed media theater," which may finally replace the earlier usage particularly as the Happening becomes more and more an event that neither needs nor want spectators.

ment. From the Dadaists, the Happening presumably got its non-linear structure and its performance conventions; from the Surrealists, its refusal to divide the animate from the inanimate, its dream content, its "symbolical and oblique treatment of sexual material." Although a number of the Dadaist and Surrealist plays have been translated and published recently, notably by Michael Benedikt and George E. Wellwarth in *Modern French Theatre* (1964) and although their influence can be seen in the work of Kenneth Koch and Lawrence Ferlinghetti, those movements are still more widely known as art movements; the unpeopled art work of pop artists and assemblagists, like Jim Dine and Claes Oldenburg, who staged some of the first Happenings, have been labeled Neo-Dada for years. Dadaist ancestry hardly contradicts the Kaprow theory of development, particularly when one recognizes that the most important inheritance from that source, shared by Happening and nontheatrical art work alike, is a distrust of art. Oldenburg in *Store Days* insists that he wants to create "Just a thing, an object. Art would not enter into it."

Among the practitioners of the new theater there is a persistent sense of release, a recognition that each has escaped from the restrictions of his own art into a new freedom or a new challenge. Kaprow (in *Assemblage*) calls the movement from painting to assemblage, "an escape hatch for others, who were looking for a new way of working that would avoid the restrictions imposed by 'pure' painting." In his statement in *Happenings*, he describes with some intensity his "disagreement with the gallery space," the feeling of being trapped by walls which finally sent him and his Happenings outdoors. Ann Halprin, in an interview in *TDR*, explains how she left the conventional modern dance world to set up an experimental workshop on the West Coast: "I didn't know what I wanted to do except to leave that scene." She no longer identifies her work with dance. Ken Dewey, who had tried to work in the conventional theater as a technician and a playwright, says (in *TDR*), "I was trying to get out. I mean that literally: out of the text, out of the building, and, most earnestly, out of theatre's way of doing things." It is tempting in the face of such statements, to ascribe the whole movement to an aesthetic respiratory problem, a discomfort in the disciplinary air of conventional art, but that would be an oversimplification. There is a certain amount of playful anarchism in the new theater, but there is also a deal of hard work (consider the way Ann Halprin's Dance Workshop spends years exploring a problem, rehearses for months and then performs infrequently) which suggests a serious (if amused) approach to new problems in aesthetics. The movement may be pervaded with rhetoric that suggests the tune-in-turn-on-drop-out slogans of the hippie world ("The enemy is bourgeois culture," writes Oldenburg in *Store Days*, and happily adds, "Bohemia is bourgeois"), but that is the language of artistic protest already familiar from the Dadaists.

Kirby also cites Antonin Artaud as an influence on the Happening and the Bauhaus theatrical experiments as, at least, an analogue. The English translation of Artaud's *The Theater and Its Double*, the most widely read (or at least discussed) theater book of the last decade, appeared in 1958, the year before Kaprow's *18 Happenings*. The social implications and the metaphysical assumptions in Artaud's book call into doubt Kirby's statement that "the general theory . . . is almost a text for Happenings," but if that "almost a text" phrase were attached to Artaud's specific suggestions about production, it would be accurate enough. The Happenings share Artaud's assumption that theater is not primarily verbal, not bound by a written text, and that words are to be used not for their meaning but for their sound. Artaud's insistence that theater must free itself from the tyranny of masterpieces should be attractive to artists committed to the impermanency of art. The publication of *The Theater of the Bauhaus*, a collection of theoretical articles dating from the early 1920's, came too late (1961) to be a formative influence on the Happening (nor did it reach the large audience that the Artaud volume did), but it shows some of the Happening techniques—most obviously, the use of the human performer as prop rather than character—in operation thirty-five years before their rebirth in the Reuben Gallery. Kirby also suggests more generalized pop-culture and literary influences, but these are too amorphous to be of value unless one is pointing to a specific artist or event; even then, the value is questionable. Red Grooms may say that his *The Burning Building* (1959) is an extension of the backyard theater he built as a boy after seeing Ringling Brothers Barnum & Bailey (as he did in *Happenings*), and Oldenburg's *Injun* (1962) may have been inspired in part by a half-remembered Wallace Beery movie (as *Happenings* says), but the crudeness of boy's theater is more important than the circus in the first instance, and the movie, in the second, has relevance only to the setting—the empty house provided by the Dallas Museum for Contemporary Arts.

The direct influence of such men as John Cage and the dancers Merce Cunningham and Paul Taylor is much clearer than that of historical movements or sister media. Cunningham has been working with chance methods since the early 1950's, and Taylor did early work with movements that were not conventionally related to one another. According to Kirby, both Kaprow and Robert Whitman attended a Taylor concert at Rutgers University, in which a girl's voice announced the time and with each tone Taylor made a movement (such as turning his head) and then returned to his original position.[6] Cage is the most pervasive influence, not only because of his own work, but because a number of the creators in the new theater—Kaprow, Dick Higgins, Jackson Mac-Low, Al Hansen, George Brecht—have been students of his; in *A Primer of Happenings*, Hansen, with all the do-you-remember enthusiasm of an old grad at Homecoming, reminisces about Cage's class at the New School in which most of these men took part. Cage can be seen most clearly in the Happening in their use of indeterminacy, which he brought to his own compositions by working with chance methods, and in their use of materials and gestures from life, the equivalent of the concrete sounds, the auxiliary noises (including silence) which he introduced into his own work. Neither of these concepts is Cage's invention; as earlier

---

[6] The dance Kirby is describing is presumably *Epic* (1957). Doris Hering's description, in her review in *Dance Magazine* (December, 1957), gives a somewhat different impression of the work.

paragraphs indicate, they came to the Happening in part through developments from painting and Dadaist borrowings.

Cage's real claim to being father of the Happening (not that he makes such a claim) lies not in his being a teacher or a theorist, but in his having staged the first Happening, seven years before Kaprow's work provided that label. This ur-Happening was performed in the dining hall at Black Mountain College in 1952. The chairs were arranged in the center of the hall under a canopy made of Robert Rauschenberg's "white paintings" ("To Whom It May Concern," Cage wrote in *Silence.* "The white paintings came first; my silent piece came later"). Each of the performers was assigned an action and, within established time brackets, was free to perform as much or as little as he wanted. Cage delivered a lecture, which included silence, from a raised lectern or a ladder (there is no very exact account of the piece). From seats among the spectators, Charles Olsen and M. C. Richards climbed ladders and recited poetry. Rauschenberg played records on a victrola. David Tudor played the piano. Merce Cunningham performed a dance in the space around the audience. A film was projected on the ceiling, showing first the school cook and then the sun, which moved across the ceiling, down the walls, and disappeared. The whole thing ended with a ritual pouring of coffee. As Kirby points out, the Cage piece may have been suggested by the publication in 1951 of *The Dada Painters and Poets,* Robert Motherwell's collection of Dada documents, which includes Kurt Schwitters' *Merz* (1920), with its description of a Happening-like theater that never got off the page. In any case, the Black Mountain performance and the Cage concerts during the 1950's, which made use of performing elements other than those traditionally identified with musicians (pouring water from one cup to another in the 1952 *Water Music*), were leading as surely to the Happenings as the concurrent development from assemblage to Environment to Happening.

Scattered through the paragraphs above are a number of references to this or that aspect, borrowing, technique of the Happening, as though it were a carefully defined art form, easily recognizable and plainly distinguishable from conventional theater. That is not the case. Most of the artists involved are not rigid theoreticians, but men working from a general sense of what they want to accomplish, which is expressed—if at all—in random jottings that sprout with contradictions. Thus Oldenburg in *Store Days* can write, "I have no desire to do environments but I will do a room," and two pages later, "it is my intention to create the environment of a store." Although Kaprow made some attempt at definition in his *Art News* article, it was Michael Kirby, in his introduction to *Happenings*, who made the first consistent effort to define the elements that make up the genre. The scripts and the descriptions that provide the bulk of Kirby's book cover what might be called the classic period of the Happening—the work of Kaprow, Oldenburg, Jim Dine, Red Grooms, Robert Whitman (all once connected with the Reuben Gallery) between 1959 and 1963, work which at every turn seems to contradict Kirby's neat definitions. Still, if the Happening is to be discussed at all, one must begin with at least tentative definitions.

Since Happenings are sometimes thought to be spontaneous creations, improvisations growing out of a happy confrontation of performer with prop and setting, it might be best to begin by recognizing that they are performances based on scripts or scores, usually rehearsed (to some extent), in which—however uncontrolled the details—the final pattern reflects the creator's conception. The score can range from a single sentence of description in a performance in which there is a high degree of indeterminacy to a complex set of directions, such as the six-foot scenario for 4/66 (1966), which was designed, as Richard Schechner told me in a letter, so that "we knew at each minute exactly what was happening or where it would happen or what situation it might present to the audience." The group in New Orleans, of which Schechner was a part, was working in a much more formal way than was the case with the early Happenings.

Indeterminacy was a part of the Happening from the beginning. The performer was often given an area of choice: to perform or not to perform within a given time, to determine the duration of his assigned task, to do the task in the manner that he found most congenial. In "The New Theatre," his essay in *TDR*, Kirby makes an attempt to differentiate between improvisation, which he sees as a creative process, and indeterminacy, which involves only the performer's option within assigned limitations. In the case of simple decisions (when to move, in what direction), his definitions may make sense; in more complicated instances the line of demarcation disappears. In Oldenburg's *World's Fair II* (1962), for instance, two men placed the inert body of a third on a table, climbed up beside him and methodically searched him, emptying his pockets, and secret hiding places of all manner of small objects. Since Oldenburg did not prescribe the objects, the hiding places, or the search routine, the two performers were forced to invent and, as the description in *Happenings* indicates, became competitive in their attempt to startle the audience. When one of the performers pulled from the shirt front a rubber glove that for a moment looked like viscera, a creative improvisation was in process, however it fitted in with Oldenburg's general intention at that moment.

Accident, like indeterminacy, plays a part in the Happening and has, I suppose, since the dog that is said to have followed Merce Cunningham in his dance around the audience was accepted as part of the performance at Black Mountain. The description (in *Happenings*) of Robert Whitman's *The American Moon* (1960) says that "Whitman considered all sounds that occurred, whether intentional or 'accidental,' part of a noise pattern that was an integral element of the Happening," an acceptance that is a direct inheritance from John Cage, whose silent piece absorbed the rustle of programs and the scrape of chairs. A form which works so closely with the audience, which asks it to perform if only to the extent of standing or moving in a certain way, has to face the possibility of unpredictable reactions which the unconventional structure of the form must then absorb, largely by refusing to recognize that anything unexpected is going on. I assume that I witnessed such an unacknowledged accident when I saw Yvonne Ranier's *Carriage Discreteness* (1966) at the

Armory. It is a "dance" in which Miss Ranier (the choreographer with the walkie-talkie) directed the movements of a number of performers who walked about the Armory floor, carrying or stepping on materials of various sizes, shapes and consistencies. At one point in the midst of this relentlessly tiresome piece, a girl in ordinary street clothes (the performers were wearing rehearsal tights) and without a two-way wrist radio walked out onto the floor, picked up a piece of the foam rubber bric-a-brac, carried it to a new location, turned, and left. The general assumption—judging by the whispers around me—was that she was simply a bored spectator; if so, the "dance" made room for her, in fact went its methodical way, stifling the hint of conventional dramatic interest that her entrance had provided.

In his attempt to narrow definitions in *Happenings*, Kirby separated the Happening from chance theater. This last, however, is very much a part of the new theater movement, as the special issue of *TDR* illustrates. As early as 1951, Merce Cunningham used chance methods in devising *16 Dances*; at about the same time, John Cage began to use coin tosses, dice, and number tables in composing his works. Chance theater, as it has developed since then, takes in any kind of performance in which chance methods are used (either before or during the performance) to decide the elements or the order in which they are presented. In only one instance has chance theater been offered in a conventional-theater context—when Jackson MacLow's *The Marrying Maiden* (1966) was presented off-Broadway by the Living Theatre on a double bill with Ezra Pound's translation of *Women of Trachis*. In the MacLow piece, the order and duration of speeches and the way in which they were to be read were decided by chance techniques; for instance, MacLow made up a list of five hundred adverbs which became the basis for how lines were to be spoken. The director, Judith Malina, fixed the activity of the production, but it was interrupted at random intervals when the stage director passed to the performers cards, chosen by throwing dice, which called for a new action. The general response to the evening was a warm-hearted affection for Pound and Sophocles.

Indeterminacy, accident, chance are all ways of reducing the control of the artist over his material, of demoting the poet from maker to finder. The object—as it was fifty years ago when Tristan Tzara made a poem by pulling words at random from a hat—is to rescue art from the pedestal on which—or so the avant-garde always imagines—the bourgeois keeps it, to restore art to life. La Monte Young is an extreme example of that strangely ambivalent wing of the new theater which seems to be constantly saying, *look at me, I'm not here.* His *Composition 1960, #5*, which so far as I know has never been performed (although I would dearly love to see it), consists of letting one or more butterflies loose in the concert hall. He sweetly asks that, once the composition is finished the butterfly be allowed to go free; in fact, since the piece can be any length, he suggests that it be put on in a hall with open doors and windows and be considered over when the last butterfly escapes. In "Lecture 1960" (in *TDR*), a chance creation in its own right since its pages (like those in Marc Saporta's novel, *Composition No. 1*) can be shuffled and read in any order, Young quotes a friend of his who wants to improve on #5: "Maybe the butterfly piece should begin when a butterfly happens to fly into the auditorium."

To work my way back from the never-never land of La Monte Young's butterflies to the very real—if a little indeterminate and occasionally accident-scarred—Happenings in verifiable locations, let me report an item of gossip. Claes Oldenburg, also an advocate of the artist as finder, is said to have been very upset that his gigantic ice cream cone got so dirty when the Sculpture of the Sixties show was shipped from Los Angeles to Philadelphia. Such concern—even if it is apocryphal—presupposes a degree of artistic control that makes it possible to talk about the other elements that go into Happenings. The materials (which make sense of the phrase "collages in action") are those of the conventional theater—light, sound, physical properties, movement—but they are to be used, as in Artaud's "theater of cruelty," not as contributive elements to a text-bound production, but as events in their own right. If a performer marches across the gallery floor while Christmas tree lights flash and a record player churns out "Celery

Stalks at Midnight" on a 78 played at 33 speed, the marcher, the flashers, and the massacred song each makes an equal sensory claim on the spectator. The sound can be anything from conventional music to unidentifiable noise. Even words are possible, but the essential nonverbal character of the Happening demands that they be freed of meaning. Thus speeches may be obscured by mechanical means (at *Carriage Discreteness,* the recorded dialogue was wrecked by feedback, but since there were a number of mechanical hang-ups that evening—it was a typical bad night for the Bell Labs—it may not have been intentional) or by having performers speak at the same time; when the words are clear, they are ordinarily not relevant to anything going on or are meaningless. In Jim Dine's *Car Crash* (1960), one girl recited a long speech beginning. "The car in my life is a car with a pole in the harm of my soul which is a pretty clank . . . ," which does at least suggest the kind of implicit communication that one finds in Kenneth Koch's less rational plays. The physical properties may be anything at all, but they tend toward things that are pourable, stuffable, portable, inflatable, useable in some action or another, or noise-making things that can be kicked, dropped, pounded, rolled. Junk of all kinds is particularly popular, in part because it is easily and cheaply available, but more importantly, as Kaprow says of objects that go into assemblages, for the "high degree of associational meaning," because it possesses "a post-Surrealist nostalgia, a mood of reverie and gentle humor or irony." To put it less positively, most of the Happenings makers are camp sentimentalists. Aside from the materials mentioned, Happenings make extensive use of slides and movies. And, of course, live performers, but, as Michael Kirby says, "the performer frequently is treated in the same fashion as a prop or a stage effect."

The difference between the performer in the Happening and in the conventional play is that the latter portrays a character, the former simply carries out a task. The favorite example of the Happening task (both Kirby and Kaprow have used it) is sweeping. A performer may be asked to sweep a certain part of the performing area; he may or may not be told how (briskly, lethargically) or how long to sweep. Of course, sweeping can be a characterization device in conventional theater. In the production of *The Merchant of Venice* at Stratford, Connecticut (1967), Jerry Dodge established his conception of Lancelot Gobbo (Robert Morse as Peck's Bad Boy) in a sweeping bit worked into his first scene; his laziness, his cheekiness, his distaste for Shylock were all made clear by the way in which he used his broom. No Happening performer would do such a thing because he never sweeps as a character (an underpaid janitor, a kindly shopkeeper) but as himself. That is the theory, at least. In fact, since sweeping is an activity quite likely to induce reverie, daydreams in which mugging is appropriate, the Happening performer sweeps not as himself but as a creature totally absorbed in the act. With rare exceptions (Kaprow asked the girl in *The Courtyard*—1962—to assume the standard starlet pose for the photographers), Happenings performers are asked to remain expressionless while they carry out their tasks. It is the activity, the thing done that is important. The performing is "nonmatrixed," to use Michael Kirby's term, unattached to a character who can be defined in terms of time and place and psychology.

The nonmatrixed performing, to stick with Kirby's terminology, goes on within a compartmented structure. A Happening is not linear, as a play is, does not assume that there is a developing relationship between one section and another, that a cough in Act I must lead to a consumption death in Act V. In *Store Days*, Claes Oldenburg says that "plot to me is sentimentality, predetermination, an arrogance on the part of an author, a harmful fabrication which creates a residue of sentimental patterns that keeps men from perceiving experience." A Happening, then, has no plot, tells no story. It is a number of events, units which are complete in themselves, presented sequentially or—more often—simultaneously. Although presumably not linked in a conventional way, the compartments may be connected by a number of devices. Images may be repeated, such as those of emptying out and growth which recur so often in Robert Whitman's *Flower* (1963) that the description (in *Happenings*) suggests a definite symbolic pattern.

The compartments may be held together by the basic material used in most of the tasks, as in Whitman's *Water* (1963); by an environment which imposes its limitations on the tasks, as in the swimming-pool setting for Oldenburg's *Washes* (1965); by re-curring figures, such as the little girl in Oldenburg's *Gayety* (1963), who in one compartment enters on guarded skates and wearing a moustache, in the next removes skates and moustache and does a bit with a mirror, and for the rest of the Happening quietly covers herself with foil.

The circus provides the favorite structural analogy for the Hap-pening. One act follows another in rapid succession, doing its own business in one ring while simultaneous acts vie for audience at-tention in another. None of them are related, yet all add up to the total sense of circus. So the analogy goes, but it goes in a direction that the Happening theorists—who may not have looked closely enough at circuses—do not intend. I am not raising a quibble about the relatedness of circus acts. It is true that the two end rings in a three-ring circus usually have the same kind of act, often one that is related to the center-ring specialty in a way that will set it off as a star turn, but that fact does not kill the analogy. These are connections between compartments, such as those I have de-scribed in the paragraph above, and not the kind of communica-tion between units that one gets in a conventional play, where an action is fully perceivable only in terms of what has gone before. The circus analogy is dangerous to the Happening purist because a circus pulls an audience into conventional dramatic contexts. There is no overall plot, of course, but each act is conceived not as a task performed nor a skill displayed, but as a tiny drama. There is conventional suspense in the tight-rope walker's act as the performer (often playing a stereotypical role: the tramp, the drunk) weaves his way to safety on the far side of the ring. There are recognizable antagonists facing the protagonist in the lion-taming act and an implicit antagonist in the "death defying" trapeze act. There is even psychological characterization. The last time I saw the Ringling circus, the star clown happily stopped where I could see him and patiently, laboriously worked with a coke bottle and a box, a problem-solving routine that established a character (total absorption which suggested genius or madness) and, because of the intensity with which it was performed, turned the chaos of circus noise and movement into a protective wall. Admittedly, the clown was working to achieve this effect, and he was certainly no amateur (as the little girl in *Gayety* presumably was), but it is difficult to imagine that the performer in the Olden-burg Happening, however carefully she was programed to do tasks and however conscientiously she tried not to play a part, could escape becoming a character—at least for any member of the audi-ence who kept his attention on her.

It is impossible to free Happenings of conventional dramatic context—as the paragraphs on artistic response early in this chap-ter suggest—because neither the artist nor the spectator is willing (or able) to shake off habitual modes of reaction. The creators of Happenings, having grown up in a psychologically oriented society and been fed on plot-bound pop culture, cannot banish character and plot from their work. Some do not intend to. Red Grooms rightly calls *The Burning Building* a "play," for, despite the inci-dental detail (the girl's face becoming a clock and saying *tick-tock*), it was essentially a slapstick chase in which the pasty man was a firebug, alternately teasing and escaping from the firemen. It seems likely that Grooms, who was to do the masks for the 1964 production of Kenneth Koch's *Guinevere*, was as much influenced by Koch's early theatrical experiments (*Guinevere* must have been written about the time *The Burning Building* was performed) as by the Happenings of the other Reuben Gallery artists. If *The Burning Building* was a kind of slapstick movie on stage, Jim Dine's *The Smiling Workman* (1960), the Happening which I most regret not having seen, was a black-comedy vaudeville blackout. It consisted of a single performer (Dine) painting the message "I love what I'm doing" on a canvas. As he neared the end of the sentence, he painted faster and faster and, as if pro-pelled by the creative (destructive) impulse, drank down one jar of paint, poured the other two over his head and then dived through the canvas. Al Hansen did a more conventional black-out bit in *Parisol 4 Marisol* (1963), in which a man kissing a girl was tapped on the shoulder by another man; it was not until the third tap that the kisser turned and got a pie in the face. Dine's joke was more serious than Hansen's, however, as Hansen implies when he calls *The Smiling Workman* Dine's "first psycho-drama," probably aware that Dine used that word to describe *Car Crash* in a remark quoted by Janis and Blesh in *Collage*. In his statement in *Happenings*, Dine admits that his piece was probably funny to see, "but I do not think obsession is funny." What is clear is that Dine—not only in *The Smiling Workman* but in his other Happenings—is, like Grooms, close to conventional theater; he admits as much when he says (in *Happenings*) that his theater pieces are extensions of his habit of "acting out everything in everyday life."

The more confirmed antidramatic artists succumb—if a little less obviously—to the blandishments of plot and character. In *Injun*, plot-hating Oldenburg fabricated something very like the old Western kidnaping plot. In *Store Days*, he speaks of "my characters" and describes them in stereotypical terms as "the city-bird-child (chick) and the beggar. innocence and experience." He had a sequence in *Washes* in which two girls, in a *noli-me-tangere* confrontation, and two boys, fighting, presumably for the attention of the girls, were involved in a psychological drama, rich with implication, short on specific definition, that Harold Pinter might have conceived—had he been considering a nonverbal play to be performed in a swimming pool. Dick Higgins, commenting (in *TDR*) on the production of his chance-theater piece, *The Tart, or Miss America* (1965), says that there was "no psychological empathy" in the production and on the next page praises Letty Eisenhauer for playing the Tart as "an urban-minority trollop who was 'going places.'" In his statement in *Happenings*, Kaprow lists four levels on which he works (or worked in the days when his Happenings still were aimed at audiences), one of which—symbolic or suggestive meaning—traps him into statements which convert his performers from doers into characters. He calls the girl in *The Courtyard* (1962) variously Mother Nature, Aphrodite, and Miss America, any of whom would have to be recognized intellectually (perceived in dramatic context) rather than felt sub-liminally (a dozen or so spectators assured Kaprow later that they "sensed . . . that there was something like that going on"). If her "listening to the rock-and-roll music on the radio . . . was . . . the beautification of her own internal rhythms," then it was not an action "with no more meaning than the sheer immediacy of what is going on," which is what one of Kaprow's other levels of crea-tion calls for. When John Cage brought up "this symbol business" in the interview in *TDR*, Kirby explained that "most of *The Courtyard* I consider an alogical play rather than a Happening." He may keep his terminology intact that way, but he cannot hide the fact that Kaprow, like the rest of the Happening makers, has a way of mislaying tasks and slipping compartments, stumbling his way back into conventional drama.

Where the maker of the Happening does not lead, the spectator will find his own way. It is a simple matter to watch a task performed—two girls having a picnic in Robert Whitman's *Mouth* (1961)—and convert it into a drama. A good many of the ac-tions, even those in which a performer confronts a prop, certainly those in which more than one performer is involved, are implicitly dramatic, perceivable not as experience (the act of sweeping) but as a psychological situation (the sweeper). In *18 Happenings in 6 Parts*, for instance, there was an action in which two men worked together, moving blocks on a board, following directions given by a phonograph; it is just as likely that a spectator would see that action psychologically (a contest between the two men) or intel-lectually (humans controlled by a machine) as experientially (the movement of blocks on a board). In watching even so austere a work as *Carriage Discreteness*, which tries to avoid what Yvonne Ranier (in *TDR*) calls "theatrical bloat with its burden of dra-matic psychological 'meaning,'" I found that as soon as two per-formers came within hailing distance of each other I began to contemplate a relationship other than the spatial one. Lest this reaction be dismissed as a highly personal one, the response of a man with a strong allegiance to conventional theater, let me report that there were three instances in the production in which there was overt evidence of audience fascination with dramatic, psychological bloat. One was the entrance of the girl in street clothes—described above in the paragraph on accident—which set up a tension between performance and intruder, a suggestion that habitual action might be disrupted, a dramatic situation familiar to playwrights—Chekhov, for instance, who used it in most of his plays. The other two occurrences were events set into motion by pre-set timing stored in a memory system. At one point a man came swooping across the arena on a swing (I assume that it was the machine and not Miss Ranier's walkie-talkie that told him when to go), an event which provided the audience with an empathic situation, like the trapeze-act in a circus, designed to increase the pulse-rate, and at the same time gave the delight of surprise and the residual pleasure of recalling childhood daring. The third event was the most revealing of all. At one point, a James Cagney movie was thrown on a screen and, although there was no sound and the image was not particularly sharp, the audience turned its attention from the discrete carrying on the floor of the Armory and, familiar with the conventions of the screen, quickly placed the characters and guessed the plot; then they settled into an old-fashioned dramatic experience until the computer shut them off and forced them to look back at the "dance" or at their watches.

If the Happening seems to be at odds with itself in the matter of performance, as the concrete act shifts, sometimes unintentionally, into the dramatic scene, it is more obviously unsure of its final effect. Kirby says that the concrete details of a Happening may function as symbols, but as private, nonrational ones. Yet much of the material of the Happening is overtly satirical, and many of the makers of Happenings talk in terms of ideas about society. This implies rationality, public rather than private symbols, and a degree of informational communication. Kirby describes (in *TDR*) a chance-theater production, *The First and Second Wilderness* (1963), subtitled *A Civil War Game*, which is plainly a pacifist play in its totality and is harshly antiwar in some of its details (the burning of cardboard soldiers while Matthew Brady photographs of the war dead were shown by opaque projectors). Wolf Vostell,[7] the German artist (he calls his Happenings "decollages"), wrote (in Kaprow's *Assemblage*) of *You*, which he staged on Long Island in 1964: "The public is brought face to face, in a satire, with the unreasonable demands of life in the form of chaos, and is confronted by the most absurd and repugnant scenes of horror to awaken consciousness." Al Hansen, whose response to *You* was highly ambivalent, judging by his description in *A Primer*, says, "In Vostell's happenings one infers immediately the terror and depravity and awfulness of the concentration camp, of the dictatorship, of the monolithic state stamping on the individual." Hansen is given to old-fashioned responses (he finds *Car Crash* "poignant," the dance sequence in *Washes* "lyrical," Kaprow's work full of "pathos"), but his description of *You* does indicate how strongly it functions in terms of traditional theatrical communication. Claes Oldenburg calls his *Gayety* "a civic report on the community of Chicago" but "mine is poetic/satiric/symbolic." Dick Higgins in *The Tart* directs that "Performers offstage should laugh softly frequently and comment and whisper together, in such a way as to stress the moral values involved." This sounds like a joke, a parodic comment on social significance in drama, but I suspect Higgins is in earnest. I doubt the sense of humor of anyone who can expound on the value of a boxing ring as a stage (*The Tart* was played in a gym), as Higgins does in *TDR*, just as though Bertolt Brecht had not already made that speech. Higgins does know Brecht, as *Postface* indicates; in fact, Higgins' criticism of conventional theater tends to lapse into Brechtian distrust of the Aristotelian situation and psychological rigidity of characters. Although not a Brechtian in his works, Higgins is obviously the most didactic of the artists working in the new theater.

[7] Vostell is coeditor with Jürgen Becker of *Happenings* (Hamburg, 1965), a collection of scripts and commentary (in German, of course) and photographs which give a better idea of the international scope of the Happening and of the centrality of the American artist in the movement than do any of the American books with the possible exception of Kaprow's recent volume. Like the Happenings issue of *Kalender* (February, 1965), a much less useful volume although it contains good photographs, the Vostell-Becker book treats Happenings in a context which includes pop art and *nouveau réalisme*.

"I may have things to say about US and many other matters," says Oldenburg in *Store Days*, "but in my art I am concerned with perception of reality and composition." This is the other, the more doctrinaire, explanation of what Happenings are about. Events are to be seen not for their content, but for themselves. The spectators are to experience the concrete act, not an abstract idea that adheres to it. The value of the form—since the Happening, too, believes in art for health's sake—is that for creator, performer, and spectator the production is a seductive device that leads him to see more clearly. It "sharpens one's perceptions," says Schechner in the Cage interview, "simply because it makes one pay attention." I am highly suspicious of this rationale, for a number of reasons. For one thing, it presupposes a lack of awareness of the reality of activities in ordinary life. I have never seen George Brecht's *Three Aqueous Events* performed, but I find it difficult to believe that my perception of pouring as an activity would be heightened in any way by watching (or taking part in) a performance that consisted of placing three empty glasses on the floor and filling them with a pitcher. When I reach the bottom of this page, I am going into the kitchen and pour myself a cup of coffee, a space/time event that I will perceive visually and kinesthetically, in no way hampered by the fact that the activity has a practical end (getting me the coffee) rather than a celebratory one. To be fair to Brecht, who, as a member of the Fluxus group, makes no differentiation between art and nonart and finds the artist dispensable, he would probably consider my coffee routine as acceptable as any Fluxus event. In general, however the assumption of the Happening maker is that the concreteness of objects and activities is emphasized by their use in Happenings. I find it ironic that men who take such a high moral tone about conventional artists (see Oldenburg's remarks on the arrogance of the plot-maker, quoted a few paragraphs back) can operate so comfortably on the assumption that they can see a bundle of rags, a saluting woman, or the act of eating with a special clarity (there goes the artist back up on the pedestal) which they can somehow communicate by placing the act or the object in an unfamiliar context. John

Cage, who seems both to accept and to be suspicious of this mission of the new theater, told the *TDR* interviewers that Alan Watts once came to a concert of his and left almost immediately, saying, "I can hear this sort of thing outside, I don't need to be here."

It is quite possible that what I am doing in the paragraph above is playing a superiority game of my own ("I can see better than you can"), but even if I were to accept the validity of the general assumption, I would doubt the sharpening powers of the Happening simply because there seems to be a limited repertory of activities. Performers in Happenings are forever dressing and undressing, being wrapped up or unwrapped, walking, marching, saluting, carrying things, eating, smearing paint, pouring a liquid into something or over themselves. The list can be extended by introducing more equipment (automobiles in Oldenburg's *Autobodys*, 1963) or juicily tactile material (raw chickens, mackerel, and hot dogs in Carolee Schneemann's *Meat Joy*, 1964), but unless the activity is structured into a psychological or informational situation (as it obviously was in the Schneemann Happening), it is minimally interesting. After all, these activities are structured in real life, and the Happening creator who hopes to narrow the line between art and life actually widens it by putting a "real" activity in a situation which renders it "unreal." My perception of the act of pouring is much deeper after watching Laurence Olivier, as Astrov in *Uncle Vanya*, pour himself a glass of vodka (even though I know Olivier is not Astrov and the vodka is not vodka) than it is after watching a frozen-faced girl in black tights (who is really in black tights but is probably not frozen faced) pour herself a glass of real water, for pouring becomes a revelatory act in the first case. It is customary, on the analogy of *musique concrète*, I suppose, to use the word *concrete* to describe an activity divorced from contexts of meaning, but the terminology is misleading; surely a movement that might be concrete observed on the street becomes an abstraction when it is reproduced, unrelated to real (or fictional) character or social situation.

This is not intended as a definitional quibble. What I want to suggest is that the Happening, in its attempt to bring life into art, tends (except when it slips and falls into conventional drama) toward dehumanization. This is obvious both in the technique of performing Happenings (the nonemotive, automation-like doing of tasks) and in the fondness for obliterating the human shape (one event in Whitman's *The American Moon*—1960—is described in *Happenings:* "the three figures could be surmised to be costumed performers, but their shapes and movements were decidedly nonhuman"). In her Notes to *Meat Joy* (in Michael Benedikt's *Theatre Experiment*), Carolee Schneemann explains that she moved from painting to the theater, attracted by the "unlimited range of materials," and she lists, in this order, "objects, people, lights, sounds." The artists-turned-theater-men tend to think of the human being simply as another substance with a usable tactile surface and a bulk that can be maneuvered in space. I found frightening the double-page spread in Kaprow's *Assemblage, Environments & Happenings* in which the label "People Inside" (illustrated by George Segal's *Dinner Table*, 1961) faced the label "Statues Inside" (illustrated by a photograph of the wine pourers from Kaprow's *Eat*—1965—who were directed to remain motionless except when a spectator-consumer asked for wine). Kaprow may have intended this as a visual joke or as an insight that recognizes that man, too, is an object. To me, it looked like a denial that man is more than that. The antihuman elements in a number of the Happenings are really extensions of the attack on rationality implicit in the nonverbal quality inherent in all of them.

It is interesting that the artist, supposedly setting out to strengthen man's self-awareness, manages to display an obvious contempt for man. An ugly manifestation of this can be found in the open aggression of many of the pieces, so obvious that Susan Sontag identifies the abusive treatment of the audience as "the most striking feature of the Happening." At the simplest level this may be no more than an attempt to force the audience to perform, as in the production of Ken Dewey's *Action Theater* (New York, 1965), described so enthusiastically by Al Hansen, in which Dewey—like a YMCA director at a community sing—bullied everyone into taking part. John Cage told the *TDR* interviewers that he resented Kaprow's telling him (the audience) to move from one room to another in 18 *Happenings in 6 Parts*. Commenting on the audience's reluctance to take part and their occasional destructive reactions to a work, Kaprow (in *Assemblage*) admits that the latter may be "caused by the latent sadism in the action." *Latent* is an odd word to use in this context, particularly for Kaprow, whose A *Spring Happening* (1961) is the classic aggressive Happening. The spectators were herded into a long, dark tunnel with peepholes at eye level through which they could see very little of what was going on. The primary assault was aural, with violent sounds that could not be identified or placed in space. Great metal barrels were thrown down from a catwalk; recorded tapes growled menacingly; two performers—who could be seen in a mock, soundless fight with eight-foot tree limbs—pounded the walls with their clubs when they were unseen; a power mover was run over the roof of the audience enclosure. Finally, the end of the tunnel toward which the audience was facing opened, and an expressionless man began to move toward them, pushing the mower; as they backed toward the entrance, it opened, and they found themselves stopped by a large fan. Caught between the machines, the audience was bunched together until the walls of the tunnel fell away and let them escape.

If this is the best example of a physical assault on the audience, Robert Whitman's *The Night Time Sky* (1965) provides the best symbolic one. It ends with a film in which the camera is the toilet bowl, looking up as a cigarette is thrown in, as a man urinates, as a man defecates. Despite Whitman's admittedly "ponderous description" of the whole Happening (in *TDR*) and his assertion that he thought it funny, it is difficult to escape the implication that the artist was shitting on the audience. In part, this is the old bourgeois put-down that the avant-garde has practiced for years; it is a little ironic in the context of the Happening, where the small audiences tended to be made up of friends of the performers and admirers of the form. Since audiences have a tendency to accept anything that is done to them, it is comforting to know that they occasionally fight back. In one part of Oldenburg's *World's Fair II*, the section called "Walls," two performers pressed large sheets of cardboard against the standing audience; during one performance, according to the description in *Happenings,* a knife blade was thrust through the cardboard, presumably by a member of the audience who wanted the option not to be a wall.

My attempts to characterize the new theater and to quarrel with it in the paragraphs above are hampered by the fact that it is too inchoate a form to rest comfortably under a specific label. A theorist like Michael Kirby—whose definitions have often been my starting point—is too precise; he tends to sound prescriptive when what he intends is presumably description. The dissimilarities aside, however, two tendencies emerge from the Happening so far—or at least from my discussion of it above. On the one hand, it seems to want to be informational, even didactic, to communicate ideas and attitudes, and in the attempt it uses, either by design or by accident, the traditional devices of plot and character, although it tries to disguise this fact with multiple activities, with fragmentation, with chance techniques. On the other hand, it seems to want to present the objects and activities of ordinary life as entities, calling attention to them by placing them in unfamiliar contexts that heighten our awareness of them not as art objects but as life objects. The first of these is self-defeating because it does little more than present amateurish bits which are attractive because they recall familiar dramatic experiences or intellectual fragments which hint that the artist has a mind as stocked with clichés as that of any Broadway formula playwright. The second is self-defeating because—for all the talk of erasing the line between life and art—the presented activities and objects are wrenched out of life and stuck into art without the comfort of art, the pattern imposed on life. This pattern, incidentally, is not the dictatorial thing the practitioners of the Happening sometimes take it to be. Shakespeare never imposes on his audience at *Hamlet* as Ken Dewey did at *Action Theater.* The ironic thing is that the men who want to turn art into life never recognize that the work of art itself—an organized reflection of the disorganization of life which, in the theater at least, allows the audience to respond intellectually, emotionally and kinesthetically—is absorbed into life, is used by the spectator (as Oldenburg used the Wallace Beery movie to get to *Injun*) in ways that could never have been envisaged by the creator.

It would be foolish to make predictions about the future of the Happening. It seems obvious that experimentation will continue and that the likely direction will be that indicated by the *Nine Evenings* at the Armory, the wedding of art and technology in a way that will extend the range of performer tasks. Two other developments within the Happening are of particular interest: one is the movement out of the theater altogether, and the other is the movement (of ideas if not personnel) into conventional theater. When Allan Kaprow wrote his article for *Art News* back in 1961, he defined Happenings as "essentially theater pieces, however unconventional." Six years later, in *Assemblage, Environments & Happenings,* he offers seven rules, almost all of which convert the Happening from a theater event into a ritual for participants; the most obvious is his injunction to eliminate audiences. Unless one accepts John Cage's definition of theater ("something which engages both the eye and the ear," he told the *TDR* interviewers, ". . . one could view everyday life as theatre"), a definition as meaningless as it is arbitrary (why should taste, touch, and smell be ruled out?), what Kaprow is now involved in—Happenings only for performers—is no longer theater. Of course, Kaprow is a little too theatrically inclined to make a clean break. In *Calling* (1965), for instance, some of the participants were wrapped in muslin and left at the Information Booth in Grand Central Station; others were wrapped in foil and left sitting in cars parked in ordinary metered spaces. This is a private activity rather like that of the exhibitionist on the subway, but Kaprow offers a definition by way of excuse; passersby, momentarily involved as observers, he says in *Assemblage,* are "authentic parts of the environment." Perhaps George Brecht's *Direction* is a better example of a non-theatrical Happening, a totally private activity involving initiates. "Arrange to observe a sign indicating direction of travel," says the Brecht score, included in *Assemblage;* the participants, who receive their instructions by mail, have two choices: "travel in the indicated direction" or "travel in another direction." Kaprow admits that "there are few who could appreciate the moral dignity of such scores, and fewer still who could derive pleasure from going ahead and doing them without self-consciousness." Such activities fall short of the purity achieved by Marcel Duchamp, who resolved the Dadaist conflict of the artist with an anti-art commitment quite simply by ceasing to work. Only Dennis Johnson has come up with a work that embodies all that Duchamp has managed not to do in the last forty years. La Monte Young reports (in *TDR*) that Johnson offered him the score to a completely indeterminate work in which the composer was finally discarded. It said, "LISTEN."

Insofar as conventional theater is moving toward mixed-media production, it may be said to be borrowing some of the impetus, the techniques, the material of the Happening. Two other phenomena of the 1960's—the emergence of Marshall McLuhan as a prophet and the psychedelic explosion—are contributive factors. All three are essentially nonverbal, antitext. As I understand McLuhan, his basic point was originally a simple, probably defensible contention that, in the long run, technology creates environment, that the means of communication is finally more formative than the ideas communicated. His lapel-button slogan for that argument, "the medium is the message," has come to mean (even for McLuhan, one sometimes suspects) that "content is of no importance." The quotation is from John Cage (in *TDR*), who attributes the idea to McLuhan, but the sentiments are on the lips of every artist, man and boy, who wants to avoid the trap (that is, the challenge) of content and does so by muttering the magic word—McLuhan. The medium is certainly the message in psychedelic shows (I do not mean LSD trips, which are popularly presumed to be the mind-blowing model for the drugless substitute) in which the assault on the senses—flashing lights in clashing colors, music that increases in sound as the distinguishability of its elements decreases, film clips that are being used only because

they provide moving images, incense—not only presupposes absence of content, but inhibits the perception of the senses except
as a kind of immersion. The result is a fashionable chaos which is
supposed to heighten reality.

The use of borrowed shock techniques in the production of
plays which are texts and have content—even when Artaud,
rather than McLuhan, is invoked—is an unfortunate development.
For years, light, sound, film, costume have been used to enrich a
text in production, but the use of these elements in competition
with the text is part of the antirational, anti-intellectual attitude
implicit in Happenings, psychedelic doings, and the public image
of McLuhan. Beyond that, they represent, as directorial inventions
often do, a distrust of the material with which they are working.
Sarah Caldwell, the artistic director of the American National
Opera Company, told an interviewer (*The New York Times*, September 10, 1967), that their production of Alban Berg's *Lulu*
would use television, movies, psychedelic light, that they were
"trying to find ways of bringing this piece to life so that it will
have meaning to us today." The implication is that the opera
cannot be expected to get by on what it has to say, in music and
text, and that media have to be substituted for message (here
meaning dramatic effect); Raymond Ericson's review (*The New
York Times*, October 8, 1967) complained of the "tricked up"
staging, which got in the way of the opera for him. Two examples
from productions I have seen—both done in 1966 by Andre
Gregory at the Theatre of the Living Arts in Philadelphia—indicate how superficial and annoying such borrowings can be. At the
beginning of what turned out to be a conventional and quite good
production of Jean Anouilh's *Poor Bitos*, a spotlight was flashed
into the eyes of the audience (a very "now" effect used by Francis
Picabia in *Relâche* in 1924), presumably to shock them into the
realization that the play is immediately relevant to the world in
which they live; since the play's relevance—it *is* a contemporary
play—is quite obvious, all that the light did was distract the audience and draw their attention away from the opening scene. When
the audience entered the theater to see Rochelle Owens' *Beclch*,

they found the auditorium draped with the kind of decorations one might find in the school gym if the prom committee decided to use a jungle theme; the effect was heightened by twittering noises and scarcely visible slides, set to change automatically. It was obviously an attempt at an Environment, but it was so ludicrous that it did not bring the audience closer to the play; it made *Beclch*, which had problems enough of its own, seem even more like an awkward teenager, uncomfortable in her miniskirt but determined to be mod at any cost. Although my misgivings about the Happening are apparent and my attraction to the psychedelic occasion is minimal, both seem to me genuine attempts at nonverbal theatrical expression. Whatever is valid in the "other" theater, however, seems to disappear when conventional productions begin to feel its influence. Too often, as the examples above indicate, borrowings are made on the assumption that a colored light, a slide, an abusive sound effect are evidence that the director is up-to-date.

If the Happening is finally absorbed into the dramatic mainstream—and drama does have a way of eating its revolutionary offspring—it will probably be because playwrights have found a way to use Happening elements to further their own work. There is already evidence of such borrowing or at least of accidental similarities. Commenting on the motelkeeper's play-length monologue in *Motel*, Jean-Claude van Itallie told an interviewer (*The New York Times*, November 27, 1966), "I'd like the audience to be assaulted with the *sound* of these words, not particularly with their meaning." In her Production Notes for *Comings and Goings*, Megan Terry explained that when the play (game) was performed at La Mama, a wheel was spun by "a disinterested party" to choose the name of the actor or actress to send in as a momentary replacement for one of the couple on stage. Sam Shepard's *Icarus's Mother* provides a more doubtful example since it was the director, Michael Smith, rather than the author, who worried in his Notes to the play about the smoke-signal sequences: "How could I get them simply to *do* it, not to *act* it?" Although many of the younger playwrights are not as protective about text as some of the older ones are and although they are using action and character—or they think they are—in a new way, it should be clear that the effects mentioned above are not used for their own sake (as they are in the Happening), but in the service of a presumed total artistic effect. Since so many of the theories and devices of the Happening were borrowed from early avant-garde experiments and from theorists such as Artaud, it is not surprising to find them being passed on to the still unconventional wing of the conventional theater. It is too early to say what that means for the Happening at a moment when so much of the "other" theater is becoming something other than theater.

Postscript

A book that deals with the contemporary theater is automatically dated as soon as it reaches the printer. This one was written, for the most part, in 1967, although a few additions were made during the spring of 1968. Now in the fall, with the galleys in front of me, I want to add a few comments.

After a spring premiere at the Buffalo Festival of Arts Today, Albee's most recent work, a connected pair of one-acters, *Box* and *Quotations from Chairman Mao Tse-Tung*, came to Broadway in September. Another experiment in form, it is interesting not only in its own right but for what it suggests about Albee's attitude toward his past work. *Box* consists of a thirteen-minute taped monologue, at once an evocation of nostalgia and a lecture in aesthetics, spoken to an audience with only the frame of a gigantic box to concentrate on. The arts are gone, the voice says, and crafts have come if not to replace them, then to occupy the vacant space. Art that hurts by telling us of our losses is the final corruption in a corrupt world, but there is still room to move around in the box and the possibility of some kind of artistic order, always on its own terms. When the voice stills, *Mao* begins. The title character, who prowls the theater quoting his Marxist platitudes, shares the stage (the box) and the contrapuntal pattern with an old woman who does nothing but recite Will Carleton's "Over the Hill to the Poorhouse" and a long-winded lady, as the program identifies her, who insistently tells a mute clergyman about the time she fell or jumped or was pushed off an ocean liner. Mao's quotations, all jargonesque abstractions, and the old woman's poem, social criticism as a tear-jerker, are rhetorical devices to avoid the human situation with which they are presumably dealing. The long-winded lady is less obvious. Using most of the verbal mannerisms I described in Chapter Two, she reveals a life as meaningless as one has come to expect from an Albee heroine. Despite the fragmented style of the play, she catches the audience conventionally, asks for identification, sympathy. Yet the story she tells—the dying husband, the defecting child—is a parallel of "Over the Hill to the Poorhouse," and, even while we are being touched, we know we are being had—that her rhetoric, that of heightened realism, is also an avoidance. Contemporary drama, Albee seems to be telling us, is at its best and its most corrupt when it treats of loss, as all of Albee's work does; craft, with a little box-room and its own sense of order, can at least recognize the fact. *Box/Mao*, I suspect, is a kind of confession.

Looking less and less like front runners, several of the playwrights of Chapter Three have at least been running again. Arthur Kopit's *Indians*, a satiric attack on American racist attitudes, with Buffalo Bill as its central figure and rodeo and vaudeville as its borrowed theatrical mechanisms, was produced in London by the Royal Shakespeare Company, directed by Jack Gelber. Gelber also directed his own most recent play, *The Cuban Thing*, which lasted for one performance on Broadway, eliciting negative reviews from all the critics and a demonstration from anti-Castro Cubans who believed, wrongly, that the piece was going to be a simple pro-Castro document. Murray Schisgal's *Jimmy Shine*, which I saw in an unfinished state during its pre-Broadway run in Philadelphia, is an old-fashioned maturation play, in which the hero outgrows his love for the wrong girl and his dependence on the stifling friend, disguised as set of musical-comedy turns for its star and obsfuscated by thoughts on mortality and art. Perhaps I should also mention William Hanley's *Flesh and Blood,* since it has been dignified by publication; a dull television drama, produced early in 1968, it is unusual for only two reasons: it shows Hanley working with a cast larger than he has ever tried on stage, and it allows the soap-opera tendencies of his work to surface and finally swallow the character insights he displays.

Two comments on the playwrights discussed in Chapter Four: (1) *The Sign in Sidney Brustein's Window* was not Lorraine Hansberry's last play, only her last finished one; her *Les Blancs,* edited by Ossie Davis, has been announced for possible production later this season; (2) LeRoi Jones, appealing his sentence, is still free, still committed to black power, and still busy as a playwright, as his contributions to the Black Theatre edition of *The Drama Review* (Summer, 1968) indicate. That publication, with Ed Bullins as guest editor, offers a number of plays indicative of the politically oriented black theater. In his essay, "The Black Arts Movement," Larry Neal suggests that Jones's Black Arts Repertory Theatre was the spiritual father of the theater groups that have sprung up in the ghettos all across the country. The directory, "Black Theatre Groups," in the issue has thirty-six entries, some, such as Cleveland's Karamu House and the Negro Ensemble Company, with goals rather different from the general separatist thrust of the issue; since new groups form and old groups disappear frequently, the list is useful primarily as an indication of the extent of the dramatic activity. The plays are, for the most part, directly propagandistic and written in the tradition of American realism. Occasionally, as in Ben Caldwell's *Riot Sale,* a playwright works in terms of cartoon metaphor; Caldwell's "(anti-poverty) cannon," which fires money into the crowd, breaking up an incipient black revolution, is an image, like those of Lawrence Ferlinghetti, designed to make a simple didactic point.

Howard Sackler's *The Great White Hope,* a success on Broadway following a première at Washington's Arena Stage, is the only interesting new play by a white man on the Negro situation. It is a combination of old-fashioned chronicle play and Brechtian epic theater, which uses the story of a Negro boxer, based on Jack Johnson, to show a racist white America destroying a man who looks too much like an image of black superiority. At the same time, Sackler refuses to sentimentalize his hero, avoiding both easy pathos and cardboard heroism, and criticizes a Negro community willing to settle for the comfort of a surrogate success in the white world.

The publication of plays by young dramatists has so increased since Chapter Seven was written that there is no point in trying to cope with it here, but a few interesting on-stage developments should be mentioned. A number of new playwrights have turned up to command at least momentary attention: John Guare (*Muzeeka*), Ron Cowen (*Summertree*), Mart Crowley (*The Boys in the Band*). Rochelle Owens' *Futz*, a play about community reactions to a man who falls in love with a pig, has created the kind of stir that has made her this year's avant-garde playwright. Tom O'Horgan's direction of that play and of Paul Foster's *Tom Paine* has called attention to the newest ensemble practice, the compulsive touching which presumably conveys some ideational sense of the oneness of the troupe (and perhaps of society), but which wreaks havoc with plays written with some attention to idea and character. An extension of the anti-intellectual, anti-verbal tendency described in both chapters Seven and Eight, its effects were best illustrated, for me, by a ludicrous production of Georg Büchner's *Woyzeck* which I saw in a relentlessly touchy production in a coffee house in Montreal. The off-Broadway and, then, Broadway success of *Hair*, subtitled "an American tribal love-rock musical," is supposed to have sounded the death-knell of the conventional Broadway musical, but it is doubtful that the likable Gerome Ragni–James Rado show, with its sentimental book and its pseudo-rock score, can manage to ring that particular bell.

From my standpoint, the most interesting new development is the emergence of Israel Horovitz. His *The Indian Wants the Bronx*, in which two bored young toughs tease then torture an East Indian who speaks no English and can judge their intentions only

by their shifting tones of voice, is a depiction of casual violence
as ugly as it is effective. It was coupled off-Broadway with the
less interesting *It's Called the Sugar Plum,* an amused approach
to violence that is the logical lead-in to *Indian.* The indication of
talent in the double bill was confirmed by *Rats,* Horovitz' contribution to *Collision Course,* a well-acted but generally undistinguished evening of sketches contributed by many of the playwrights discussed in the body of this book: Jean-Claude van
Itallie, Lanford Wilson, Rosayln Drexler, Terrence McNally,
Martin Duberman, Jules Feiffer, Leonard Melfi. *Rats,* which had
point and style enough to stand out from the rest of the work,
used a quarrel between two rats over a black baby to make an
effective comment on the prevailing attitude in the Negro community against protective paternalism from outside. A book of
Horovitz' plays, *First Season,* is scheduled for publication this
fall and, as I write this, his *Line* is tentatively listed for Broadway
production during the 1968–69 season.

November 1968

Index